ams

mom + Da

Bought you a little
pressie - thought it
may come in useful

love

Narusha + Berenice

amsterdam

a pocket guide

Virgin

First published in 2001
Virgin Publishing Ltd, London w6 9HA
Copyright 2001 © Virgin Publishing Ltd, London

contents

Written by 20 contributors in-the-know, this guide gives the inside take on Amsterdam. The focus is on having fun; where to hang out, shop, eat, relax, enjoy and spoil yourself. And there's a selection of the top cultural hot spots...

area lowdown

A selection of Amsterdam's key areas.

buitenveldert & amstelveen ♯off map

The Netherlands' biggest Japanese community lives here. Few nonresidents ever venture to this district, except to visit the CoBrA Museum.

the canals ♯map 12

The picture-perfect canals that form a horseshoe around the Old Centre save Amsterdam from having a purely notorious reputation. Built during the height of the Golden Age, they provided a scenic setting for the building of elegant homes for the emerging class of wealthy merchants in the 17th- and 18th-centuries, and they are still the most sought-after addresses in town. The opulent mansions on the *Goude Bocht* (Golden Bend) stand out from the rest, and dispel the myth that the Dutch don't show outward signs of success. While many businesses, hotels and shops have moved in, the city's respect for its monuments has ensured that most of the buildings retain a sense of old school grandeur. The streets that link the canals – built originally for workers and artisans – tend to act as a cozy counterbalance, with neighbourly cafés and small specialty shops. As the city's shopping central, the tendency is to consume, consume, consume. But remember the more romantic option and stroll the watery arteries, letting your eyes roam upwards to admire the gabled façades, and down to trip on the shimmering reflections – which adds to the area's somewhat seedy fascination.

de pijp ♯map 14

Like many stories, it all began with a beer... when in 1865 Grandad Heineken bought some boggy land on which to build his brewery. A working-class neighbourhood of tall houses and 'pipe'-like narrow streets grew up around the factory. The cheap rents also attracted a fair share of radicals, students, and later-to-be-acclaimed writers, performers, and painters – along with many bars and brothels to serve them. It was only after WWII, with immigration from the likes of Indonesia and Surinam, that there was a stronger sense of community, with cheap, cosy restaurants replacing older, more dubious ones. While the brewery now only dispenses tours, the true heart of the area remains the Albert Cuyp Markt, the nation's largest. With a metro line due – theoretically – within a decade, De Pijp is going through some gentrification, but the harsher trends are mellowed with long-established neighbourly vibes.

haarlemmer ♯map 2

With a history that includes being the supply road to Haarlem during the 80-year war of independence against Spain; a favoured residence for retired sailors; and a prime strip for squatters during the 80s and early 90s, Haarlemmerstraat and

Haarlemmerdijk are now officially scrubbed clean and revitalised as quirky shopping streets. West, beyond the imposing 1840-built city gate, Haarlemmerport, lie monuments to the area's industrial past. The most notable is the former gas complex of Westergasfabriek, whose land and buildings are now being transformed into a centre for the arts with a film house, a happening café, studios for artists and theatre groups, and many unique spaces for parties, fashion shows, and cutting-edge exhibitions. This is definitely an area that's busting loose...

joordan $map 6

The picturesque labyrinth of small streets and densely packed houses that make up the villagey Jordaan were originally inhabited by the workers of industries previously banned from the city centre (like tanners and metal workers). The architecture and chaotic town planning was in total contrast to the majestic geometry of the neighbouring grand canals, exaggerating the differences in wealth of the two areas. Jordaaners are the locals' locals – and a true Jordaaner must be born within earshot of Westerkerk's bells. But today's inhabitants, many of whom are writers, artists, and boho types, come from all over. Characterful brown bars, clusters of *hofjes* (garden courtyards), and bustling markets are the legacy of the area's working-class roots. In the last few years, there's been an outbreak of classier restaurants and higher-end stores to cater for the influx of more chichi residents, but the old still happily mixes with the new. And even Amsterdammers visit the Jordaan at weekends.

noord $off map

This dull, modern residential area is punctuated by corners of centuries-old wooden houses and rambling parkland. Because you get there by ferry from behind Centraal Station, the north seems cut off from the rest of the city.

old centre $map 7

Flanked to the north by Centraal Station, and encompassing the focal point of Dam square, the Old Centre is cheek by jowl trash and treasure. It's a real mixed bag, with everything from old-world charm to in-your-face commercialism. A good chunk of the area's old buildings have been encrusted with neon, extolling the virtues of sex, shopping, gambling, and greasy food. But to get away from it all, Spui square and the adjoining courtyard of Begijnhof present a more gracious contrast. Similarly, the middle-of-the-road shopping that reigns supreme along Damrak, Rokin, and Kalverstraat is balanced by earthier examples of Amsterdam's 'merchant spirit' at the many outdoor markets – especially Waterlooplein, devoted to all things dusty and delightful. And by night, choose between atmospheric cafés, the bright lights of Rembrandtplein, or the arty bohemia along Nieuwezijds Voorburgwal. Ah, variety is indeed the herb of life.

oost
off map

The 'East' offers a mixed bag: gracious Plantagebuurt, with its flourishes of art nouveau, was once the city's smart Jewish neighbourhood; whilst Oosterpark has a multi-cultural, middle-eastern air.

oosterdok
off map

Renzo Piano started the craze, with an impressive building that looks like a giant sailing ship. Now all the developers want to jump on board, so the once dismal Eastern Docks look set to get a giant alternative music complex, and a host of other culturally oriented goodies to turn it into a prime hot spot. The Eastern Islands are being developed into a prime residential area, featuring some bravura modern architecture.

oude west
off map

One of the main focuses of the Moroccan and Turkish communities, but a good mix of other nationalities too. The friendly neighbourhood market and the myriad shops catering to different ethnic foibles help give the Old West its charm.

red light district & nieuwmarkt
maps 7 & 8

Since the beginning of Amsterdam's docking days, ladies of the night have entertained the sailors and travellers of the world, making this the most famous Red Light District of all. Around 5000 legal prostitutes (who conveniently group together by similar nationality and service speciality) create an annual turnover of millions of guilders. Despite the sleazy image, the area is less threatening than you'd expect. Previously seedy streets like the Zeedijk and Nieuwmarkt have cleaned up their act and now bow to the other basic instincts of hunger and thirst. This is an area of contrasts: the oldest profession happily trades next door to the Oude Kerk; funky fashions lie on the same streets as sleazy sex shops; and hip drinking spots sit next to grungy headshops. The high tack factor is a source of amusement and amazement to the many voyeurs, but look past the red lights and up to the beautiful canalhouses that line the *walletjes* ('little walls') to discover a finer side to the neighbourhood.

museum district & vondelpark
maps 9 & 11

As Amsterdam marched towards the 20th century, more housing for the rich was built up on this formerly boggy land. And even today, this area remains a centre of elitist living, designer shopping, and, of course, museum-hopping. Formerly sporting what used to be known as the nation's 'shortest motorway', the newly revamped Museumplein now harmonizes nicely with the three bordering must-see art museums and the elegant Concertgebouw. But the true green heart and people's park of Amsterdam is the Vondelpark – named after 'the Dutch Shakespeare', Joost van den Vondel. No longer the crash pad of the love generation, it still holds on to its hippie past on sunny days – complete with armies of bongo players – as the most popular park in the city.

watergraafsmeer   *off map*

Once considered far flung, Watergraafsmeer has magically moved closer to town. The reason: rising house prices in the centre. Over the past few years, artists and style-setters have opted for its 30s apartments, and the area is on the up. Neighbouring Betondorp (concrete town) is an unaltered 20s garden suburb.

westerdok   *off map*

The Western Docks is enjoying a rehab. The converted warehouses on the islands around Prinseneiland, especially, are the territory of media and advertising types. But the quarter retains much of its romantic seafaring air.

westerpark   *map 3a*

A former gasworks rejuvenated as an arts centre, and acres of new environmentally right-on houses are gradually transforming a dull corner of town.

zuid   *off map*

This refined quarter of old villas lets its hair down a little as you move east into the Rivierenbuurt, which is becoming a popular address for journalists and other media folk.

zuid oost & bijlmermeer   *off map*

Bijlmermeer is a 60s dream-turned-nightmare, the concrete forest of high-rises has turned very un-des res. But the tower blocks are being revamped, and a flash new entertainment boulevard is in the making. Zuid Oost is also getting a make-over, and is now the home of a flashy new business park development.

area index

SHOPPING

SIGHTS, MUSEUMS & GALLERIES

BARS & CAFÉS
Café Krull (club/bar) 87
Carel (club/bar) 87
Gambrinus
(brown café) 85
Jan Steen (club/bar) 87
O'Donnells (Irish bar) 92
Pilsvogel (brown café) 86
Quinto (club/bar) 88

COFFEESHOPS
Katsu 98

RESTAURANTS & EETCAFÉS
Albine
(Chinese) 63
Aleksandar
(Yugoslav) 83
Bagels & Beans
(eetcafé) 66
Balti House (Indian) 73
Cambodja City
(oriental & southeast Asian) 78
De Duvel (Dutch) 65
District V (French) 69
Eufraat (Middle Eastern) 77
Falafel Dans
(Middle Eastern) 77
Kingfisher (global & fusion) 71
L'Angoletto (Italian) 74
Lokanta Ceren
(Middle Eastern) 77
Ondeugd (global & fusion) 71
Volendammer Viswinkel
(herring stall) 72
Yamazato (Japanese) 75
Zento (Japanese) 75

SHOPPING
Abracadabra (gifts) 42
Albert Cuyp Markt
(market) 48
Casa Molero (food) 38
De Aanzet (food) 38
De Emaillerkeizer (interiors) 44
De Peperbol (food) 38
The Filipino Foodstore & Toko
(food) 39
Kinderfeestwinkel (toys) 58
Kniphal (fabrics) 37
La Tienda (food) 39
Okado (gifts) 42
Runneboom (food) 40
Tjin's Toko (food) 41
Van Moppes (diamonds) 34

SIGHTS, MUSEUMS & GALLERIES
Ciel Bleu Restaurant
(viewpoint) 122
Heineken Brouwerij
(one-off) 135
Sarparthipark
(green scene) 138

delft

RESTAURANTS & EETCAFÉS
Kleyweg's Stads-Koffyhuis
(out of town) 79

SIGHTS, MUSEUMS & GALLERIES
Koninklijke Porcelyne Fles
(out of town) 140
Stedelijk Museum Het
Prinsenhof (out of town) 141

den haag

RESTAURANTS & EETCAFÉS
De Wankele Tafel
(out of town) 78
Greve (out of town) 79

SIGHTS, MUSEUMS & GALLERIES
Haags Gemeentemuseum
(out of town) 140
Mauritshuis
(out of town) 140
Panorama Mesdag
(out of town) 141
Vredespaleis
(out of town) 141

area index

haarlemmer &
westerpark

havens west

jordaan

leiden

old centre

SIGHTS, MUSEUMS & GALLERIES

area index

area index

shops

The world's uncontested capital of anything risqué, Amsterdam's also hot on the fun, the funky – and the downright bizarre. The wackiest of wares are sold in tiny boutiques lining streets steeped in 17th-century charm. Downtown (especially around politically correct Hooftstraat) it's all sass and class, as international designers open flagship stores. What's more, it's all so compact, you can walk from one good shopping street to another. So put those trainers on, and get shopping!

antiques

☆ ANTIEKHANDEL LEBBING   *♯D11*
If you haven't been able to find what you're looking for, you're sure to here. Chocka with all sorts of collectables from furniture to vases and mirrors to razor kits.
Prinsengracht 805–807, The Canals ☎ 624 1253

☆ ARONSON ANTIQUAIRS   *♯D11*
For old Delft tiles, ranging from the 15th to the 20th centuries and costing anything from a few guilders to the price of your airfare home.
Nieuwe Spiegelstraat 39, The Canals ☎ 623 3103

Bits & Pieces   *♯ off map*
Classic pieces for the old-moneyed set, including antique furnishings and the occasional painting.
Overtoom 441, Museum District & Vondelpark ☎ 618 1939

De Brocanteurs   *♯ off map*
Feast your eyes on wonderful classic antiques.
Overtoom 179, Museum District & Vondelpark ☎ 616 8949

Golden Bend   *♯A12*
A charming assortment of ceramics and pottery.
Herengracht 510, The Canals ☎ 627 7784

Heinen   *♯A11*
Delftware is the bread and butter of the Dutch antique trade, and this is the official dealer of Royal Delft and Makkum pottery, with pieces dating back to the 17th century.
Spiegelgracht 13, The Canals ☎ 421 8360

Klevering *♭B5*
Specializes in salvaged interior and exterior treasures from old Dutch buildings.
Bloemgracht 175, Jordaan ☎ 422 0397

Mieke Zilverberg *♭E7*
Part with your dosh in genteel surroundings: ring the bell, lower your voice, and step in for antiques and silverware at daunting prices.
Rokin 70, Old Centre ☎ 625 9518

Polak Kunsthandel *♭D11*
Best known for its European and oriental antiques, but be warned, *objets d'art* from this gallery are purchased by museums around the world, so line your pockets.
Spiegelgracht 3, The Canals ☎ 627 9009

☆ PREMSELA & HAMBURGER *♭E7*
Of the super-smart establishments along the Rokin, this, with its wondrous array of classy old silver, is the most visitable.
Rokin 98, Old Centre ☎ 624 9688

☆ THOM & LENNY NELIS *♭B11*
Sells odd and alarming medical antiques.
Keizersgracht 541, The Canals ☎ 623 1546

☆ VAN DREVEN & TOEBOSCH *♭D11*
Try Van Dreven & Toebosch for clocks (from towering tickers to delicate travel clocks) musical boxes, and barometers.
Nieuwe Spiegelstraat 33–35, The Canals ☎ 625 2732

art

☆ AKINCI *♭F5*
One of six adjacent canalside galleries – you can go from one to another without going outside – which all show interesting work. Akinci has been known to show nude performances.
Lijnbaansgracht 317, Jordaan ☎ 638 0480

☆ CONSORTIUM *♭ off map*
Large projects can be accommodated in this converted dockside warehouse, which features work by up-and-coming international artists.
Oostelijke Handelskade 29, Oosterdok ☎ 421 2408

☆ DE PRAKTIJK
♭D5

Run by an art-loving ex-dentist, De Praktijk focuses particularly on contemporary Dutch figurative paintings and photography.
Lauriergracht 96, Jordaan ☎ 422 1727

Donkersloot
♭F9

For an arty buzz, hit on this rather commercial collection of modern prints and original paintings, with up-and-coming Dutch artists on show.
PC Hooftstraat 127, Museum District & Vondelpark ☎ 572 2722

☆ ELISABETH DEN BIEMAN DE HAAS
♭D11

For that little Picasso or Matisse.
Nieuwe Spiegelstraat 44, The Canals ☎ 626 1012

☆ FONS WELTERS
♭D5

Worth looking up, this gallery 'stocks' mainly well-known Dutch artists like Aernout Mik, Rob Birza, and Merijn Bolink. Less likely to feature big names.
Bloemstraat 140, Jordaan ☎ 423 3046

☆ FOTOGALERIE 2 BIJ 4
♭E6

For photography enthusiasts.
Prinsengracht 356, The Canals ☎ 626 0757

☆ GALERIE OELE
♭C11

One of the most innovative galleries within this Jordaan art complex.
Lijnbaansgracht 314, Jordaan ☎ 627 8628

☆ GALERIE PAUL ANDRIESSE
♭A6

Specializing in abstracts.
Prinsengracht 116, The Canals ☎ 623 6237

☆ JASKI ART GALLERY
♭D11

Features CoBrA artists as well as contemporary pieces.
Nieuwe Spiegelstraat 27–29, The Canals ☎ 620 3939

☆ LUMEN TRAVO
♭F5

Another innovative gallery housed in this art complex.
Lijnbaansgracht 314, Jordaan ☎ 627 0883

☆ MELKWEG GALLERIE
♭D9

If photography is more up your street, go see the exhibitions at the Melkweg Gallerie.
Marnixstraat 409, The Canals ☎ 531 8181

☆ **MONTEVIDEO** ♫C6
The place for zany video installations.
Keizersgracht 264, The Canals ☎ 623 7101

☆ **NANCY DE VREEZE** ♫C11
Predominantly abstract art.
Leidsedwarsstraat 198–200, The Canals ☎ 627 3808

Reflex Modern Art Gallery ♫E11
Purveyors of contemporary art whose exhibits feature photography,
paintings, sculpture, and installations by renowned and up-and-coming
international artists alike.
Weteringschans 79a, The Canals ☎ 627 2832

☆ **ROB JURKA** ♫F5
Shows big-name, arty photographers as well as conceptual art.
Singel 28, The Canals ☎ 627 6343

☆ **SERIEUZE ZAKEN** ♫F5
Renowned for its gay proprietor, Rob Malasch, a highly critical journo
with a preference for theatrical shows. He is dedicated to promoting the
causes of young artists and has been known to bring over Brit-pack
artists like Gavin Turk and Sarah Lucas.
Flandsstraat 90, Jordaan ☎ 420 5252

Song Lines ♫C11
Learn the stories of an ancient people where aboriginal sculpture and
paintings teach of times gone by.
Prinsengracht 570, The Canals ☎ 422 2212

☆ **TORCH** ♫D5
The trail-blazing Torch veers toward the novel, with shows on the
strangest subjects like 60s cult sex-goddess Betty Page.
Lauriergracht 94, Jordaan ☎ 626 0284

☆ **W139** ♫C7
While this gallery started out as a squatters' art-space, W139 is now one
of the bigger spaces in Amsterdam, so can exhibit large installations. It
is renowned for its wow opening parties as opposed to the quality of
the work.
Warmoesstraat 139, Old Centre ☎ 622 9434

Sotheby's and **Christie's** each have a branch in Amsterdam, but you need truckloads of guilders to buy anything at either. More affordable are the household clearings and antiques sold at **De Eland** and **Veilinghuis de Nieuwe Zon**. Or the city pawn shop, **Stadsbank van Lening**, auctions unreclaimed objects on a regular basis. Anything can be found here, from silverware and furniture to stereos and CDs.

Christie's $E10
Cornelis Schuystraat 57, Museum District & Vondelpark ☎ 575 5255

De Eland $F5
Elandsgracht 68, The Canals ☎ 623 0343

Sotheby's $ off map
De Boelelaan 30, Buitenveldert ☎ 550 2200

Stadsbank van Lening $E7
Oudezijds Voorburgwal 300, Old Centre ☎ 622 2421

Veilinghuis de Nieuwe Zon $ off map
Overtoom 197, Museum District & Vondelpark ☎ 616 8586

bags

☆ **CELLARICH CONNEXION** $A3
The hippest hold-alls in town. Funky bags from Vivienne Westwood, arty attachés by Antoni Allison, and a variety of purses from France, Spain, and the Netherlands too.
Haarlemmerdijk 98, Haarlemmer & Westerpark ☎ 626 5526

☆ **DE GROTE TAS** $D7
Hide your clutter in leather totes: functional briefcases, wallets, and shoulder bags plus an assortment of lightweight rucksacks and suitcases. Nothing too shocking.
Oude Hoogstraat 6, Red Light District & Nieuwmarkt ☎ 623 0110

☆ **HESTER VAN EEGHEN** $D6
Primary colours, soft leather, geometric designs, and surprising elements characterize these distinctive bags and wallets. Lovingly crafted, and now sold around the world, it all started here.
Hartenstraat 1, The Canals ☎ 626 9212

beauty supplies

BODY SHOP   ♯E7
Crammed with Anita's successful marketing ploys, fruit-flavoured shower gels, cosmetics, and smelly gunk for the new man and woman.
Kalverstraat 157, Old Centre ☎ 623 9789

LE SAVONNEREA   ♯E6
Homemade soaps galore, which can even be inscribed with your own text. Assorted bathtime accessories include ginseng shampoo and tools for the art of massage.
Prinsengracht 294, The Canals ☎ 428 1139

RED EARTH   ♯A11
An Australian enterprise which has recently peeled off its facial masks, oils, and accessories lines to concentrate on cheep 'n' cheerful cosmetics. One of its 300 lipsticks should match any new outfit.
Leidsestraat 64, The Canals ☎ 638 9700

SHU UEMURA   ♯A7
These trend-setting, no-frill cosmetics from Japan are complemented by deep sea minerals, traditional Japanese bath oils, Tweezerman tools, and scrubs and creams from their New York health spa. Bliss...
Magna Plaza, Nieuwezijds Voorburgwal 182, Old Centre ☎ 638 8127

books, newspapers & magazines

AMERICAN BOOK CENTER   ♯E7
The big selection is bolstered by funky staff who know their stuff, and give 10% discount to students.
Kalverstraat 185, Old Centre ☎ 625 5537

ART BOOK   ♯D10
Strong on primitive art, new media, photography, and fashion. The reading table, balcony, and exhibition space make it a place to linger.
Van Baerlestraat 126, Museum District & Vondelpark ☎ 664 0925

ATHENAEUM BOEKHANDEL & NIEUWSCENTRUM   ♯F6
The *boekhandel* (bookshop) stocks fiction, philosophy, and art. For your monthly glossy magazine fix, don't bother going anywhere else. If they don't have your mag of choice here, nowhere will.
Spui 14–16, Old Centre ☎ 622 6248

☆ **BOEKIE WOEKIE** ₡E(
Their claim to fame is their limited edition illustrated art books.
Berenstraat 16, The Canals ☎ 639 0507

☆ **BOOK EXCHANGE** ₡F,
For cheap travel reading, where the stacks of second-hand paperback
and quality non-fiction hardbacks scream for space.
Kloveniersburgwal 58, Old Centre ☎ 626 6266

☆ **BOOK TRAFFIC** ₡A(
Particularly good for used books on esotericism, sci-fi, and literature.
Leliegracht 50, Jordaan ☎ 620 4690

☆ **DE SLEGTE** ₡E,
Serious browsers could spend a day in De Slegte. Not exclusively English
language, it's still your best bet for out-of-print editions and publishers
remainders.
Kalverstraat 48–52, Old Centre ☎ 622 5933

☆ **NIJHOF & LEE** ₡F,
Stocks new and out-of-print books on art, architecture, and graphic
design as well as reference works.
Staalstraat 13A, Old Centre ☎ 620 3980

☆ **WATERSTONE'S** ₡E,
Hushed and carpeted, Waterstone's is big on biographies and special
offer paperbacks.
Kalverstraat 152, Old Centre ☎ 638 3821

cds, records & tapes

Boudisque ₡B,
Walk away with your favourite CD, and score tickets to gigs at the same time
Haringpakkerssteeg 10–18, Old Centre ☎ 623 2603

☆ **CONCERTO** ₡F12
Shifting vinyl since the 50s, the city's best one-stop shop for new and
used CDs, LPs, MCs, CD-Is, and videos. Almost anally ordered, it's a cinch to
find your second-hand surf, Carl Cox, or Carl Orff – whatever turns you on
Utrechtsestraat 52–60, The Canals ☎ 623 5228

☆ **DANCE TRACKS** ₡A,
For local club mixes, hard house, and big beat as well as 70s funk classics
Nieuwe Nieuwstraat 69, Old Centre ☎ 639 0853

☆ GET RECORDS ♪F12
Specialist in non-commercial pop, Get Records is a cool and friendly option.
Utrechtsestraat 105, The Canals ☎ 622 3441

☆ MUSIQUE DU MONDE ♪D6
Here they burn to the beat of a different drum: an Hawaiian one maybe, or a Celtic flute – this cozy store stocks CDs of traditional music from around the world.
Singel 281, The Canals ☎ 624 1354

☆ RUSH HOUR RECORDS ♪A7
DJ fodder only – Mo' Wax, dub, plus floor-fillers from the 8os.
Spuistraat 98, The Canals ☎ 427 4505

Soul Food Records ♪A7
A clubbers' delight, where local DJs find the hottest new soul, hip-hop, and R&B vinyl imports. Staff here are ultra-knowledgeable.
Nieuwe Nieuwstraat 27c, Old Centre ☎ 428 6130

☆ SOUND OF THE FIFTIES ♪A11
50s floor-fillers have been drawing doo-wop die-hards here for two decades. The followers are still there, shuffling through the rock 'n' roll, R&B, and soul for rare recordings and bargains – all there, on CD and vinyl.
Prinsengracht 669, The Canals ☎ 623 9745

☆ VIRGIN MEGASTORE ♪D6
Covers classical through country to charts and boasts a videodrome, games centre, books, and accessories.
Magna Plaza, Nieuwezijds Voorburgwal 182, Old Centre ☎ 622 8929

children's wear

☆ OILILY ♪F9
Oilily takes its clients very seriously, even if they are only five years old. The clothes sold at this wonderful shop are created in vibrant colours children adore, and wearing them is as comfortable as can be.
PC Hooftstraat 131, Museum District & Vondelpark ☎ 672 3361

Storm ♪D6
Storm specializes in well-made, trendy clothes and shoes. In addition, the shop offers angel wings and Batman suits to dress up in, and hip presents such as inflatable aquariums. While adults shop, kids can cycle around the store on steady three-wheelers.
Magna Plaza, Nieuwezijds Voorburgwal 182, Old Centre ☎ 624 1074

Teuntje *♀C*
More down-to-earth goods can be found at Teuntje, including bab
clothes, accessories, and furnishings.
Haarlemmerdijk 132, Haarlem ☎ 625 3432

't Schooltje *♀C9*
Mum and dad are going to need a fat wallet to shop here as the clothe
in this shop (Armani, Versace, and Replay) ain't cheap. But they can take
their time looking for suitable togs as there are two great pedal cars to
keep the kids amused.
Overtoom 87, Museum District & Vondelpark ☎ 683 0444

cigars

☆ **PGC HAJENIUS** *♀E*
Even the most avid non-smoker would want to take in a lungful of the
hushed art deco ambience of cigar specialist Hajenius. Short fillers
panatellas, pipes, smoking accessories, and a tiny, mezzanine museum.
Rokin 92–96, Old Centre ☎ 625 9985

clubwear

☆ **ANGEL BASICS** *♀F12*
A bubbly little boutique full of fringes, sequins, and patchwork shaped
into girlie get-ups by the likes of Betsey Johnson, Cinnamon, and Wild &
Lethal Trash. If you don't know what you want, you'll find it here – with
shoes and bags to match.
Utrechtsestraat 132, The Canals ☎ 624 1348

☆ **CLUBWEAR HOUSE** *♀C6*
Furnishing local catwalks with nine-speed flashing T-shirts by Ligh
Attack, dare-to-be different designs by British Cyberdog, and their own
head-turning creations, this is a dynamic, happening place. Good for
tickets for in-crowd-only parties.
Herengracht 265, The Canals ☎ 622 8766

☆ **HENNES EN MAURITZ (H&M)** *♀E7*
The knowledge that they'll fall apart after a season won't stop you
snatching up handfuls of these cut-price clothes from Sweden: casuals
clubwear, and pretty party accessories. The racks seem to hold twice the
amount they were made for.
Kalverstraat 200, Old Centre ☎ 556 7777

☆ HOUSEWIVES ON FIRE ♭B6

A hothouse for local club culture, a select crop of offbeat outfits for exhibitionists only is strung out on chains in the spacious basement. Upstairs it's haircuts, henna tattoos, and pierced wenches exchanging club-floor gossip.
Spuistraat 130, Old Centre ☎ 422 1067

Somewear-else ♭F6

Owned and run by two Italians whose grasp of Dutch is poor, but taste in womenswear cutting edge. Here you'll find treasures from W&LT, Vivienne Westwood's Anglomania line, and wild wear from E-pure and Yunk.
Spuistraat 242, Old Centre ☎ 428 8422

department stores

☆ DE BIJENKORF ♭A7

Five floors of luxury loot for true fashionistas in Amsterdam's largest department store. The Bijenkorf (it means beehive) is especially good for quality kitchen equipment and home furnishings – from designer bed linen to tasteful trivia for spare shelves. All departments (including hi-fi, luggage, toys) cover a broad price range and the café, La Ruche, is an excellent place for lunch. There are masses of clothes, too. Designer outlets include Benetton, DKNY Jeans, and French Connection. Chill Out, on the top floor, has lost its edge but is still good for club gear and wacky accessories.
Dam 1, Old Centre ☎ 621 8080

☆ HEMA ♭B11

Stocks cheap 'n' cheerful basics displaying more than a passing hint of current design trends. One floor only, it carries no-nonsense beauty products, stationery, kitchen accessories, and underwear – all displayed in a clean-lined interior. Prices may be low but quality here is high. Hema (with stores throughout the city) has a reputation for value for money and is famed for its high-quality wine and cheese selection.
Kalvertoren, Old Centre ☎ 422 8988

☆ MAISON DE BONNETERIE ♭A12

Luxuriate in the abundance of chandeliers, wooden banisters, and the sumptuous grand café in this most upmarket of Amsterdam stores. No longer the exclusive haunt of rich old ladies, it now carries Tommy Hilfiger, Paul Frank, and W&LT, as well as Polo Ralph Lauren and Armani. The designer labels extend to its delicious bed and bath linens on the ground floor, while the second floor is devoted entirely to golf.
Rokin 140–142, Old Centre ☎ 626 2162

☆ METZ & CO
βB

Avant-garde is the *raison d'être* for a store providing one of the city's mos
elegant shopping environments – its seven floors are an indulgence fo
top designers. Pick up glassware from the likes of Alessi, Cartier, Starck, o
Lalique, and designer threads from Helmut Lang, Alexander McQueer
Nicole Farhi, or New York Industries. There are regular art exhibitions or
the top floor and the café here has great views of the city.
Leidsestraat 34–36, The Canals ☎ 520 7020

Oininio
βC

Visit New Age department store, sauna, and restaurant Oininio whos
uncertain future rests in the hands of financiers.
Prins Hendrikkade 20–21, Old Centre ☎ 553 9334

☆ VROOM & DREESMANN
βC

Nothing chic or outrageous here, but it's a great place for both trendy an
affordable accessories and lingerie. The top floor is hot on electrica
equipment; they have their own line in children's wear; and it's good for
basic raincoat or swimsuit. The good piazza-style restaurant is always busy
Kalverstraat 201, Old Centre ☎ 622 0171

designer clothes

☆ AZZURO
βF

Two floors of this season's staples from Gaultier, Versace, Moschino, an
Mugler: sleek separates for about-town sophisticates, and price
bodywarmers for the Alpine ski slopes. The diffusion store, a few door
down, features funkier lines by Anna Sui, D&G, and Philosophy.
PC Hooftstraat 142a, Museum District & Vondelpark ☎ 671 6804

☆ CORA KEMPERMAN
βA

It might present a similar challenge to putting up your first tent, but onc
you've figured out which limb goes where, Cora Kemperman's layered lool
will fix you firmly between Yamamoto and young urban traveller.
Leidsestraat 72, The Canals ☎ 625 1284

☆ CUM LAUDE
βF

A seductive souterrain crammed with whimsical creations particularl
suitable for a night at the opera. Lots of pleated and puckered silk, velve
appliqued voile, and evidence of startling creativity with a sewin
machine. Scarves by ZAZ and bags by Vivienne Westwood.
PC Hooftstraat 106, Museum District & Vondelpark ☎ 676 3970

☆ DKNY   ♭E11

The ingenuity of all-American designer Donna Karan seems to know no bounds. Her impertinent approach to fabric and funky use of colour extends across all lines here – Essentials, Classics, Jeans, and Kids.
PC Hooftstraat 60, Museum District & Vondelpark (branches also on Kalvertoren & Leidsestraat) ☎ 671 0554

☆ EMPORIO ARMANI   ♭E11

Top-notch tailoring from the master of Italian minimalism. Alongside quality men's suits and row upon row of silk ties are easy evening pieces for women – often sprinkled with a handful of glitter – and understated casuals for both sexes.
PC Hooftstraat 39–41, Museum District & Vondelpark ☎ 471 1121

Giamboi   ♭C6

Sleek and superbly cut separates from up-and-coming Italian designers.
Hartenstraat 20, The Canals ☎ 638 1744

Gianni Versace   ♭F9

The hottest in Eurotrash clothing and the home signature collection. If the price tags are out of your league, check out the wild Versace experience.
PC Hooftstraat 97, Museum District & Vondelpark ☎ 662 3588

☆ KHYMO   ♭E11

Ambitious garb for the avant-gardia. This is the place to pick up a backless rabbit-skin top, cowhide two-piece, or sequin-studded mohair. The directional designers responsible include Gaultier, Plein Sud, Bill Tomade, and Amaya Arzuaga. Lots of black.
Leidsestraat 9, The Canals ☎ 622 2137

Local Service   ♭C8

Two shops bursting with men's and women's flirty rock star-style togs, from velvet suits by Paul Smith to sizzling separates from Gaultier, Girbaud, and more.
Keizersgracht 400–402, The Canals ☎ 626 6840

☆ RAZZMATTAZZ   ♭E6

Clothes that are hot off the catwalks – from Vivienne Westwood, Dexter Wong, Masaki Matsushima, and Geoffrey B Small, plus a host of undiscovered new talent. The personnel (who think they're works of art themselves) stride noisily through the bare-brick interior clutching yapping dogs and mobile phones.
Wolvenstraat 19, The Canals ☎ 420 0483

☆ **TURNING POINT**   *♀E8*

Lots of cobwebby lace, floaty viscose (mostly by Ghost), and a host of elegant, ultra-feminine designs from Lillith and La Fée Maraboutée. Menswear is also on the soft side and includes creations by Bruun Bazaar and John Crummay.

Sint Antoniesbreestraat 126–128b, Red Light District & Nieuwmarkt
☎ **420 5179**

☆ **VAN RAVENSTEIN**   *♀C8*

The best of established Belgian design. Chic, understated, and classically cut, the clothes still display an edgy hint of the hip and happening. Designers include Dries van Noten, Dirk van Bikkembergs, and Lieve van Gorp.

Keizersgracht 359, The Canals ☎ **639 0067**

diamonds

Though no rival to Antwerp as a vortex of the diamond trade, Amsterdam's history as a diamond-polishing centre means it's a good place for rocks on the cheap. Famous gems, such as the Koh-I-Noor, were cut here. Today, diamond-cutting works around town lure you in for a free 'tour' or 'demonstration' before propelling you on to their sales rooms. The tour usually involves explanations of the cutting and polishing process (they use olive oil), dull charts, lumps of diamond-shaped glass, and dollops of sales pitch. Then it's off to the shop, where jewellery and unmounted gems are (granted) generally cheaper than in other capitals. All the stores sell stones from a few hundred to hundreds of thousand guilders. Reputable firms include:

Amstel Diamonds   *♀ off map*
Amstel 208, Old Centre ☎ **623 1479**

Costers   *♀A13*
Paulus Potterstraat 2–6, Museum District & Vondelpark ☎ **305 5555**

Van Moppes   *♀D13*
Albert Cuypstraat 2–6, De Pijp ☎ **676 1242**

drink

☆ **DE BIERKONING**   *♀D6*

Witches brew, chocolate ale, and mussel beer are some of the most intriguing-sounding of some 850 different beers from around the world. Also stocks a selection of unusual glasses and tankards.

Paleisstraat 125, Old Centre ☎ **625 2336**

☆ GEELS & CO $B7

Chrysanthemum tea, Arabic coffee, along with sweets such as traditional Dutch fudge and toffee are all sold here in the store's steamed, aromatic, 17th-century interior. This is also the place to buy tea- and coffee-drinking accessories which are trad and trendy. There is even a mini-museum.
Warmoesstraat 67, Red Light District & Nieuwmarkt ☎ 624 0683

Oekie Delicatessen $D12

Wine and cheese specialist extraordinaire. Over 100 European cheeses, 10 types of port, some wicked Dutch wines, peppery homemade pâtés, and succulent salads.
Utrechtsestraat 57, The Canals ☎ 624 3740

☆ WATERWINKEL $E13

Bottled water from all over the world: whether it be fruit-flavoured, sex-enhancing, or hangover-soothing, it's all sold in an aqua-tint interior to the sound of a waterfall.
Roelof Hartstraat 10, Museum District & Vondelpark ☎ 675 5932

erotica

☆ ABSOLUTE DANNY $D7

Cross the threshold into the leopard skin and leather boudoir of Absolute Danny and you're greeted by the vivacious owner herself. Beaming and friendly, she will help you choose second-skin rubber and latex fetish wear which she'll happily accessorize with the perfect paddle, whip, or toy to suit.
Oudezijds Achterburgwal 78, Red Light District & Nieuwmarkt ☎ 421 0915

☆ CHRISTIANE LE DUC $E7

This store has well-thumbed mags along with a regular visitation of raincoats. This is the place to buy your bang cock penis cream, cat masks, and red lace undies.
Spui 6, Old Centre ☎ 624 8265

☆ CONDOMERIE HET GULDEN VLIES $C7

Alongside tested condoms and flavoured dental dams, there are condoms marked in inches, glow-in-the-dark grow-bags, and hand-painted penis protectors.
Warmoesstraat 141, Red Light District & Nieumarkt ☎ 627 4174

☆ **DEMASK**   *♫A*
Here, nipples exist to be clamped – or reinforced in rubber. They do the
own line in latex – dresses, T-shirts, corsets, and G-strings, and have
basement full of bondage gear. This is the place to find flyers for sex partie
Zeedijk 64, Red Light District & Nieuwmarkt ☎ 620 5603

☆ **FEMALE & PARTNERS**   *♫A*
Stocks more standard sex-wear: glossy black PVC and stilettos and zippe
leather shorts for men. Accessories explore the lighter side of bondag
and a range of vibrators, books, and videos.
Spuistraat 100, Old Centre ☎ 620 9152

☆ **STOUT**   *♫E*
Positively chic. Sartorial invitations to intimacy include Swiss lace corset
black bodies, and candid, kooky evening wear. The videos are on Tantric a
opposed to thrusting sex and lubricants have lost out to massage oils.
Berenstraat 9, The Canals ☎ 620 1676

eyewear

☆ **DE JONGEJAN**   *♫D*
Everything from pre-war to glam rock: vintage frames and sunglasses fo
those with their sights set on something different.
Noorderkerkstraat 18, Jordaan ☎ 624 6888

☆ **MARCEL BARLAG EYEWEAR**   *♫A*
Inspired window displays will draw even the most short-sighted to view
spectacular designs by Marcel's brother Gabriel, fun frames from LA
Eyeworks, and classics by Zeiss, Armani, and Robert La Roche.
Nieuwezijds Voorburgwal 129–131, Old Centre ☎ 622 1777

☆ **VILLA RUIMZICHT**   *♫F12*
Want contact lenses with dollar signs or a new cornea colour for the
evening? No problem. Ruimzicht is a lens specialist, and also sells
designer glasses by Gucci, Calvin Klein, Emmanuelle Kahn, and Matsuda
Utrechtsestraat 131, The Canals ☎ 428 2665

fabrics

☆ **CAPSICUM**   *♫D7*
The city's classiest fabric emporium – natural threads only. Deck yoursel
out in shot silk from Thailand; smother your sofa in an Asian ikat, or trea
your kitchen table to crisp Belgian linen.
Oude Hoogstraat 1, Red Light District & Nieuwmarkt ☎ 623 1016

Kniphal *C14*

This store sells fabrics with international flair, from saris to silks, and even funky fake furs. Patterns from the likes of Vogue and Butterick are also available.

Albert Cuypstraat 162, De Pijp ☎ 679 5831

☆ MCLENNAN'S *C6*

Beaded brocades, velvets, and organza from India – it's all silk and all sold by the metre. From heavier stuff to add snazz to your sashes to ephemeral threads for a night at the opera.

Hartenstraat 22, The Canals ☎ 622 7693

flowers & plants

Bloemenmarkt *B11*

The Bloemenmarkt (flower market) on the Singel is a bit touristy, but the cut flowers are cheap and there's a great selection.

Singel, The Canals.

Fleuremonde *C3*

Show someone you love them with a striking bouquet.

Haarlemmerdijk 49, Haarlem ☎ 623 3727

Gerdas Bloemen en Planten *E6*

Add the crowning touch to the perfectly laid table with an exotic centrepiece. Any hostess worth her salt wouldn't dream of going anywhere else for flowers.

Runstraat 16, The Canals ☎ 624 2912

food

☆ ALBERT HEIJN FOOD PLAZA *D6*

Holland's number-one supermarket, this store is well-stocked for busy professionals with a taste for all things fresh and foreign. Sushi, *burritos*, and onion *bhajis* vie for shelf space along with hot Dutch cinnamon bread.

Nieuwezijds Voorburgwal 226, Old Centre ☎ 421 8344

☆ A TASTE OF IRELAND *D6*

Hunkering for the home country? Check out the homemade soda bread and Guinness. Other imports – from the whole of the British Isles – include haggis, pies, and sausages.

Herengracht 228, The Canals ☎ 638 1642

Casa Molero
♯D1

Where borders merge to bring the best of Spain and Portugal, and the most difficult choice is deciding which type of sausage to go for: *chorizo* or *linguica*.
Gerard Doustraat 66, De Pijp ☎ 676 1707

De Aanzet
♯B1

For the health-conscious, this tiny biodynamic health food cooperative offers old-world charm and good wholesome food.
Frans Halsstraat 27, De Pijp ☎ 673 3415

De Kaaskamer
♯E6

Beat the Dutch record of an annual 14 kilos of cheese per person with this selection of local and international cheeses.
Runstraat 7, The Canals ☎ 623 3483

☆ DE NATUURWINKEL
♯F11

Health food heaven. Alongside organic alternatives to regular supermarket products, you'll find sediment-rich beers, spicy samosas, sugar-free chocs plus cosmetics, incense, and candles.
Weteringschans 133, The Canals ☎ 638 4083

☆ DE PEPERBOL
♯C14

Spice up your rice and free up your tea. Hundreds of herbs, condiments, and flavoured brews, all labelled in a variety of languages. Plus accessories to squeeze, grind, and shake them up.
Albert Cuypstraat 150, De Pijp ☎ 673 7519

De Pepperwortel
♯C9

Picnic baskets of goodies in the summer, and great deli food and wines all year round.
Overtoom 140, Museum Districts & Vondelpark ☎ 685 1053

De Thai Shop
♯C8

Every ingredient for turning out fabulous Thai food at home.
Koningsstraat 42, Red Light District & Nieuwmarkt ☎ 620 9900

☆ EICHOLTZ
♯A11

Specialists in imported products from America, England, France, and Germany. Especially hot on cereals and chocolate, there's a useful range of edible Dutch souvenirs like tiny homemade Edams.
Leidsestraat 48, The Canals ☎ 622 0305

he Filipino Foodstore & Toko   ♫D14

xotic ingredients and takeaway. Filipino classics like *pansit* (noodles)
nd handmade *loempias* (egg spring rolls).
e Sweelinckstraat 20, De Pijp ☎ 673 4309

endrikse Le Confiseur   ♫ off map

inish off the perfect alfresco dining experience with handmade
onbons and extravagant patisserie.
vertoom 448–450, Museum District & Vondelpark ☎ 618 0260

G Beune   ♫B2

crumptious handmade bonbons.
Haarlemmerdijk 156–158, Haarlem ☎ 624 8356

☆ KWEKKEBOOM   ♫A12

ou can find a *kroket* (croquette) in every fast-food joint in the city, but
his baker does the best ragout-filled snack around. Also good for
ausage rolls, sweet pastries, and chocolate.
eguliersbreesstraat 36, Old Centre. ☎ 623 1205

☆ LE MARCHÉ   ♫C7

he Vroom & Dreesmann in-store bakery (with separate entrance),
vhose panini, pizzas and mini-quiches – all cooked on the spot – are a
odsend for busy shoppers who appreciate wholesome, flavoursome
ood. Crusty breads (with olives, garlic, and thyme) and nutbread can be
avoured later.
Kalverstraat 201–203, Old Centre ☎ 622 0171

a Tienda   ♫B14

ry the sensational sausages, wine, and pastas. Brings locals a great
election of Spanish and Italian treats.
e Sweelinckstraat 21, De Pijp ☎ 671 2519

☆ LOEKIE DELICATESSEN   ♫D12

Wine and cheese specialist extraordinaire. Over 100 European cheeses,
10 types of port, some wicked Dutch wines, peppery homemade pâtés,
and succulent salads.
Utrechtsestraat 57, The Canals ☎ 624 3740

☆ MEEUWIG & ZOON   ♫D3

f you're low on edible oil, head here for a refill. There's bottles of the stuff
– olive, coconut, pumpkin seed, and pricey ones that have been in vats for
50 years or more – plus vinegar spiked with saffron.
Haarlemmerstraat 70, Haarlemmer & Westerpark ☎ 626 5286

Olivaria's
$F

Foodies should investigate this mind boggling selection of olive oils from all round the world.

Hazenstraat 2a, Jordaan ☎ 638 3552

☆ ORIENTAL COMMODITIES
$F

Busy Chinatown *toko* for eastern exotica such as dried jellyfish, water chestnuts, frozen lime leaves, and ginseng. Non-food items include *sake* sets, chopsticks, and kites.

Nieuwmarkt 27, Red Light District & Nieuwmarkt ☎ 626 2797

☆ PASTA PANINI
$D

A busy spot for all things Italian: packaged *panforte* from Siena, ready-to-eat roast artichokes from Rome as well as Vin Santo, ricotta, and Amaretto. Plus fresh-filled ciabattas to take away.

Rozengracht 80, Jordaan ☎ 622 9466

☆ PAUL ANNEE
$E

This is your best bet for bread fashioned from exclusively organic ingredients, sticky, sugar-free apple cakes, and preservative-free pizzas.

Runstraat 25, The Canals ☎ 623 5322

☆ POMPADOUR CHOCOLATERIE
$E

Designer chocolates and cakes to savour in the restful refinement of this tiny teashop, or to take away for a later indulgence.

Huidenstraat 12, The Canals ☎ 623 9554

☆ PUCCINI BOMBONI
$B

Chic chocolates in a stylish, modern interior. They all look good and taste even better, even if they do contain some weird ingredients like thyme and lemon grass. There's another branch on Staalstraat.

Singel 184, The Canals ☎ 427 8341

Ron's Groenten en Fruit
$E

For the best fruit and veg, Ron's Groenten en Fruit is where it's at. American ex-pat Ron also has great takeaways, from chocolate mousse to pasta with a porcini sauce.

Huidenstraat 26, The Canals ☎ 626 1668

Runneboom
$A14

Bread to accompany all cultural cuisines can be found at this, the UN of bakeries. Selections from Russia, Turkey, and Ireland, as well as the Netherlands.

1e Van der Helststraat 49, De Pijp ☎ 673 5941

in's Toko
♭A14

...nown locally as a *toko*, stocks mainly Indonesian specialties like *nasi*- ...ice) or *bami*- (noodle) based dishes; it also has strange crossover items ...ke American candy and Hellman's mayonnaise, as well as all the bits ...nd pieces to make sushi.

Van der Helstraat 64, De Pijp ☎ 671 7708

Wah Nam Hong
♭A8

...n Asian supermarket that spans the full range of Chinese and Japanese ...aples as well as bits and bobs from Asia.

eldersekade 90, Red Light District & Nieuwmarkt ☎ 627 0303

☆ YOLANDA & FRED DE LEEUW
♭D12

...ine meats for the connoisseur: Japanese *kobe* beef, pata *negra* ham, ...rench *gascon* (pork), and salami from the best Italian smoking houses. ...us magic mushrooms of a different kind – morels, *ceps*, and truffles.

trechtsestraat 92, The Canals ☎ 623 0235

urniture

☆ MANUFACTURED ORIGINALS
♭E6

...dark showroom at the forefront of Dutch new minimalist design, the ...oberly shaped furniture bears the trademark of local architect Jen ...lkema. All the pieces on show here are Alkema, hence the name ...Manufactured Originals.

erenstraat 11, The Canals ☎ 620 0677

☆ POL'S POTTEN
♭ off map

...Housed in an old cocoa warehouse, Pol's Potten is chock-a-block with its ...wn-label furniture called 'Wood', together with tables made out of ...frican woods, multicoloured glassware, and quality toys like small ...vooden scooters. It is a real Aladdin's cave.

KNSM-laan 39, Oosterdok ☎ 419 3541

gay shops

☆ BLACK BODY
♭F5

...overs of latex mustn't miss this, the biggest collection of rubber ...etishwear in Europe.

ijnbaansgracht 292, Jordaan ☎ 626 2553

☆ INTERMALE GAY BOOKSTORE
♭F6

...Carries more highbrow stock – next to the erotica, there are shelves of ...poetry, plays, and art.

puistraat 251, Old Centre ☎ 625 0009

☆ **MR B**   *$E*

Specializes in stylish accessories for piercings, postcards, magazines, an
prints.

Warmoesstraat 89, Old Centre ☎ 422 0003

☆ **ROB AMSTERDAM**   *$E*

To get studs, spikes, or strategically placed zips on your leathers head this wa

Warmoesstraat 32, Old Centre ☎ 420 8548

☆ **ROBIN & RIK**   *$E*

Jackets, trousers, caps, and belts – all crafted on the spot – kit out many
local leather boy.

Runstraat 30, The Canals ☎ 627 8924

☆ **VROLIJK GAY & LESBIAN BOOKSHOP**   *$E*

Offers a varied browse, from novels and biographies to travel guide
comic books, and popular non-fiction

Paleisstraat 135, Old Centre ☎ 623 5142

☆ **XANTIPPE UNLIMITED**   *$E*

More of a women's pot of gold than a gay store, Xantippe Unlimited ha
a lot of lesbian literature and the top floor is devoted entirely to women'
studies. It also stocks girlie glossies, feminist postcards, and books t
interest boys.

Prinsengracht 290, The Canals ☎ 623 5854

gifts

Abracadabra   *$C1*

Grown-ups who like to escape into fantasy worlds stock up on Indiar
treasures like glittering jewellery and wildly kitsch Ganesh and Shiv
lamps here.

Sarphatipark 24, De Pijp ☎ 676 6683

Blue Gold Fish   *$D*

Specializes in goofy, one-of-a-kind gifts like quasi-religious lamps, pin-u
girl cuff links, and dazzling diamante jewellery.

Rozengracht 17, Jordaan ☎ 623 3134

Okado   *$D1*

Truly unique gifts are harder and harder to come by these days, but here
everything is hand-crafted and lovingly painted by handicapped people.

1e Sweelinckstraat 18, De Pijp ☎ 690 9491

Unique, whimsical one-offs from international artists. Clocks, jewellery, lamps – all inspired creations combining magic and fun. Ask to put a coin in the Marilyn and leave with a smile on your face...
Rusland 22, Old Centre ☎ 420 2813

hats

☆ DE HOED VAN TIJN
F7

Alongside the Stetsons, Borsalinos, and berets, you'll find vintage headgear and inspired one-offs. Plus felts, feathers, and sequins to tart up your own titfer.
Nieuwe Hoogstraat 15, Red Light District & Nieuwmarkt ☎ 623 2759

☆ HOEDEN M/V
B11

Quality headgear in a classy canalhouse interior. The hand-stitched leather creations by Patricia Underwood are to die for (and your wallet will); Orla Kiely's designs cater for a clubbier crowd, and loads of other designer lids for anyone weakened by whim.
Herengracht 422, The Canals ☎ 626 3038

headshops

☆ CONSCIOUS DREAMS KOKOPELLI
B7

For the style-conscious user, this place is a trip in itself. In this psychedelic cavern, you can pick up herbal Es, peyote, and sex stimulants, check your hotmail, and plug into a brain machine in a chill-out space overlooking a canal.
Warmoesstraat 12, Red Light District & Nieuwmarkt ☎ 421 7000

☆ THE HEADSHOP
F7

A throwback to the 60s that still reeks of patchouli. This is the place for hash pipes, papers, bongs, and even buddhas. It also does a sideline in quick-hit tool kits for perfect powder preparation.
Kloveniersburgwal 39, Red Light District & Nieuwmarkt ☎ 624 9061

☆ INNER SPACE
B6

Inner Space offers henna tattoos, live DJs on Thursday evenings, and a fridge full of high-energy beverages.
Spuistraat 108, Old Centre ☎ 624 3338

☆ INTERPOLM
F3

Caters for the sophisticated traditionalist – seeds, hardware, and advice for successful home cannabis culture, plus recipe books to blow your dinner guests' minds.
Prins Hendrikkade 11, Old Centre ☎ 627 7750

☆ **SENSI SEED BANK** *♭F7*
There's a staggering selection of seeds at the Sensi Seed Bank as well as books, videos, T-shirts, and cosmetics.
Achterburgwal 150, Red Light District & Nieuwmarkt ☎ 624 0386

interiors

☆ **BINNENHUIS** *♭E6*
The multi-storey Binnenhuis majors in sober design and subtly coloured fabrics. It stocks Faas Van Dijk, one of the Netherlands' most popular designers; has its own home decoration collection, and an assortment of unique accessories like Vietnamese *objets*, African Ashanti statue-stools, and hand-blown glassware.
Huidenstraat 3–5, The Canals ☎ 638 2957

Colorique *♭E6*
Swathe your home in bejewelled lamps, hot pink mosquito nets, and mountains of satiny pillows in every colour of the rainbow.
Huidenstraat 30, The Canals ☎ 626 1632

De Emaillerkeizer *♭B14*
Carry the Asian theme into the whole house by decorating it like an Indian bazaar, complete with giant pink plastic chandeliers, enamelled pots, and plastic wicker chairs from De Emaillerkeizer.
1e Sweelinckstraat 15, De Pijp ☎ 664 1847

Dom *♭F6*
For a modernist experience at a minimalist price. Mass-produced up-to-the-minute interior *objets* at jaw-dropping prices.
Spuistraat 281, Old Centre ☎ 428 5544

For Ever *♭D5*
This shop verges on the weird, with things like transparent toilet seats filled with pasta, and dead butterflies in toothbrush handles. They'll cast anything in acrylic for you and posterity.
Rozengracht 51, Jordaan ☎ 423 3388

☆ **FROZEN FOUNTAIN** *♭A11*
The place for up-and-coming designers, Frozen Fountain is the showground for all things new, and is great for original pressies. It has its own fabric department, ceramics from Hell Jonerius, and jewellery by Ben Hucklesby. Once a year it has an exhibition of wacky work by promising design students.
Prinsengracht 629, The Canals ☎ 622 9375

☆ KASSTOOR   ♯D5
This mega-store for interior design (with the same owner-buyer as Koot Light Design) has furniture by all the big names: Corbusier, Rietveld, Citerio, and Sipek.
Rozengracht 202–210, Jordaan ☎ 521 8112

☆ KIS   ♯D6
All the objects on display at Galerie KIS are handmade – they call it 'craft-design'. The slick pieces are by both students and self-taught enthusiasts. The lamps, furniture, and accessories, like small candleholders, are all unique, but can be reproduced on request.
Paleisstraat 107, Old Centre ☎ 620 9760

☆ KITSCH KITCHEN   ♯A6
Resembling a Mexican *mercado*, Kitsch Kitchen stocks multi-coloured plastic bits and pieces for the kitchen as well as religious kitsch, colourful bead curtains, Ghanaian cupboards of recycled cans, and strangest of all, old wallpaper. If it's weird, it's here.
1e Bloemdwarsstraat 21, Jordaan ☎ 622 8261

☆ KOOT LIGHT DESIGN   ♯D6
Hot on lighting, Koot carries everything from modern chandeliers to clean structurist standard lamps.
Raadhuisstraat 55, The Canals ☎ 626 4830

Nic Nic   ♯D6
A jumble of housewares, and small furnishings, with the very best of kitsch.
Gasthuismolensteeg 5, The Canals ☎ 622 8523

☆ OUTRAS COISAS   ♯E3
At Outras Coisas you'll find garden furniture from France, earthenware from southern Europe, and cast iron tables from Holland. Some things are old, some new, but always – as the name suggests – different.
Herenstraat 31, The Canals ☎ 625 7281

The Present   ♯C11
Ceramics and *tchotchkes* from the 50s to the 70s abound.
Prinsengracht 750, The Canals ☎ 622 6635

☆ SCANDINAVIA FORM   ♯D11
This basement interiors store promotes the work of over 30 Scandinavian designers and craftspeople. Ice-cold colours and textures predominate in the stock of sculpture, painting, textiles, glass, and ceramics.
Spiegelgracht 2, The Canals ☎ 622 3088

☆ **TRUNK**   *♂F6*

A rather magical mixture of a Moroccan-Indian bazaar, with a hint of Thailand, where lanterns sit next to earthenware, toothpicks next to aluminium ricepots. Photographers and stylists flock here to see what's new on the scene.

Rosmarijnsteeg 12, Old Centre ☎ 638 7095

☆ **WONEN 2000**   *♂D5*

This huge design shop sells lots of furniture from international names and loads of accessories by Dutch designers like Vincent Van Rijk and Marcel Wanders. Philippe Starck and other classics can also be found here. Prices vary, but Starck chairs go for around ƒ200 and limited editions for up to ƒ7500.

Rozengracht 219–223, Jordaan ☎ 521 8710

☆ **WORLD OF WONDERS**   *♂F9*

Dedicated to Asian as well as European products, this shop carries major brands like Versace and Fendi. It also has a range of more affordable gifts like Japanese incense, seashell spoons, furry cushions, and cutesy tea-sets.

PC Hooftstraat 129, Museum District & Vondelpark ☎ 470 7332

jewellery

Anneke Schat   *♂C11*

Just as enticing is a one-off from local artist Anneke Schat, who sells her original jewellery and paintings at her tiny workshop-boutique.

Spiegelgracht 20a, The Canals ☎ 625 1608

☆ **BEAUFORT**   *♂E7*

Minimal contemporary designs in 18-carat gold and silver by Burgersdijk and Peters, who are happy to leave their workshop to serve and advise. Innovative and bold pieces, including unusual wedding rings.

Grimburgwal 11, Old Centre ☎ 625 9131

☆ **BIBA**   *♂F7*

Novel jewellery from America, France, Thailand, Denmark, and South America including Scooter, JP Gaultier, Bronti Bay, and – Hillary Clinton's favourite – John Hardy. Bags and belts too. If it's hot, it's here.

Nieuwe Hoogstraat 26, Red Light District & Nieuwmarkt ☎ 330 5721

BLGK Edelsmeden   *♂C6*

Give one of these talented Dutch jewellers free rein to design your wedding ring or get a lovely Byzantine one from their ready-to-wear collection.

Hartenstraat 28, The Canals ☎ 624 8154

shops

☆ CHRISTOPHER CLARKE ⌖B6
Designs range from lightweight lacquered aluminium earrings – organic and shell-like – to more trad 22-carat gold necklaces dripping with Austrian crystal.
Molsteeg 4, Old Centre ☎ 620 0017

Galerie Ra ⌖D11
Collect, exhibit, or just be plain flashy in these stunning artworks. This extravaganza of jewellery by international designers ranges from wearable to downright futuristically sculptural.
Vijzelstraat 80, The Canals ☎ 626 5100

☆ GOLDLIEF ⌖C7
Whimsical and sparkly originals from Israel, San Francisco, France, and Italy – plus its own innovative designs. An eclectic collection in a tiny shop behind the Nieuwe Kerk.
Nieuwezijds Voorburgwal 143, Old Centre ☎ 622 4876

☆ INEZ STODEL ⌖D11
A treasure trove of beautiful old jewellery,
Nieuwe Spiegelstraat 65, The Canals ☎ 623 2942

lingerie

☆ ROBIN'S BODYWEAR ⌖F7
Sleek and sporty, but not shy of an occasional frill, this is an accessible store stocking Calvin Klein, Aubade, Naf Naf, and more. Unobtrusive service and big fitting room.
Nieuwe Hoogstraat 20, Red Light District & Nieuwmarkt ☎ 620 1552

☆ SALON DE LINGERIE ⌖D12
This is a classy joint for classy ladies, and is the place to pick up a feather-fringed negligee or silk suspenders. Popular lines are: Nina Ricci, Christian Dior, Wacoal, and Millesia.
Utrechtsestraat 38, The Canals ☎ 623 9857

maps

Jacob van Wijngaarden ⌖C9
For those venturing further afield, this store has a dizzying array of travel guides, nautical charts, and maps.
Overtoom 97, Museum District & Vondelpark ☎ 612 1901

shops

☆ ALBERT CUYP MARKT   ♫C14
For regular fruit and veg, head to the biggest (it stretches a kilometre) and noisiest general market in town – food, cheap and cheerful clothing, repro antiques, bits and pieces from the Dutch colonies, and the odd off-the-back-of-a-lorry bargain. While ogling the fresh fish displays to a soundtrack of salsa and reggae, make sure you try a hot, sweet 'n' sticky *stroopwafel* (treacle waffle), griddled on the spot.
Albert Cuypstraat, De Pijp

☆ BLOEMENMARKT   ♫A12
Busy, but fragrant, is the Bloemenmarkt (flower market) on the Singel – a bit touristy, but the cut flowers are cheap and there's a great selection.
Singel, The Canals

☆ BOEKENMARKT   ♫F6
Peeling paperbacks, on a wide variety of subjects, collectors' tomes, and that copy of *Life* from the year you were born can be found at the Boekenmarkt on the Spui. As with most book collections in Amsterdam, the English is mixed in with the rest.
Spui, Old Centre

☆ BOERENMARKT   ♫E3
The Boerenmarkt is Amsterdam's Saturday farmers' market. All the produce (bread, cheese, pâtés, and pickles) is organic and both hawkers and punters are an alternative lot which makes for a laid-back, New-Age atmosphere (a smaller version can be found at the Nieuwmarkt on Saturdays).
Noordermarkt, Jordaan

☆ DE ROMMELMARKT   ♫ off map
Rommelmarkt (jumble market), in front of the city hall, has a fleamarket atmosphere, with piles of old LPs, 60s kitsch, and chunky glassware.
Waterlooplein

☆ KUNSTMARKT   ♫F6
Treasures with broad appeal can be found at the Kunstmarkt (Art Market) on the Spui, where local artists display pretentious pottery and overpriced jewellery – but you might find something that appeals.
Spui, Old Centre

☆ LINDENGRACHT ♭D2
Saturday is the day for Amsterdam's coziest general market.
Lindengracht, Jordaan

☆ MARKT OP DE AMSTELVELD ♭ off map
A horticultural hang-out, where amateur gardeners stock up on geraniums, rose bushes, and fresh herb plants in one of the most secluded squares in town.
Amstelveld, The Canals

☆ NIEUWMARKT ♭C8
For a junk fix on a Sunday (summers only), explore a motley collection of antiques and curiosa.
Nieuwmarkt, Red Light District & Nieuwmarkt

☆ NOORDERMARKT ♭E3
Dedicated browsers stroll amongst deco-to-60s paraphernalia before meeting for coffee and apple pie in one of the cafés round the Noorderkerk.
Noordermarkt, Jordaan

Oudemananhuispoort Boekenmarkt ♭F7
A secluded spot, deep in the heart of Amsterdam academia, the Oudemanhuispoort Boekenmarkt is a covered walkway where old books and prints are set out for leisurely perusal.
Oudemananhuispoort, Old Centre

☆ POSTZEGELMARKT ♭A7
Men in raincoats pore over plastic-covered coin and stamp collections, intent on their precious treasures.
Nieuwezijds Voorburgwal, Old Centre

☆ WATERLOOPLEIN MARKT ♭ off map
Dealing in sought-after junk for over a century. Despite the recent influx of imported crafts from Thailand and Indonesia, there's still room for plenty of hip gear, most of it secondhand. Great for cheap clubby stuff, leather jackets, and kitsch Dutch bric-a-brac.
Old Centre

☆ WESTERSTRAAT ♭F2
General market goods and fabrics appear along here on Monday mornings.
Westerstraat, Jordaan

shops

Didato
♭F9
Men into utility wear and crisp clean lines hit Didato.
PC Hooftstraat 94a, Museum District & Vondelpark ☎ 671 9283

☆ HUGO BOSS
♭F9
Clean lines, bold colours, and luxurious fabrics distinguish this German design house from the best of the rest. Essentially a menswear outfit, Boss fashions some surprising twists on classic looks and sportswear for both sexes.
PC Hooftstraat 49–51, Museum District & Vondelpark ☎ 364 0412

☆ MAN TALK
♭B11
This is the place to find the trendiest and most complete collection of men's underwear and swimwear in town. Rubbing shoulders with Calvin Klein, D&G, Versace, and Armani are hot Dutch designers Xcitement and I'll Dress U.
Reguliersdwarsstraat 39, Old Centre ☎ 627 2525

☆ 2 π R
♭D7
Two adjacent, designer-driven stores for lads with a need to look good. One carries cutting edge clubwear – from Vivienne Westwood's Anglomania, D2, and Helmut Lang; the other stocks more street-oriented threads by Psycho Cowboy and Suspect.
Oude Hoogstraat 10–12, Red Light District & Nieuwmarkt ☎ 421 6329

night shops

☆ DE AVONDMARKT
♭A2
Especially good for hot baguettes, cheese, and wine.
De Wittenkade 94, Haarlemmer & Westerpark ☎ 686 4919

☆ DOLF AVONDVERKOOP
♭D2
Small, but with all the basics – including hot snacks.
Willemsstraat 79, Jordaan ☎ 625 9503

☆ STERK
♭ off map
Along with all the emergency late-night essentials, it's hot on champagne.
Waterlooplein 241, Old Centre ☎ 626 5097

☆ BETSY PALMER
C7

Hip and chaotic, this funky local initiative specializes in keenly priced, own-label footwear: fluffy mules, jelly bean sandals, and other fun treats for feet.

Rokin 9–15, Old Centre ☎ 422 1040

Dr Adams
F9

This store is a down-to-earth, local favourite – Dr Adams sells sassy shoes at a good price.

PC Hooftstraat 90, Museum District & Vondelpark ☎ 662 3835

☆ FRED DE LA BRETONIÈRE
D12

Nothing extreme, but stylish and hip nonetheless. The natural-look interior hints at the untreated leather used in the sophisticated but chic shoes, bags, and accessories by this Dutch designer with a French-sounding name.

Utrechtsestraat 77, The Canals ☎ 626 9627

Free Lance Shoes
E7

If you require a bit more from a shop than clinical rows of shoes on shelves, let the twisty wrought-iron interior by English designer John Eager distract you from the prices; their footwear is stylish, utilitarian, and modern.

Rokin 86, Old Centre ☎ 420 3205

Gucci
F9

Gucci's one-stop accessory heaven for pricey but ultra-cool shoes, belts, and bags.

PC Hooftstraat 56, Museum District & Vondelpark ☎ 470 4269

Mare
A11

Three floors of seductive shoes make even hardened fashionistas drool.

Leidsestraat 79, The Canals ☎ 620 1564

☆ PAUL WARMER
A11

This stylish minimalist interior invites leisurely browsing of the latest from Gucci, DKNY, Sergio Rossi, and D&G with lots of innovative fastenings. Glamour rules here.

Leidsestraat 41, The Canals ☎ 427 8011

shops

Sacha
♭E7
Funky shoes for slaves of fashion.
Kalverstraat 161, Old Centre ☎ 627 2160

☆ SEVENTY FIVE
♭F7
Sneakers – for clubbin' and cruisin' rather than runnin' – are displayed for
quick, easy selection in one of the leanest interiors in town. Choose from
Aussie label Royal Elastics, classy Italian LFP and Diesel, Converse, Nike,
Puma, and Acupuncture.
Nieuwe Hoogstraat 24, Red Light District & Nieuwmarkt ☎ 626 4611

☆ SHOEBALOO
♭B11
Designer wearables by Prada, Patrick Cox, Miu Miu, and Girbaud – plus
the store's own more affordable, but still trendy line. You might need to
tear the staff away from their regular preening sessions to be able to see
a mirror though.
Koningsplein 7, Old Centre ☎ 626 7993

souvenir shops

☆ HET KANTENHUIS
♭E7
This is the place for linen and lace – for your windows and tables. Much
of it with a Dutch touch (windmill and tulip motifs). The fabrics are both
tasteful and traditional.
Kalverstraat 124, Old Centre ☎ 624 8618

☆ THE MILL SHOP
♭E7
One of the oldest souvenir shops in the city. Alongside the usual fridge
magnets, tankards and tulip-tipped umbrellas are antique dolls and very
pricey Delft porcelain originals.
Langebrugsteeg 2, Old Centre ☎ 627 6774

☆ 'T KLOMPENHUIS
♭F7
Tired of tulips? Cheesed off with cheese? Then get kitted out with clogs:
cow-hide, coloured leather, plain, painted, or for kids.
Nieuwe Hoogstraat 9a, Red Light District & Nieuwmarkt ☎ 622 8100

speciality stores

☆ ART UNLIMITED
♭B11
Thousands of postcards by artists and photographers, and on a variety of
subjects – all arranged alphabetically. Calendars and posters too.
Keizersgracht 510, The Canals ☎ 624 8419

Backstage *D5*

If it's faces you're painting, Backstage supplies stage make-up, wigs, brushes, and wild-coloured hair dyes.

Rozengracht 68–70, The Canals ☎ 622 1267

☆ **CHRISTMAS WORLD** *B7*

Four floors of year-round Christmas kitsch – from singin', hip-shakin' Santas to luminous icicles and mini-Mondrians for hanging on your tree. Such wintry wonders are imported from around the world, but the focus is definitely Dutch.

Damrak 33, Old Centre ☎ 420 2838

☆ **COPENHAGEN 1001 KRALEN** *D5*

Decorative fare for the nimble-fingered. Thousands of beads in wood, plastic, bone, original Venetian glass, and genuine medieval trade beads. Plus assorted jewellery-making accessories.

Rozengracht 54, Jordaan ☎ 624 3681

☆ **DE KNOPENWINKEL** *E6*

A pearly emporium to the humble button. Handmade, vintage, mother-of-pearl, bone, brocade, and Chanel – all displayed in this store's warm, welcoming interior.

Wolvenstraat 14, The Canals ☎ 624 0479

☆ **DE KRAMER KAARSEN** *C6*

Smelly candles, decorative candles, even birthday candles.

Reestraat 18-20, The Canals ☎ 626 5274

☆ **DE WITTE TANDENWINKEL** *E7*

Serious and silly things for teeth: from toothcare sets for travellers to glow-in-the-dark, natural wood, and cartoon-character brushes.

Runstraat 5, The Canals ☎ 623 3443

For Ever *D5*

This shop verges on the weird, with things like transparent toilet seats filled with pasta, and dead butterflies in toothbrush handles. They'll cast anything in acrylic for you and posterity.

Rozengracht 51, Jordaan ☎ 423 3388

☆ **FREUD & CO** *E6*

Sharpen up your kitchen skills with knives by Global, pans by All-Clad and Fissla, and terracotta ovenware from Spain. A small selection of quality, good-looking kitchen tools, and accessories.

Runstraat 2, The Canals ☎ 624 5407

Greenlands *♭D12*
Earth-friendly hemp clothes.
Utrechtsestraat 26, The Canals ☎ 625 1100

Intertaal *♭B10*
If you want to learn the local lingo while you're on your travels, Intertaal has rows and rows of dictionaries and language aids from Albanian to Zulu.
Van Baerlestraat 76, Museum District & Vondelpark ☎ 575 6756

☆ JOE'S VLIEGERWINKEL *♭F7*
Go buy a kite – or a boomerang, a frisbee, a diabolo, or, well, anything that flies really. Racers, stunt kites, and kites for kids – ready-mades, and raw materials. Plus tips from the pros.
Nieuwe Hoogstraat 19, Red Light District & Nieuwmarkt ☎ 625 0139

La Botanica *♭C3*
At the top end of the mystical/wacky scale, La Botanica specializes in white magic and herbal remedies.
Haarlemmerstraat 109, Haarlem ☎ 622 2917

☆ LAMBIEK *♭A11*
This is the place to find underground and mainstream comic strips and related trivia. Indulge your penchant for Popeye or your soft spot for the Simpsons in this award-winning store/gallery – it's been a scene since the 60s.
Kerkstraat 78, The Canals ☎ 626 7543

Quadra Original Posters *♭B11*
For the very best in posters from the turn of the last century to the present, from magical old circus posters to lurid B-movie schmaltz.
Herengracht 383, The Canals ☎ 626 9472

☆ SANTA JET *♭E3*
Electric-coloured crafts from Mexico: mirrors with gaudy hammered tin frames, travelling altars (pricey originals and cheaper modern fakes), and kitsch, religious car accessories are displayed in a vibrant, mosaic-decorated interior. Some serious art too.
Prinsenstraat 7, The Canals ☎ 427 2070

Schaak En Go Het Paard *♭C3*
If you prefer sedate activity, choose from the fab selection of games.
Haarlemmerdijk 147, Haarlem ☎ 624 1171

A Space Oddity _C6_
Although specializing in _Star Wars_ artefacts, fans of _Star Trek_, _Batman_, _Spiderman_, _James Bond_, _the Muppet-show_, _Love Boat_, or _Charlie's Angels_ shouldn't miss this shop either. The owner stocks as much film and TV merchandise as possible. Space toys, robots, and action figures from comics and films abound.
Prinsengracht 204, The Canals ☎ 427 4036

Van der Linde _D5_
Artists can find all their supplies to paint, sculpt, draw, and more at Van Der Linde
Rozengracht 36–38, Jordaan ☎ 624 2791

sportswear

Aqua Diving _C3_
Get yourself decked out for a day of diving, ice skating, or roller-blading. Supplying everything you'll need to look and act the part, they both hire and sell the essential gear.
Haarlemmerstraat 165, Haarlemer & Vesterpark ☎ 622 3503

☆ DUO INTERSPORT _D6_
Amsterdam's biggest sports store. Whether you like to skate, hike, run, or snowboard – or just want to look like you do – this is the place.
Raadhuisstraat 30–40, The Canals ☎ 530 4160

☆ RDLF'S _off map_
For serious skaters (fitness, aggressive, distance) and BMX-ers (flatland and street), there are skateboards, longboards, accessories, clothes, and flyers for all local events. Europe's first skate specialists now have three city outlets (smaller branches in Magna Plaza and Utrechtsestraat).
Sarphatistraat 59, Oost ☎ 622 5488

Tom's Outlet _F7_
Skateboards can be found at Tom's Outlet, which also carries a cool collection of clothes and shoes for an all-in-one stopover.
Nieuwe Hoogstraat 13, Red Light District & Nieuwmarkt ☎ 428 2101

stationery

☆ ORDNING & REDA _D6_
Simple, bold, and colourful stationery styles that haven't stood still. This Swedish paper chain blends trend with tradition in fun and functional products to sass up the dullest of desks.
Magna Plaza, Nieuwezijds Voorburgwal 182, Old Centre ☎ 422 8366

Benetton ♯B11
Familiar favourites in every colour from this Italian chain.
Kalverstraat 19, Old Centre ☎ 626 9150

Claudia Strater ♯E7
Stark wardrobe staples in sumptuous fabrics.
Kalverstraat 179, Old Centre ☎ 622 0559

☆ ESPRIT ♯E7
Sharp coordinates from the States: sporty essentials, smart accessories, and timeless, conservative classics. The minimalist interior includes a popular café.
Spui 10, Old Centre ☎ 626 3624

Guess? ♯B11
For luscious Lolitas who favour second-skin jeans and fluffy sweaters.
Kalvertoren, Singel 457, Old Centre ☎ 427 9051

☆ HENXS ♯F7
A hip (hop) hangout for fashion-conscious graffiti artists, complete with cans of spray paint and insider mags. Hooded jackets and baggy trousers by gsuss (design duo breaking into the big time); accessories by Carhartt; and even live DJs upstairs.
Sint Antoniesbreestraat 136, Red Light District & Nieuwmarkt ☎ 416 7786

☆ LAUNDRY INDUSTRY ♯E7
Minimalist Dutch design is distilled here into both clothes and decor. The stark separates are equally at home in clubs, media workplaces, and other hip haunts and are executed in quality fabrics only – lambswool, cashmere, and fine cottons. The austere interior conceals surprising visual elements (like mini aquariums).
Spui 1, Old Centre ☎ 420 2554

Mango ♯D6
Funky day and evening separates.
Magna Plaza, Nieuwe-zijds Voorburgwal 182, Old Centre ☎ 422 9500

Marks & Spencer ♯E7
Everyone's favourite ever-reliable store.
Kalverstraat 66–72, Old Centre ☎ 620 0006

shops

Mexx Lifestyle ♭F9
If your budget is tight, but you're willing to pay that bit extra for quality and style, try this store for cool, clean, modern clothes and accessories.
PC Hooftstraat 118–120, Museum District & Vondelpark ☎ 675 0171

Oilily ♭B10
Breakaway from black and get into colourful coordinates from this successful Dutch label. And don't be put off by the predominance of pink and orange – a purchase from this store will do wonders for flagging spirits, especially if it's accompanied by something from their toiletries line.
Van Baerlestraat 26, Museum District & Vondelpark ☎ 400 4543

Reflections ♭F9
Men and women with more conservative tastes look to these rails for classic clothes.
PC Hooftstraat 66–68, Museum District & Vondelpark ☎ 664 0040

☆ REPLAY ♭D6
Middle-of-the-road mode from Italy. Lots of denim and nothing very outrageous, though the e-play label does cater to customers with a funky streak. Accessories include sunglasses, and the kooky Japanese-themed decor embraces the polarity of Zen.
Magna Plaza, Spuistraat 137, Old Centre ☎ 638 8737

☆ SISSY BOY ♭B11
Own-label basics in regular styles and regular colours – for regular guys 'n' gals. An Amsterdam initiative, it stocks street clothes, smart gear, and nothing too shocking. Also carries French Connection and Migel Stapper.
Kalverstraat 199–210, Old Centre ☎ 638 9305

☆ STILETT ♭C7
T-shirts printed with tongue-in-cheek takes on well-known logos, and witty ways with words are tacked floor-to-ceiling on the walls of this streetwise store. The music's loud, the personnel chilled, and most designs original.
Damstraat 14, Red Light District & Nieuwmarkt ☎ 625 2854

toys

Bam Bam ♭D6
Looking for tasteful babyclothes or cuddly toys? Try Bam Bam, where a range of great baby accessories is offered, including bibs, bells, and rattles.
Magna Plaza, Nieuwezijds Voorburgwal 182, Old Centre ☎ 624 5215

☆ **DE BEESTENWINKEL** *♦F7*
Lots of toys can be found in this tiny animal theme store, but there are also chairs, tattoos, and jewellery too – all of which feature wacky representations of beasts.
Staalstraat 11, Old Centre ☎ 623 1805

Kinderfeestwinkel *♦A14*
The Kinderfeestwinkel sells everything to make a kids' party swing: from singing candles and small fountains that will brighten up a birthday cake, to materials to make masks for a party. The selection of fun clothes means kids can be transformed into a Peter Pan, witch, princess, pirate, or a fairy.
1e van der Helststraat 15, De Pijp ☎ 470 4791

Mechanisch Speelgoed *♦F2*
Nostalgic-looking toys can be found at this shop, including humming tops, kaleidoscopes, and other old-fashioned playthings. It also houses a large collection of brand new tin toys which appeal to kids and grown-ups alike and have the look of a different era altogether.
Westerstraat 67, Jordaan ☎ 638 1680

Pinokkio *♦D6*
Beautiful dolls' houses modelled on Amsterdam canalhouses can be found here. Kids can become proud house owners for a mere ƒ260. The store also sells mini furniture to go inside, as well as many other wooden toys.
Magna Plaza, Nieuwezijds Voorburgwal 182, Old Centre ☎ 622 8914

vintage clothes

Bis *♦D7*
This store is the place to go for Jackie-O style cocktail dresses, stacked shoes, and fabulous missile-coned bras and corsets, all from the 50s and 60s.
Sint Antoniesbree-straat 25a, Red Light District & Nieuwmarkt ☎ 620 3467

Exota *♦B5*
Funks things up with a mix of flashback fashion and modern streetwear and accessories for women.
Nieuwe Leliestraat 32, Jordaan ☎ 420 6884

shops

☆ JO JO OUTFITTERS $E6

Vintage menswear, most of it in pristine condition, kits out downtown dudes in vexed flying jackets, tailored suits with winkle-pickers, and 70s wing-collared shirts; two-tone cuff links optional.

Huidenstraat 23, The Canals ☎ 623 3476

☆ LADY DAY $C6

American separates, both worn and (never-before-worn) deadstock, from the 50s to the 70s, form the mainstay of this collection for men and women. Particularly good for plain white shirts, leather jackets, suits, and dresses.

Hartenstraat 9, The Canals ☎ 623 5820

☆ LAURA DOLS $E6

Lovers of lace, frills, and all things sparkly can rummage through rails of cocktail dresses from the 20s, pearl-buttoned blouses from the 30s, and Dior's numbers from the 40s. Plus dinky pillboxes, beaded evening bags, and second-skin gloves.

Wolvenstraat 7, The Canals ☎ 624 9066

Moriaan $F2

Hipper than thou vintage gear. Costs a bit more, but the garments are 'modern' vintage and usually in perfect condition.

2e Anjeliersdwaarsstraat 19, Jordaan ☎ 620 4798

☆ PUCK $F7

The classier, pricier end of the market. Pre-war wedding dresses, silk blouses from the 30s, and kimonos from Japan are just as popular as the bijoux, lace, and antique linen.

Nieuwe Hoogstraat 1a, Red Light District & Nieuwmarkt ☎ 625 4201

Wini $F3

Groovy secondhand clothes, ranging from the 50s to the 90s, for both men and women.

Haarlemmerstraat 29, Haarlem ☎ 427 9393

☆ ZIPPER $F7

A regular weekend haunt for a young crowd wanting affordable club gear. Two floors of colourful cardis, tank tops, fake fur, petticoats, masses of coats, and jeans, most from the 60s and 70s. Plus funky jewellery, cheap new accessories, and party flyers.

Nieuwe Hoogstraat 10, Red Light District & Nieuwmarkt ☎ 627 0353

Antiekhandel Lebbing ♯D11
Chocka with all sorts of collectables from furniture to vases and mirrors to shaving kits.
Prinsengracht 805–807, The Canals ☎ 624 1253

☆ BEBOP DESIGN INTERIORS ♯C11
Step into this store if you want to slip back into the 50s: slide into an easy chair, listen to the jukebox, and marvel at the patterned furniture. This store is a mini time warp selling period design classics from the 50s to the 70s.
Prinsengracht 764, The Canals ☎ 624 5763

☆ DE LOOIER ♯F5
Indoor antiques market offering anything from an art deco brooch to old Dutch lace.
Elandsgracht 109, Jordaan ☎ 624 9038

Keystone Novelty Store ♯E6
For more collectable madness. Not only do they sell vintage housewares, but owner Marlene also has a great selection of classic toys and board games.
Huidenstraat 28, The Canals ☎ 625 2660

Ritornare ♯A3
This is the place to find classic gear for your home. Ritornare carries vintage furnishings from the 50s on, including Versace dinnerware and Alessi's madcap kitchen gadgets.
Haarlemmerdijk 119, Haarlem ☎ 428 2548

Toetie Froetie ♯ off map
Where every corner holds secret delights.
Waterlooplein 175, Old Centre ☎ 625 6494

☆ WATERLOO WAREHOUSE ♯E8
Dig up the odd gem from among the piles of genuine junk.
Jodenbreestraat 144, Old Centre ☎ 420 7508

watches

☆ SWATCH STORE ♯B11
If you want to make sure your Swatch is the latest, make time for this tiny store – full of sassy straps and bright, funky faces.
Kalvertoren, Singel 457, Old Centre ☎ 422 8878

restaurants & eetcafés

The cynic would thank colonialism for the culinary state of Amsterdam. When Napoleon ruled this land, he stirred in a few palate-jolting southern European subtleties. When the Dutch ruled Indonesia, they added its spices and exotic recipes. And with the last decades of immigration and travel, they've resolutely embraced more than just the cow, the carrot, the potato, and the herring.

african & caribbean

De Tropen *♫D2*
Focuses on the cuisines of the Tropics, be it Cajun, African, or Caribbean, and offers a colourful rattan backdrop in which to savour such treats as red snapper baked in ginger.
Palmgracht 39, Jordaan ☎ 421 5528 *ff*

☆ ETHIOPISCHE RESTAURANT GENET *♫ off map*
After a sweat purge at the Fenomeen squat sauna around the corner or a bit of sport in the Vondelpark across the street, you can maintain a sense of health by coming here for the vegetarian-friendly Ethiopian food in an amiable and folkloristic atmosphere. With the thin and spongy *injera* (a kind of pancake) functioning as not only a staple food but as edible cutlery and plate, enjoy the variety of subtly spiced complex vegetable (there are also meat options) compounds that are piled liberally on top.
Amstelveensweg 152, Buitenveldert ☎ 673 4344 *f–ff*

☆ INDABA *♫D12*
Hurry to this beautifully designed South African restaurant/gallery where they grill a refined tribute to nature's most efficient chicken: the ostrich. They also serve other such free-range critters as zebra, springbok, and crocodile (the wine rule being: red with reptile), along with less surprising vegetarian and fish options. As an ancient crossroads and colony, South Africa has evolved true fusion cookery which combines the gentler tastes of Africa, India, and Europe. On Sundays and Mondays they host a *braai* when masses of meat is barbied over specially imported fragrant wood.
Utrechtsestraat 96, The Canals ☎ 421 3852 *ff–fff*

☆ KILIMANJARO
♫ off map

One can toss back palm-infused Mongozo beer from a calabash or sip on Ethiopian honey wine at this relaxed pan-African eatery, with a patio placed on a quiet square near the harbour. While their ever-changing menu tends to focus on *injera* (pancake-based) dishes of Ethiopia, they also serve favourites from Tanzania, Senegal, Kenya, South Africa, and Morocco. At the end, you'll have to be patient for your coffee: the beans and herbs are roasted specially for each pot.

Rapenburgerplein 6, Oosterdok ☎ 622 3485 *ff*

Lalibela
♫ off map

Cozy and folkloric, an Ethiopian specialist, serving delicious spiced veg and meat combinations on *injera* (pancakes). The incense smoke can get a tad pungent, but the financially challenged leave feeling sated and smug.

Eerste Helmersstraat 249, Vondelpark ☎ 683 8332 *ff–fff*

☆ RIAZ
♫A9

Ruud Gullit and many others score food from this utilitarian but comfy Surinami restaurant (the oldest and best in town), where the Caribbean gets touched up with Eastern spices. Meat and/or veg go along with rotis, rice and beans, *nasi* (spiced and herbed-up rice), and *bami* (spiced and herbed-up noodles). If packed, you can do a take-away to the nearby Vondelpark.

Bilderdijkstraat 193, Oude West ☎ 683 6453 *f–ff*

breakfast & brunch

☆ BARNEY'S BREAKFAST BAR
♫C3

International fry-ups are high up on the menu, as can be your state of mind since Barney's multi-tasks as a coffeeshop. An alternative way to start the day.

Haarlemmerstraat 102, Haarlemmer & Westerpark ☎ 625 9761 *f*

☆ CAFÉ PRINS
♫A6

Most brown cafés serve a selection of sandwiches (*broodjes*) and fried eggs (*uitsmijters*), but this one has a trad and true Dutch breakfast special: a variety of breads, a selection of toppings, a boiled egg, and a glass of freshly squeezed juice. Canal-side patio.

Prinsengracht 124, The Canals ☎ 624 9382 *f*

De IJsbreker
♫ off map

The place for breakfast/brunch malingerers as well as wine lovers, It is actually a low-key contemporary music centre and venue by night, but it's the terrace with Amstel riverside views that really sells the place by day. The calm is broken only by the rustle of broadsheets and the chink of white crockery.

Weesperzijde 23, Oost ☎ 668 1805 *ff*

☆ GREENWOODS   ⌖A7
Pressing all the Brit breakfast buttons: fry-ups, scones, crumpets, and a library of teas. Service can be slow due to its popularity. Canal-side patio too.
Singel 103, The Canals ☎ 623 7071 *f*

Lime   ⌖A7
The latest arrival on the scene promising regular sushi nights among its ambitions. But otherwise, its Sunday brunch, designer sandwiches, art-dotted minimalist decor, sofas, long hours, and open kitchen contrast heavily with the rest of the area, making it seem destined to become a local favourite among the chilled and arty.
Zeedijk 104, Red Light District & Nieuwmarkt ☎ 639 3020 *f*

't Balkje   ⌖A11
This restaurant, where you get served by charmingly loud and obnoxious Amsterdammers, is speedy in dishing out breakfast/brunch/lunch.
Kerkstraat 46–48, The Canals ☎ 622 0566 *f*

chinese

Albine   ⌖D13
A Suri-Indo-Chin snackbar where the Chinese influence wins out, staff can slide a quality and laughably cheap *roti* into a bag at lightning speed – or you can eat in, under the garish fluorescent lighting.
Albert Cuypstraat 69, De Pijp ☎ 675 5135 *f–ff*

Dim Sum Court   ⌖D7
Chooses to attract the punters on pure economics, offering all-you-can-eat-in-an-hour dim sum for a mere *f*15.
Zeedijk 109, Red Light District & Nieuwmarkt ☎ 638 1466 *f*

Lotus   ⌖C8
An impeccable reputation for quality, elegant stylings together with a happy hour (4–6.30pm), which gets you a plate full for *f*18.50.
**Binnen Bantammerstraat 5–7, Red Light District & Nieuwmarkt
☎ 624 2614** *f–fff*

☆ NAM KEE   ⌖D7
A universal favourite of cheap Chinese food lovers who don't seem to mind that they're dining in a white-tiled box with few pretensions towards the ornate. The friendly enough service can be occasionally slow due to sheer demand – but only because they obviously want to

maintain consistency in quality. Aphrodisiac lovers should try their sexily presented steamed oysters. They also do takeouts. Second location in the Red Light District at Geldersekade 117 (639 2848).
Zeedijk 111–113, Red Light District & Nieuwmarkt ☎ 624 3470 *f*

☆ **ORIENTAL CITY**   ⊘D7
While enjoying some of the city's best and most authentic dim sum, rest your bleary eyes on the bird's-eye view of the canal, Royal Palace, and Damstraat. But you don't have to be hung over: Chinese locals, romantic couples, and a scattering of tourists also seem to enjoy the food from the monolithic menu (with sub-volumes for wine and champagne).
**Oudezijds Voorburgwal 177–179, Red Light District & Nieuwmarkt
☎ 626 8352** *f–fff*

chips

Vlaamse Friteshuis   ⊘F6
Chunkier and crispier Belgian chips, best sampled while lurking with the pigeons on the cobblestone street outside
Voetboogstraat 31, Old Centre ☎ no phone *f*

club/restaurants

West Pacific   ⊘A2
Cool, calm and collected, this restaurant serves great food early on – think grilled bream topped with pepper and *schoog* (a spicy herbal mix) – before the tables are kicked back for a double helping of funky pie.
Haarlemmerweg 8-10, Haarlem & Westerpark ☎ 597 4458 *ff*

delivery

☆ **MOUSAKA EXPRESS**
Greek treats delivered to your door.
☎ 675 7000 *f–fff*

☆ **NEW YORK PIZZA**
Because most purveyors of Amster-pizza rely on a flimsy wet crust, we recommend this chunkier New World model.
☎ 445 0000 *f*

☆ **ONTBIJTSERVICE**
'Breakfast Service' brings you breakfast in bed – with a bubbly pseudo-champagne Henkell Trocken option. Must be ordered one day in advance.
☎ 669 3834 *ff–fff*

☆ **SUSHI KINGS**
ƒ32 gets you a solid and sating box of Dutch-touched sushi.
☎ 675 4836 *f–ff*

dutch

De Duvel *♯C14*
The well-dressed but style-free thirty-something crowd come back again and again for their grilled red snapper in white wine within its shrunken opera house-like interior.
1e Van der Helst-straat 59, De Pijp ☎ 675 7517 *f–ff*

De Roode Leeuw *♯C7*
Battle through Damrak's crowds into the unaltered classicism evoked by this time warped brasserie. It has the city's oldest heated terrace, an impressive champagne list, and serves up posh native fare on even posher silverware.
Damrak 93–94, Old Centre ☎ 555 0666 *ff–fff*

☆ **D'VIJFF VLIEGHEN** *♯F6*
Business folk in search of something 'different' are regular visitors to 'The Five Flies'. Head for this sprawling Golden Age envisioned dining institution – complete with a Knights' Hall and a Rembrandt Room with bona fide sketches – that will entertain chubby-walleted connoisseurs of kitsch. Serving well-prepared but slightly overpriced Dutch cuisine with a penchant for such ingredients as pigeon and pickled lamb's tongue, it's more about the atmospherics, which can be enhanced by the gargantuan wine list.
Spuistraat 294–302 (entrance at Vlieghendesteeg 1), Old Centre
☎ 625 8369 *fff*

☆ **KEUKEN VAN 1870** *♯F3*
For pure, unadulterated domestic Dutchness, don't miss this tile-and-wood, high-ceilinged former soup kitchen which has changed little in the past century: with the right lighting, it could be the setting of a Vermeer painting. Even the staff has probably only been replaced once. Chances are you'll be sharing a table, so be sure to say *eet smakelijk* (eat tasty!) when your dining companions tuck in. The bold and honest menu is made up of the Netherlands' favourite home-cooked victuals: meat (liver, beef, smoked sausage, chicken), veg (it varies, but count on carrots and peas), and potato (boiled or baked). Dead cheap mussels are seasonally available.
Spuistraat 4, Old Centre ☎ 624 8965 *f*

☆ **MOEDERS** ♪C5

If stomach and heart strings are tugging you homewards to mother's home-cooking, then why not try some typically Neder-mother dishes? And if you're feeling particularly sentimental, you can even leave a picture of your own Mother amongst the hundreds that decorate the walls of this cozily laid out café. The food groups (meat, veg, and potato) are approached with love and an honestly refined gusto, and served up by friendly young ladies that would make any mother proud.
Rozengracht 251, Jordaan ☎ 626 7957 ff–fff

☆ **PANCAKE BAKERY** ♪F2

As a well-honed art form which delicately balances thinness with belly-packing power, one can't really go wrong with Dutch pancakes. But the Pancake Bakery rises above the pack with its medieval vibe, canal-side patio, and a mammoth menu with over 70 choices of sweet and savoury toppings. They also do a convincing take on the folk dish of *erwtensoep* (a smoked sausage-imbued peasoup that's so thick you can eat it with a fork).
Prinsengracht 191, The Canals ☎ 625 1333 f

't Swarte Schaep ♪E11

For a dose of old world swank, choose the Royal family favourite, whose entrée of goose liver prepared in five different ways gives you an idea of what's on the rest of the menu.
Korte Leidsedwarsstraat 24, The Canals ☎ 622 3021 fff

eetcafés

Bagels & Beans ♪D13

Patioed and popular with students, the menu includes muffins and fresh juices.
Ferdinand Bolstraat 70, De Pijp ☎ 672 1610 f

Begijntje ♪F6

Hidden in a courtyard of the Amsterdams Historisch Museum, the perfect place for a scenic and restful *broodje* – or French country dish – any time of day.
Begijnensteeg 6–8, Old Centre ☎ 624 0528 ff–fff

Café Loetje ♪A13

Typically 'brown' – but sunny in the afternoon. Primary attraction on its long menu is the celebrated steak (with all the fixings). It attracts a media and advertising crowd
J Vermeerstraat 62, Vondelpark ☎ 662 8173 ff

Eat at Jo's
D9

If you happen to be in the 'hood for a show at the Melkweg, go to their own café/restaurant. Not only does it feature a cook who is rumoured to have been formerly employed at the Playboy Mansion, but it is also where the Melkweg's performers are probably already enjoying the bargain-priced world-embracing daily specials.

Marnixstraat 409, the Canals ☎ 638 3336 *f–ff*

1e Klas
D4

Surprisingly few people know it is possible to kill time in grand art nouveau style in this former first class waiting room in Centraal Station, where you can linger over a beverage, snack on a *broodje* (sandwich), savour a vaguely French meal, or try the highly rated (and priced) hamburger.

Centraal Station, Old Centre ☎ 625 0131 *ff*

Foodism
B6

The funky student hang-out for a cheap and filling meal.

Oude Leliestraat 8 ☎ 427 5103 *f–ff*

Het Einde van de Wereld
off map

As the name ('The End of the World') suggests, this restaurant is a bit out of town, but the trip is worthwhile. It's located on a barge and the menus (which change daily) are very cheap (f7 for kids, f12 for adults).

Opposite Javakade 21, Oosterdok ☎ 419 0222 *f*

Het Dobbertje
C5

There can be no better representation of the bottom of the Neder-food chain than the *broodjes* (sandwiches) and *uitsmijters* (fried eggs with topping of your choice) on offer at this early morning drinker's den. Here, a ham sandwich is a ham sandwich... it's back to the Jordaan's working-class roots.

Marnixstraat 325, Jordaan ☎ 622 0465 *f*

Kinderkookkafé
D7

Turn the tables and get kids to run after you for a change. Kinderkookkafé is a restaurant where kids do the cooking, the waiting on, and the washing up. Each child has to take at least two guests to enjoy their culinary masterpieces.

Oudezijds Achterburgwal 193, Old Centre ☎ 625 3257 *f*

Latei
D7

Healthful sandwiches and juices can be had here in a jumble of 50s kitsch (all for sale!).

Zeedijk 143, Red Light District & Nieuwmarkt ☎ 625 7485 *f*

restaurants & eetcafés

Lunchlokaal Wynand Fockink ♂C7
A cheap option, in a peaceful inner courtyard that even goes so far as to suggest the 'great outdoors'. Serves a daily special and sandwiches ranging from the simple to the spruced up.
Pijlsteeg 31, Red Light District & Nieuwmarkt ☎ 639 2695 *f*

Spek en Boontjes ♂F6
'Bacon & Beans' is a peachy – both literally and figuratively – destination in the afternoon, with a broad selection of smoothies, shakes, international sandwiches (an Indonesian-American club sandwich, anyone?), and an old school Dutch breakfast special.
Wijde Heisteeg 1, The Canals ☎ 620 5678 *f*

fondues

☆ CAFÉ BERN ♂C8
Socially cozy Café Bern sticks to the cheese fondue's Swiss roots. Also popular is the Entrecote Café Bern, where meat is softly sautéed in a pesto-like sauce.
Nieuwmarkt 9, Red Light District & Nieuwmarkt ☎ 622 0034 *f–ff*

Crignon Fromagerie ♂A7
Students and budget travellers with an urge to indulge tend to choose this social eaterie with its light, woody interior and broad range of fondues.
Gravenstraat 28, Old Centre ☎ 624 6428 *ff–fff*

☆ GROENE LANTAARN ♂A6
An Old World setting where they have some additional odd options: what's a Dim Sum Fondue? So posh that they shred the bread for you!
Bloemgracht 47, Jordaan ☎ 620 2088 *ff–fff*

french

Amsterdam ♂A2
Eat reasonably-priced French food like *confit de canard* and steak *béarnaise*, under an industrial-height ceiling and floodlighting in this former pumping station. The punters here are a true cross-section of Amster-society.
Haarlemmerweg 8–10, Haarlemmer & Westerpark ☎ 682 2666 *f–fff*

Belhamel ♂F3
In the northern end of the canal ring Belhamel is a trad, old-world, romantic option. Its fairly standard French menu seems far superior when served in a spooky art nouveau interior.
Brouwersgracht 60, The Canals ☎ 622 1095 *f–ff*

☆ BORDEWIJK $A3

One easily imagines that an obsessive day of market-hopping has been put in before chef Wil Demandt opens the doors to his long-acclaimed restaurant. Maybe it's because the chairs are so damn comfy that the vaguely 8os designer interior melts into a pleasant background; or, more likely, it's course after course of originally refined French cuisine (with a marked truffle fetish). The service is relaxed, the wine selection intelligent and tingly, and the bill ultimately satisfying (because you know you could easily be paying twice as much for less at one of those Michelin joints).
Noordermarkt 7, Jordaan ☎ 624 3899 *fff*

☆ CAFÉ ROUX $E7

Prepared in a kitchen overseen by a living, breathing Roux brother (Albert), the three-course lunch at ƒ44.50 remains one of the French culinary deals of the city. The thoughtful service provided by penguins just adds to the fun for budgeted lovers of elegance. Much of the mixed crowd is culled from the attached (truly) Grand Hotel, which shares Roux's art deco interior design. Wine hounds should take advantage of the encyclopaedic knowledge of the enthusiastic sommelier.
Oudezijds Voorburgwal 197, Red Light District & Nieuwmarkt ☎ 555 3560 *ff–fff*

☆ DISTRICT V $E14

This relative newcomer, on a strangely Parisian square, attracts a mixture of locals and arty types who've heard the word on the streets – that District V deserves *haute* status but lacks the required pretensions and price tag. With an open kitchen, one can see the happily obsessed chefs prepare the component fish/meat/vegetarian choices on their French-inspired daily set menu. With the specially designed plates, tables, and lamps in its post-modern-meets-backwoods interior all up for sale, they even pull off being arty without inducing a grimace (the washrooms in particular are a *tour de force*). One of the best French-based culinary deals around.
Van der Helstplein 17, De Pijp ☎ 770 0884 *fff*

☆ LE GARAGE $C13

The menu speaks of 'primal' and 'culinary cross-pollination', but this former garage can perhaps be better described as French regional with virtual frequent flyer miles (for instance caviar from Iran). Regardless, this trendy brasserie has one of the highest-rated kitchens in the city, with its three-course menu du jour at ƒ55 standing out as a particular bargain. The kaleidoscope mirrored walls allow you to keep a broad anthropological eye on the schmoozing media crowd.
Ruysdaelstraat 54–56, Museum District & Vondelpark ☎ 679 7176 *fff*

restaurants & eetcafés

Nostradamus ☼*E6*
This restaurant may prove to become a millennial forerunner with its French cookery, astrologically tinged interior, and tarot-reading waiting staff.
Berenstraat 8, The Canals ☎ 624 4292 *ff*

Utrechtsedwarstafel ☼*D12*
Continues to draw the crowds with its proprietors' infectious love for French-styled Dutch produce and fine wine.
Utrechtsedwarsstraat 107–109, The Canals ☎ 625 4189 *fff*

global & fusion

☆ **BEDDINGTON'S** ☼*E13*
A watered-down term like 'fusion' does chef Jean Beddington an injustice. This is the optimum spot to experience original tastes: where something looking French will actually rocket you to Japan (or vice versa) with potential stopovers in Spain, the West Indies, and even England. The Monkfish Tandoori in particular has gained a cult following. The sleek, minimalist setting allows no distraction from the melding of food and tongue.
Roelof Hartstraat 6–8, Museum District & Vondelpark ☎ 676 5201 *fff*

Blakes Amsterdam ☼*E6*
The restaurant belonging to Anouska Hempel's new hotel on the Keizersgracht has been getting lyrical reviews for its fusion foods and old-world-meets-Zen interior.
Keizersgracht 384, The Canals ☎ 530 2010 *fff*

Garlic Queen ☼*B11*
With a name containing multiple *entendres* that reflects the general orientation of its neighbourhood, it consistently surprises with an all-clove approach to international dishes, as well as an indescribably delicious fruit-encrusted ice cream.
Reguliersdwarsstraat 27, Old Centre ☎ 422 6426 *ff–fff*

☆ **INEZ IPSC** ☼*A12*
The Roxy may have burnt down on the night of his funeral, but the legacy of its designer Peter Giele, who had a talent for making potentially garish colours soothing, lives on at Inez. With one of the best views in Amsterdam you can watch the sun set over the cityscape (which includes a view over Hotel de L'Europe, used as a set piece in Hitch's *Foreign Correspondent*). A deep-pocketed arty crowd comes to see, be seen, and eat from the (let's call it) freestyle menu that changes monthly. Starter and main can be chosen from five creative options: two meat, two fish, and one vegetarian
Amstel 2, Old Centre ☎ 639 2899 *f–fff*

Kingfisher   ƒB13

Once brown, but now infused with clean lines and lots of natural light, Kingfisher still comes across as a friendly neighbourhood café/bar but one with inventive snacks. Not to mention a set daily special, invariably a fusion dish which is guaranteed to take in a few continents. Priced at ƒ19.50, this place is sticking to De Pijp's roots: it's cheap.

Ferdinand Bolstraat 24, De Pijp ☎ 671 2395 ƒ

☆ LOF   ƒD3

The chef starts his day by buying the freshest and most enticing ingredients he can find and returning to his restaurant, which may look plain by day but by night comes alive with lighting and the servers' personalities. At work in the kitchen, he magically improvises dishes – one meat, one fish, and one vegetarian option – that straddle both Med and Oriental cuisine. His fish, in particular, has been known to make a grown-up cry with pleasure. Flashy boho types all agree: forget *haute*, long live Lof.

Haarlemmerstraat 62, Haarlemmer & Westerpark ☎ 620 2997 ƒƒƒ

New Deli   ƒD3

With a white Zen-like interior and consummately global menu, New Deli fills a unique niche.

Haarlemmerstraat 73, Haarlemmer & Westerpark ☎ 626 2755 ƒ–ƒƒ

Ondeugd   ƒB13

More international in food, and ironic in outlook Ondeugd has long been efficient in exploiting the Achilles heel of bright, young things with money to blow and desire for both sassy service and reasonably priced lobster (Mondays only). But their regular globe-trotting menu also pulls the punters the rest of the week, and hops from sushi to foie gras, from *gamba* bisque to wild duck with truffle *boudin*.

Ferdinand Bolstraat 15, De Pijp ☎ 672 0651 ƒƒ

The Supper Club   ƒC7

Creative folks have a soft spot for its wackily themed nights of arty dining.

Jonge Roelensteeg 21, Old Centre ☎ 638 0513 ƒƒƒ

☆ !ZEST   ƒE3

Slips quite a bit of lemon – and its zest – into their 'the world on a plate' dishes. The small select menu bounces from a Japanese seviche to a Thai pumpkin curry to a *nage* of smoked eel to a… well, you get the idea. All are carefully prepared and all have a perfect companion to be found in the equally select wine list. Designer food in a serenity-inducing designer wood setting.

Prinsenstraat 10, The Canals ☎ 428 2455 ƒƒ–ƒƒƒ

greek

☆ **EETCAFÉ I KRITI**   ♭E13

Not only did the Greeks lay down the foundations of the culinary arts (inventing the chef's hat in the process), but they also know how to party. I Kriti combines sublimely fine Greek eats – all the standards on the menu – with the proprietor's willingness to show off a dance move or two as the evening progresses. You can buy plates for ƒ2 per giddy throw. The later you go, the more chance the floor crunches underfoot and that some Greek musical legend has dropped by to pick some mean bouzouki....

Balthasar Floriszstraat 3, Museum District & Vondelpark
☎ 664 1445 *ƒ–ƒƒƒ*

herring stalls

The sushi of the Low Countries (and ultimate hangover cure), *haring* (herring) is kept raw and, thus, lubricant enough to slide speedily down your throat. The experience can be diluted by garnishing it with chopped onion and/or pickle, or by ordering it all within a *broodje* (sandwich). *Paling* (smoked eel) makes for a sublime treat. The many stalls dotted around town also have a selection of cooked fish. These are some of the most reliable:

Altena   ♭E11
Rijksmuseum/Stadhouderskade, Museum District & Vondelpark

Kromhout   ♭D6
Singel/Raadhuisstraat, The Canals

Volendammer Viswinkel   ♭A14
1e van der Helststraat 60, De Pijp ☎ 676 0394

Indian

☆ **BALRAJ**   ♭C3

Certainly not the fanciest or the largest (though there is a semi-hidden upstairs) Indian joint, but years of consistency goes a long way. Students and locals come here when only a quality curry (Biryani, Masala, Korma, Madras, Punjabi) can truly abate their desires. Their *Saag Paneer* and *Aloo Gobi* are known to put extra swagger in a vegetarian's steps.

Binnen Oranjestraat 1, Haarlemmer & Westerpark ☎ 625 1428 *ƒ–ƒƒ*

Balti House *♫D13*

Almost shockingly roomy for the district. While they have yet to disappoint a diner on any day, they do betray bonus refinement on Wednesdays when the proprietor cooks tandooris and variously spiced curries, as well as baltis.

Albert Cuypstraat 41, De Pijp ☎ 470 8917 *ff*

indonesian

☆ DE ORIENT *♫B10*

The *rijsttafel* (rice table) combines rice with dozens of small dishes where flavours, spices, and textures combine and play off each other in a way that induces a near-orgasmic culinary reverie. Snug with wooded comfort, this restaurant, complete with shadow puppets and the gentle sounds of gamelan gongs, is relatively mellow in the tongue-blistering department. Vegetarian and *halal* diets are particularly well-catered for.

Van Baerlestraat 21, Museum District & Vondelpark ☎ 673 4958 *ff–fff*

☆ DJAGO *♫ off map*

True Indo-epicureans would send you as far away as The Hague in search of the 'real' Indonesian kitchen, which remains unblemished by compromises to the Dutch/tourist palate. But Djago, with its simple and folksy 'Spice Islands' interior, is a more than sufficient compromise. Near the RAI Convention Centre, it has a glorious *rijsttafel* plus a tasty selection of less daunting undertakings – call them one-dish mini *rijsttafels* – such as their *Bami* (noodles) *Rames* and *Nasi* (rice) *Rames* (both bargains at *f*19.75).

Scheldeplein 18, Zuid ☎ 664 2013 *f–fff*

☆ TEMPO DOELOE *♫D12*

Take heed of the menu's spiciness rating at this slightly cramped but posh Indo-establishment that dishes out a monumental *rijsttafel*. Dishes can be f***ing hot at times, although lemon and salt can take away some of the heat, and the sweet witbier (white beer) can help douse your tongue. But this is one of the city's best.... and you can always chill with their mango dessert.

Utrechtsestraat 75, The Canals ☎ 625 6718 *ff–fff*

Tujuh Maret *♫D12*

This is a great priced Indonesian for people who don't want to make a long night of it – an eat-and-run sort of place.

Utrechtsestraat 73, The Canals ☎ 427 9865 *ff–fff*

restaurants & eetcafés

☆ IL PIACERE $D7

As the short form of an Italian phrase meaning 'for the love of the Italian kitchen', Il Piacere is well named. The love for mamma's food – irrelevant of her region of origin – is so evident here that you can imagine the excellent staff staying late to argue about whether there was a half a sprig too much tarragon on the *gamberi*. This rustic yet chic retreat from the neon Red Light District is worth a long linger: from *antipasti* all the way to *dolci* – when you can order a *grappino* or two for its icy kick.
Kloveniersburgwal 7, Red Light District & Nieuwmarkt ☎ 626 2582 *fff*

☆ LA STORIA DELLA VITA $E12

This place is about surrendering: surrendering to the grand brasserie-styled spaciousness; surrendering to the sweet tinkling of a grinning piano player; and ultimately surrendering to the personable host who, after a short chat about dietary limitations, nods his head, and goes off to place your never-placed order. It's his prerogative to select a unique combo for each diner from the endless course options of pure and delicious Italian country cooking. Trust him and he reciprocates by leaving you three large bottles of liquor with the coffee.
Weteringschans 171, The Canals ☎ 623 4251 *fff*

L'Angoletto $ off map

The Italian devotion to pasta, and convivial chaos have full effect.
Hemonystraat 18, De Pijp ☎ 676 4182 *f–fff*

Pasta di Mamma $E9

Light and bright Pasta di Mamma allows you to scoff an excellent Italian deli sandwich or tasty bowl of spaghetti.
PC Hooftstraat 52, Vondelpark ☎ 664 8314 *f–ff*

Renzo's $D10

For a more earthy Italian try Renzo's, where the espresso reigns supreme. You can pull up a crate to an outdoor table and enjoy their fresh pasta and savoury sophisto-snacks.
Van Baerlestraat 67, Vondelpark ☎ 673 1673 *f–ff*

Toscanini $D2

A highly rated (by the business-suited) Italian, ingeniously blending a remarkably spacious cantina interior with the feeling of sitting in someone's kitchen. It serves southern Italian inspired dishes, including excellent pastas and pure and simple fish and meat.
Lindengracht 75, Jordaan ☎ 623 2813 *ff–fff*

☆ JAPAN INN
♭C11

Even though a Pacific rain has recently showered this city with many slick and cheapish purveyors of sushi, Japan Inn should not feel threatened. Besides snappy service and a long list of quality *maki*, *nigiri*, and *temaki* sushis, the menu is broadly supplemented with thin sliced *sashimi* and charcoal roasted *yakitori* options. Sit at the bar to admire the techniques on display in the open kitchen or settle down on a cafeteria-style table amongst the crowds of tourists, Japanese students, and locals.
Leidse Kruisstraat 4, The Canals ☎ 620 4989 *ff–fff*

Morita-Ya
♭A8

Tiny, homey, and canalside Morita-Ya supplements excellent sushi and sashimi with karaoke – can it be a coincidence that the Schreierstoren (Weepers' Tower) is just around the corner?
Zeedijk 18, Red Light District & Nieuwmarkt ☎ 638 0756 *ff–fff*

Stereo Sushi
♭C7

A funkily laid out sushi bar with late hours and convenient location just off Nieuwezijds Voorburgwal.
Jonge Roelensteeg 4, Old Centre ☎ 777 3010 *f*

☆ YAMAZATO
♭E14

It's thanks to a few millenniums of accumulated skill that such a restaurant exists. Traditional and ultimately fresh Japanese food is sublimely presented in a restful atmosphere that combines kimonos and a tatami room with views overlooking a fountain of frolicking fish. It'll cost you (though you won't regret spending f60 on the *Shokado Bentoo* lunchbox or f33 for a light lunch).
Okura Hotel, Ferdinand Bolstraat 333, De Pijp ☎ 678 8351 *ff–fff*

Yoichi
♭F12

Excellent Japanese menu and service are on offer at this very posh establishment with its sushi bar and evocative tatami room.
Weteringschans 128, the Canals ☎ 622 6829 *ff–fff*

Zento
♭D13

Long-houred Zento is a designer sushi bar complete with conveyor belt.
Ferdinand Bolstraat 17–19, De Pijp ☎ 471 5316 *f*

restaurants & eetcafés

☆ **KAYA** *♯D12*
Strap down your tastebuds because they're going to go for a rollercoaster ride when trying the nutritious and low-cal food of Korea. If you like sour and spice and meat barbecued (on your table), this is the modern place for you. On the downside: vegetarians should seek greener pastures... but on the upside: beer lovers can ask for a table with its own tap.
Utrechtsestraat 42, The Canals ☎ 625 9251 *ff*

late-night opening

☆ **BOJO** *♯C11*
Not the height of Indonesian food, but the huge portions are more than edible.
Lange Leidsedwarsstraat 51, The Canals ☎ 622 7434 *f–ff*

☆ **GARY'S MUFFINS** *♯B11*
Excellent muffins and bagels by moonlight.
Reguliersdwarsstraat 35, Old Centre ☎ 420 2406 *f*

☆ **HET DOBBERTJE** *♯C5*
Opening at 5am makes it more 'early' eating, and its selection of *broodjes* (sandwiches) and *uitsmijters* (fried eggs) does smack more of breakfast – but then with a fully stocked bar....
Marnixstraat 325, Jordaan ☎ 622 0465 *f*

mediterranean

Christophe *♯A6*
One of Amsterdam's few Michelin-starred restaurants, continues to act as a magnet to deep-pocketed connoisseurs of light and innovative cooking.
Leliegracht 46, the Canals ☎ 625 0807 *fff*

☆ **KIKKER** *♯A6*
An art deco interior provides the romantic setting. The reasonably priced Chef Surprise menu usually features the freshest of seafood (even lobster!). On weekends the intimacy is replaced by a *bon vivant* anarchy, with magicians, musicians, and comedians darting from table to table. They also have a remarkable wine and whisky collection, taking in the best of the last century.
Egelantiersstraat 128–130, Jordaan ☎ 623 4251 *ff–fff*

Zuid Zeeland ⊘B11

A Mediterranean-Oriental slant on food makes Zuid Zeeland a current gourmand favourite in this area.
Herengracht 413, The Canals ☎ 624 3154 *fff*

middle eastern

☆ **DE FALAFEL KONING** ⊘A12

The first falafel joint in Amsterdam, it is known for its particularly tasty 'secret recipe'.
Regulierssteeg 2, Old Centre ☎ 421 1423 *f*

☆ **EUFRAAT** ⊘C14

Eat the food enjoyed by the builders of the Tower of Babel at this scrubbed clean and modern family-run restaurant. They have familiar and impeccably prepared Middle Eastern snacks, delicious soups (at *f*6!) which turn into a meal when accompanied by their home-baked bread, and a vast variety of grills, kebabs, and vegetarian oven dishes.
1e van der Helststraat 72, De Pijp ☎ 672 0579 *f–ff*

☆ **FALAFEL DANS** ⊘F13

Notable for its happy hour of all-you-can-eat falafel between 3 and 5pm daily. There's also a branch at Nieuwendijk 28 in the Old Centre.
Ferdinand Bolstraat, De Pijp ☎ 676 3411 *f*

☆ **FALAFEL MAOZ** ⊘A12

Regarded for its later hours and central locations. There are also branches on the Muntplein in the Old Centre and on Leidsestraat in The Canals.
Reguliersbreestraat 45, Old Centre ☎ 624 9290 *f*

☆ **LOKANTA CEREN** ⊘D13

Turkish hospitality is very evident in this clean, straight, and tiny eaterie. They heartily recommend the *raki* when indulging in their many tasty starters (*mezeler*), which are accompanied by an endless supply of fresh bread. If you feel the need to look further down the menu, you will find a balanced focus that includes both grilled lamb succulence and vegetarian indulgences.
Albert Cuypstraat 40, De Pijp ☎ 673 3524 *f–ff*

modern european

Zomers ⊘C6

Modern European food and decor and notable for its themed menus and a port-infused Dutch cheese terrine.
Prinsengracht 411, The Canals ☎ 638 3398 *ff–fff*

restaurants & eetcafés

restaurants & eetcafés

Vrolijke Abrikoos *♪E12*
Crafted biodynamic dishes are available at this New Agey restaurant.
Weteringschans 76, The Canals ☎ 624 4672 *ff–fff*

oriental & southeast asian

☆ **CAMBODJA CITY** *♪D13*
A large selection of dishes is lovingly prepared under the eagle eyes of a benevolent matriarch and served up in a clean and (if you except the remarkable 3D waterfall 'painting') modest atmosphere. The *Banh Xjeo*, a Cambodian pancake stuffed with shrimp, chicken, and veg served with a divine dipping sauce, must be tried. They also have complete multi-course set dinners for two to four people. A take-away service is available too.
Albert Cuypstraat 58–60, De Pijp ☎ 671 4930 *f–ff*

☆ **DYNASTY** *♪B11*
Dynasty offers artfully presented and generously portioned classics from Cantonese, Thai, Malaysian, and Vietnamese cuisine. Prime choices would be the shark fin soup, the particularly pretty Phoenix and Dragon ('duck and lobster' if you subtract the poetry), and Bangkok's Secret of the Spicy Ox. The rich palatial paradise interior with light defusing from the upside-down umbrellas on the ceiling is only superseded by their 'dream terrace' located in a majestic courtyard. Romance anyone?
Reguliersdwarsstraat 30, Old Centre ☎ 626 8400 *fff*

out of town

Annie's Verjaardag
Right on the waterside, serving filling portions of traditional Dutch fodder. In winter, skaters set off from its terrace on tours around the frozen canals.
Oude Rijn 1, Leiden ☎ (071) 512 5737 *f–ff*

De Pêcherie Haarlem aan Zee
A good bet for fish specialities.
Oude Groenmarkt 10, Haarlem ☎ (023) 531 4884 *ff–fff*

De Wankele Tafel
'The WobbEly Table' mixes brown rice and buckwheat pancakes with flair.
Mauritskade 79, Den Haag ☎ (070) 364 3267 *f–ff*

Grand Café Brinkman
Serves a mixture of international and traditional Dutch brasserie fare.
Grote Markt 41, Haarlem ☎ (023) 532 3111 *f–ff*

Greve ♯F6
A hip hangout to dance the night away at weekends. Has a superb restaurant serving set price dinners that rely on the freshest seasonal ingredients.
Torenstraat 138, Den Haag ☎ (070) 360 3919 *f–ff*

Kleyweg's Stads-Koffyhuis
For a lunchtime sandwich or filling pancake.
Oude Delft 133, Delft ☎ (015) 212 4625 *f*

Lachende Javaan
For Indonesian fare.
Frankestraat 27, Haarlem ☎ (023) 532 8792 *ff*

Loft
A Spanish tapas bar also open for breakfast and lunch.
Grote Markt 8, Haarlem ☎ (023) 551 1350 *f–fff*

Ma Brown's
Offers traditional British food.
Nieuwe Groenmarkt 31, Haarlem ☎ (023) 531 5829 *ff–fff*

Polman's Huis
A three-course set menu is served in a brasserie-like space taken from a 19th-century ballroom. The chefs have a tasty Middle Eastern-cum-Oriental take on traditional Dutch ingredients.
Keistraat 2, Utrect ☎ (030) 231 3368

Restaurant Betty Beer
The best eating option in Rotterdam, offering copious servings of quality meat dishes that can be washed down with cocktails.
Blaak 329, Rotterdam ☎ (010) 412 4741 *ff–fff*

Stadscafé Restaurant Van der Werff
Enjoy the view of De Valk windmill from the terrace or classy art deco interior and its French-influenced cuisine.
Steenstraat 2, Leiden ☎ (071) 513 0335 *ff–fff*

pasta & pizza

De Pastorale ♯B2
The basement of this large pizzeria is a reservoir of soft balls for kids to dive into. Should they want more, there are videos, a football table, and a slide.
Haarlemmerdijk 160–164, Haarlemmer & Westerpark ☎ 625 9928 *f–ff*

Goodies   *♪E6*
A young and charming folk serve up inventive sandwiches and bagels by day, and at night it offers one of the best pasta deals in the city.
Huidenstraat 9, The Canals ☎ 625 6122 *f–ff*

☆ **YAM-YAM**   *♪A5*
This snug trattoria serves tasty Italian pasta dishes. It's slightly off the beaten track but that hasn't stopped it from being the favourite to more than just the neighbourhood, with creative and clubbing folk coming from afar to talk shop and hang out. A recent expansion (complete with an authentic Italian pizza oven) might make getting a table easier.
Frederik Hendrikstraat 90, Oude West ☎ 681 5097 *f–ff*

portuguese

☆ **ALCANTARA CERVEJARIA**   *♪F2*
A former cinema oey atmosphere. Representing French and Catalan-influenced *cuisine bourgeoise*, the tastes are much softer than usual from this land of garlic and hot pepper. Portuguese diners speak of its authenticity.
Westerstraat 184–6, Jordaan ☎ 420 3959 *ff–fff*

seafood

Al's Plaice   *♪F3*
Speedily serves good old-fashioned Brit fish 'n' chips, pies, and pasties – all begging to be slathered in mushy peas, HP sauce, or Heinz ketchup (the latter two being available to buy by the bottle).
Nieuwendijk 10, Old Centre ☎ 427 4192 *f*

☆ **PIER 10**   *♪A4*
Book a table in their 'Glass Room' in order to gander at the wonderful watery vista afforded from this former shipping office behind Centraal Station (including the frolicking herons) as you enjoy innovative fish dishes from the able hands of the chefs. Start with monkfish cheeks and finish with their white chocolate soup with fresh strawberries – this should have you seeing romance through the candlelight.
De Ruijterkade, Old Centre ☎ 624 8276 *ff–fff*

☆ **VIS AAN DE SCHELDE**   *♪ off map*
You might have to compete for a table with the already established regulars at this backwater fish paradise. Their luxuriate French approach – praise for their *bouillabaisse* being universal – includes visionary side-steps to Japan and into the world of the Thai fish fondue. Choose between dining on a white tablecloth in an understated art deco interior or outside on the patio.
Scheldeplein 4, Zuid ☎ 675 1583 *ff–fff*

Vishandel Zeedijk   *D7*

Head up Zeedijk to these friendly and well-stocked fish folks.
Zeedijk 129, Red Light District & Nieuwmarkt ☎ 624 2070 *f*

☆ VISRESTAURANT LE PÊCHEUR   *B11*

The marble and mural interior may be elegant, but when there's sun, it's the terrace, placed as it is within a Golden Age courtyard, that will have you sitting smug without a care in the world. Both the clientele and the service are thoughtfully mature. Choose à la carte or from the menu of the day, but rest assured: the mussels and oysters are divine, the salmon home-smoked to perfection, and the *crème brûlée* (with honey and saffron) to die for.
Reguliersdwarsstraat 32, Old Centre ☎ 624 3121 *fff*

south american

☆ EL HUASO   *D5*

If you're used to having access to good cheap Mexican food, the best advice when in Amsterdam is to go Chilean – one that serves generously spiked cocktails and ample portions of such Latin American specialities as *guacamole, tostadas, quesadillas, enchiladas, tacos, burritos*, and a mouth melting King Prawn in garlic. Some street-side tables can be used as an alternative to the basic brown bar interior.
Rozengracht 160, Jordaan ☎ 770 1904 *f–ff*

spanish

A la Plancha   *A6*

With a bull's head over the bar, this is fiesta-like on the taste buds but, unfortunately, due to its size and current acclaim, only has elbow room in the mid-afternoon or late at night.
1e Looiersdwarsstraat 15, Jordaan ☎ 420 3633 *ff*

Centra   *B7*

The perfect antidote to the inevitable crowds of voyeurs Centra offers a one-way ticket to Spain where one can hide behind their unparalleled paella.
Lange Niezel 29, Red Light District & Nieuwmarkt ☎ 622 3050 *ff–fff*

☆ PASODOBLE   *F2*

You can imagine Don Quixote himself holding up the bar at this convincing and colourfully tiled replica of an old school tapas joint – the cooks arguing in Spanish just adds to the flavour. And flavour is quite evident in its 40-plus choices of tapas. Pasodoble also passes the fundamental test: the margarita has flavour and punch. Go early to avoid the equally authentic chaos.
Westerstraat 86, Jordaan ☎ 421 2670 *f–ff*

restaurants & eetcafés

Pathum
_♭D_
The true thing: authentic, divinely prepared and well-priced dishes are
served in a sadly predictable interior.
Willemsstraat 16, Jordaan ☎ 624 4936 _ff_

Pheun Thai
_♭C_
Classy and delectable, a place for the whole family.
**Binnen Bantammerstraat 11, Red Light District & Nieuwmarkt
☎ 427 4537** _f–ff_

Sjaalman
_♭A6_
While obviously a former 'brown' bar, Sjaalman goes more for a designe
atmosphere with modern background beats and relaxed servers to
attract the hip. But this you pay extra for.
Prinsengracht 178, Jordaan ☎ 620 2440 _ff–fff_

☆ THAISE SNACKBAR BIRD
_♭A8_
You may want to dine in their new roomier restaurant across the street
but come here for a true flashback to Bangkok, where the food is
authentic, cheap, crunchy, and fresh. The menu is full of flash-fried
before-your-eyes favourites, and the setting modest but bustling.
Regulars often opt for one of their poignant _Tom Yam_ soups or have a
noodly _Pad Thai_ constructed to their specifications.
Zeedijk 77, Red Light District & Nieuwmarkt ☎ 420 6289 _f–ff_

tibetan & nepalese

☆ SHERPA
_♭C1_
Not only the food and the crowded and simple setting, but also the
menus – advertising as it does 'traditional cooking from Tibet and Nepal'
– will flash you back in time if you have ever travelled in this region. The
fundamental emphasis is on packing your belly and keeping you warm
but without sacrificing flavour. Tibetan cooking has a unique take on
variously stuffed dumplings – a _momo_ when steamed and a _kothay_ when
fried – which must be tried. Vegetarians get happy here.
Korte Leidsedwarsstraat 58, The Canals ☎ 623 9495 _f–ff_

Tibet
_♭B7_
If your stomach is grumbling later than usual, join the international
crowd or Szechuan or some nourishing _momo_-based mountain food.
Lange Niezel 24 ☎ 624 1137, Red Light District & Nieuwmarkt _f–ff_

☆ BETTY'S PETIT RESTAURANT   ⌖ off map

Vith few of the city's vegetarian restaurants offering a middle path
etween chewing on twigs and nibbling on overpriced floral
rrangements, it's worth the slight trek to Betty's, where they serve
ovingly prepared international vegetarian dishes favoured by the Jewish
iaspora. Relish huge portions of *blintzes, holishkas, falafel, empanadas,*
nchiladas, or *daal.* Wash it all down with juices, wine, or their home-
rewed *amé.* The cozy café ambience is brought a notch up the romantic
cale with white tablecloths and tasteful tunes.

ijnstraat 75, Rivierenburt ☎ 644 5896 *ff*

urger's Patio   ⌖F2

hough not strictly veggie Burger's Patio is a particularly vegetarian-
riendly purveyor of more moderately priced Italian dishes. It has a
eautiful inner courtyard hidden in its deco interior.

e Tuindwarsstraat 12, Jordaan ☎ 623 6854 *ff*

☆ DE BOLHOED   ⌖F2

)n the edge of The Canals, with a scenic canal side patio and a kitsch-
neets-Krishna interior, De Bolhoed serves up a variety of well-packed
•lates of vegan and vegetarian daily specials. Salads, stuffed bread rolls,
erbal teas, fresh pressed juices, biological Kik beer, and a mouthwatering
election of desserts round off the menu. A pleasant and mellow place.

·rinsengracht 60, Jordaan ☎ 626 1803 *f–ff*

Vliegende Schotel   ⌖B5

The Flying Saucer' attracts many students to its relaxed digs and cheap, but
arely stellar, meals. Dishes – including some vegan offerings – start at around
11, making it a cheap choice, but don't expect a culinary rollercoaster ride.

Nieuwe Leliestraat 162, Jordaan ☎ 625 2041 *f–ff*

·ugoslav

☆ ALEKSANDAR   ⌖F13

.ike many places serving recipes from the former Yugoslavia, Aleksandar is
now disguised behind the moniker 'Grill Restaurant'. They do an excellent job
)f recreating the area's passion for food and hospitality. So if you don't feel up
.o massive portions of perfectly grilled meats and fishes with flavourful veg
and potato side dishes, just drop by to sit at the bar and toss back a few of that
most soulful of hard liquors – *schljvovic.* It'll scour the palate so that you may
·njoy the earthy resonance of their reasonably priced starters.

.eintuurbaan 196, De Pijp ☎ 676 6384 *ff–fff*

bars & cafés

Amsterdam may be trumpeted as sex- and drugsville but drinking here is one of the most pleasant things life has to offer. It's simple, really: convivial locations, superior drinks, and low, low prices. Everything the serious boozer could ask for.

brown cafés

☆ CAFÉ DE SCHUTTER
♭F

A sanitized spit 'n' sawdust first floor café where the walls are thick with a decade's worth of entertainment listings. The Schutter does good cheap food and has a huge array of beers – whether that's why the place is crammed with students is open to debate.
Voetboogstraat 13–15, Old Centre ☎ 622 4608

Café de Tap
♭C

The relaxed ambience is occasionally marred by out-of-control office parties
Prinsengracht 478, The Canals ☎ 622 9915

Café Nol
♭F

This kitsch café claims to sum up the true 'spirit' of the area. It is home to a diverse cross-section of locals united in their love for the Jordaan-born oompah-pah-based drinking songs which they belt out en masse with sweat-spraying emotion. To save sliding to the bar every few minutes order their 'Pole of Pils', a tube which holds almost 15 pints of beer.
Westerstraat 109, Jordaan ☎ 624 5380

Café Welling
♭D10

Few thrills go on at Café Welling but the clientele, mostly musos who've just played the neighbouring Concertgebouw, make up for that.
**Jan Willem Brouwersstraat 32, Museum District & Vondelpark
☎ 662 0155**

☆ DE TUIN
♭F2

De Tuin has spit 'n' sawdust decor along with old tobacco signs, but also great sandwiches and a mean selection of board games. Very relaxed, and perfect for whiling away one of those Amsterdam summer afternoons when it invariably pisses down. Evenings turn it into a favoured local of the alternatively inclined young and hip denizens of the Jordaan, who hold mellow court during the week and go happily nuts on the weekend
Tweede Tuindwarsstraat 13, Jordaan ☎ 624 4559

ENGELBEWAARDER   ♭F7

This nicely eccentric brown café started life as a literary hangout – a vibe that comes alive during its jazz jam sessions (Sun). This place is beloved by old hippies who sit on the terrace-cum-barge outside – fortunately it's tethered, preventing punters floating away physically if not mentally.

Kloveniersburgwal 59, Old Centre ☎ 625 3772

Gambrinus   ♭E14

Gambrinus was one of the first bars to show a little hip. Brown in essence, with sand on the floor as proof, it's a relaxed and large-windowed corner local for a more affluent crowd, who seem devoted to their fresh-from-the-market daily specials. Service can be a tad grumpy at times.

Ferdinand Bolstraat 180, De Pijp ☎ 671 7389

Het Elfde Gebod   ♭B7

If a hearty fish and meat dish washed down with a choice of more than 80 different kinds of bottled brews, including a good selection of pretty lethal Trappist beers, is your sin, then the narrow brown café Het Elfde Gebod (The Eleventh Commandment) decrees 'thou shalt enjoy'.

Zeedijk 5, Red Light District & Nieuwmarkt ☎ 622 3577

★ KATTE IN DE WIJNGAERT   ♭D2

Occasionally used in films to portray a true neighbourhood café, this Jordaan hang-out is just that. A good selection of beers and *jenevers* (Dutch gin) is served in a homey setting where everyone's made to feel welcome. With an age range of up to 80 years at any given time – you might even catch a grandad and grandson doing battle on one of their chessboards. But time hasn't completely stopped here: they have come to recognize the hangover-curing properties of an English breakfast fry-up which they serve on Sundays.

Lindengracht 160, Jordaan ☎ 622 4554

Molenpad   ♭A11

One of the best brown cafés which gets everything right: canalside setting, friendly crowd, good food, and jazz.

Prinsengracht 653, The Canals ☎ 625 9680

Orangerie   ♭C3

For a more trad 'brown' sense of coziness, plump for Orangerie, with its ancient jukebox playing the tunes of yesterday and nicotine-stained interior ideal for quiet conversation.

Binnen Oranjestraat 15, Haarlem ☎ 623 4611

Pilsvogel

♭C

Scruffier in clientele, and attitude, the always personable Pilsvogel ('bee bird') has a relaxed brown-bar-meets-cantina scene going which is on enhanced by the serving of tapas. It also has a great terrace to observ the chaos that is Albert Cuyp Markt.

Gerard Doustraat 14, De Pijp ☎ 664 6483

☆ T' SMALLE

♭A

Probably the most scenic canalside patio, where, during the summe many boaters tie up for a revitalizing coffee or beer. Otherwise, the wel stocked bar itself acts as a beacon to a suited after-work crowd attracte to its doll's house-sized antique interior and friendly service – making a prime representative of an old school 'brown café'.

Egelantiersgracht 12, The Canals ☎ 623 9617

Thijssen

♭C

Another bar known to break out in raucous song – but mostly just o weekends when the frat boy regulars completely take over. Relativel large, and recently renovated, it is still decidedly 'brown' by night, bu infused with light from its large panoramic windows by day – really th best time to visit, especially when the patio is open and you can munc on designer sandwiches and gaze introspectively out onto the canal.

Brouwersgracht 107, Jordaan ☎ 623 8994

chess café

☆ SCHAAKCAFÉ HET HOK

♭C

There's a chess board on every table, but the café might be a bit noisy fo the serious player who likes the only sound to be of mental straining.

Lange Leidseswaarsstraat 134, The Canals ☎ 624 3133

club/bars

☆ CAFÉ COX

♭D

In the same building as the Stadsschouwburg, is the city's premier pre and post-theatre bar. It's best visited during a performance, when fewe thespians are hanging out and you're more likely to get a seat.

Marnixstraat 429, The Canals ☎ 620 7222

☆ CAFÉ CUBA

♭C8

Designer commie hangout, the Hemingway-esque Café Cuba is hidde behind a narrow façade. This heavily wood-panelled 40s bar is an authentic American jazz ghetto, with its fair share of old timer characters

Nieuwmarkt 3, Red Light District & Nieuwmarkt ☎ 627 4919

CAFÉ KRULL
C14

tterly dedicated to the powers of light: both indoors and on its patio. It's
e perfect daytime stop for a coffee and a cruise through their
agazine selection.

arphatipark 2, De Pijp ☎ 662 0214

CAFÉ LUX
D9

ard-drinking Café Lux, with funky projections adding to an already
esigner interior, is a million miles away from the ladled-on tack of the
earby Leidseplein. Wednesdays to Sundays sees the young hard-
rinking, trendsetting crowd enjoying DJs who stress the mellower
angents of drum 'n' bass.

arnixstraat 403, The Canals ☎ 422 1412

CAREL
D13

ttracts local gangs of youngish *bon viveurs* – cheap whisky and cognac
erhaps acting as an extra lure – but its earlier opening time and woody
trium also make it a prime daytime retreat.

rans Halsstraat 76, De Pijp ☎ 679 4836

DE DUIVEL
A12

ip-hop central, De Duivel (that's right: the devil) is famous throughout
urope. It is impossibly small with impossibly good DJs most nights. It's
ot just that it's good (although it is), it's more that there's nowhere else
ke this in town. Beer and weed form the diet of its regulars.

eguliersdwarsstraat, Old Centre ☎ 626 6184

HET BLAUWE THEEHUIS
E9

 cool summer hang-out for those not offended by dope smoke. Since the
ysterious (now solved) murder of the last owner, it has meta-
orphosed into Amsterdam's premier club/bar. The surrounding park
hills the terrace out nicely but the upstairs dancefloor, which affords a
reat view, does anything but.

ondelpark, Museum District & Vondelpark ☎ 662 0254

JAN STEEN
D13

eflects the area's grittier, browner past. Thanks to government funding,
t is geared to support the local ex-con community, so it serves the
heapest beer in the city. Luckily, the local clientele's brand of 'rowdy' is
ust so damn neighbourly that it never comes close to a bona fide brawl.
n fact, by day, with a pool table, a canalside patio, and an equally econo
offeeshop next door, it rates as an officially mellow hangout.

Ruysdaelkade 149, De Pijp ☎ 671 7392

☆ MAXIMILLIAAN

$D

A former cloisters dating from 1544. Nuns used to brew their own beer here and this rather chic brewery-cum-bar-restaurant carries on the tradition, producing 10 different kinds of the amber nectar. Glasses are filled directly from huge copper vats at the end of the bar.
Klovieniersburgwal 6–8, Red Light District & Nieuwmarkt ☎ 626 6280

☆ MORLANG

$A

Slightly more cosmopolitan (and expensive) than most, but in a stunning location and with quality designer café food (read: pesto on the sandwiches, salmon in the pasta) to match.
Keizersgracht 451, The Canals ☎ 625 2681

☆ QUINTO

$B

Quinto has a framed personal letter of compliments from a Saudi prince for its international food. Hide in huge stained-glass booths or join the friendly fray on the many wooden tables.
Frans Halsstraat 42, De Pijp ☎ 679 6848

☆ RUM RUNNERS

$A

Benefits from a prime canalside position, but it eschews the sophistication in favour of a cocktail-fuelled fiesta: a big hit with students.
Prinsengracht 277, The Canals ☎ 627 4079

☆ SCHILLER

$B1

This bar is Rembrandtplein's one truly redeeming feature. It has a faded glory and a real sense of history that the other grand cafés would sell their souls for. Though its a bit on the tatty side, it has a typical *fin de siècle* wooden interior. As well as this, Schiller has real charm, and, away from the hubbub, its atmosphere befits its surroundings: quiet, assured and calm.
Rembrandtplein 26, Old Centre ☎ 624 9846

☆ SEYMOUR LIKELY LOUNGE

$D

Amsterdam's original kitsch-inclined club/bar has been overshadowed by the competition of late and has doubled its efforts to capture past glories. Ironically, the place is now more palatable than in its snotty heyday with a far more jovial crowd and a funky laid-back choice of the latest dance sounds.
Nieuwezijds Voorburgwal 250, Old Centre ☎ 627 1427

☆ TUINFEEST

$C8

Just off the square, at the cozy, split-level Tuinfeest (garden party), a trendy crowd devours delish food, like goat's cheese salad, and grooves to cool beats.
Geldersekade 109, Red Light District & Nieuwmarket ☎ 620 8864

VAAGHUYZEN
#A7

favourite of Amsterdam's DJ fraternity, Vaaghuyzen feels and looks
ore like a locals' bar. It achieves club status with its nightly DJ sets –
me impromptu courtesy of visiting 'names' – which, depending on the
y, may focus on rare grooves, trip-hop, drum 'n' bass, and even techno.
eck their schedule...

ieuwe Nieuwestraat 17, Old Centre ☎ 420 1751

VOC CAFÉ
#A8

is Café, in the Schreierstoren, has a maritime history all of its own. A wicked
never is served while accordionists play to the lively weekend crowd. Others
ck back in the literary-edged room at the rear, or on the terraces.

**chreierstoren, Prins Hendrikkade 94–95, Red Light District &
ieuwmarkt ☎ 428 8291**

☆ WINSTON KINGDOM
#B7

ne Winston was formerly content with the suffix 'Hotel' until a major refit
aw it redesigned as one of the Red Light's few bars with its finger on the
ulse. A big artist hang-out that also attracts a lively mixed crowd, it plays
ost to live bands, poetry nights, DJs, and a popular Sunday club night.

Varmoesstraat 123–129, Red Light District & Nieuwmarkt ☎ 625 3912

rand cafés

afé Fonteyn
#C8

ther favourites on the square include Café Fonteyn with its genteel
adies' drawing-room feel.

ieuwmarkt 13, Red Light District & Nieuwmarkt ☎ 422 3599

☆ DE BALIE
#C11

his large, austere and quietly regal café is truly 'grand' in scope: not only
oes it provide refuge from Leidseplein for a post-film and theatre crowd,
: also has a media centre with highbrow programmes of film, lectures,
xhibitions, and multimedia presentations. Sip a cognac, then nip to the
ext room to check your emails...

leine Gartmanplantsoen 10, The Canals ☎ 553 5310

☆ DE JAREN
#E7

contemporary take on the grand café, with a high-ceilinged, spartan
modern white interior. It has pricey but fantastic food – focusing on
andwiches and sporting one of the city's few salad bars – plus a great
vaterside terrace, which is understandably popular and can get crowded.

ieuwe Doelenstraat 20, Old Centre ☎ 625 5771

☆ DU LAC

Du Lac has the most bizarre interior; half grand café and half biblic
allegory, much of it taken from a demolished church. The populace of [
Lac are a friendly and unassuming bunch and any artistic pretensio:
engendered by the decor are dispelled by the pool table.
Haarlemmerstraat 118, Haarlemmer & Westerpark ☎ 624 4265

☆ EBELING

Ebeling is a very refined, ever-so-slightly trendy bar and one of the fe
non-Irish drinking spots to serve draught Guinness. Its design
'grandness' hides its former function as a bank – except the toilets, whic
are in the original vaults complete with massive steel doors.
Overtoom 52, Museum District & Vondelpark ☎ 689 1218

☆ GRAND CAFÉ DE KROON

Housed in the same building as several TV and radio stations, De Kroon
a haunt for media dahlings. High ceilings, chandeliers, and faux Louis X
furniture contrast with bright modern colours and contemporar
paintings. The mood changes nightly: Saturdays are hip and buzzin
whilst Mondays are tango central.
Rembrandtplein 17, Old Centre ☎ 625 2011

Huyschkaemer

Its reputation for personable service, worldly experimental café food, an
a wackily designed split-level interior, has led to the broadening of it
predominantly gay clientele with local hetero couples settling in for
romantic night out.
Utrechtsestraat 137, The Canals ☎ 627 0575 *f–ff*

☆ L'OPERA

The fusion of art nouveau and art deco styles create an opulenc
reminiscent of early European grand cafés. A large terrace and sedat
atmosphere attract a mixed crowd. Just the place to while away a Sunda
with a newspaper, coffee, and cake.
Rembrandtplein 27, Old Centre ☎ 627 5232

hip hangouts

☆ BEP

By night, this place fills up quickly with young, hip, and media-savvy crews
so you'll only be able to truly appreciate the clean-lined and pristine whit
lounge interior if you visit by day: dip into their collection of internationa
mags while enjoying a cappuccino and an excellent designer sandwich.
Nieuwezijds Voorburgwal 260, Old Centre ☎ 626 5649

☆ CAFÉ SAS ♭B2

Stepping into Café SAS is like being on acid. It's that bizarre… With the upstairs bar under constant evolution, artists and the politically active gather to drink on the spray-painted sofas. In the basement, cheap veggie food is served up in less visually fraught surroundings.
Marnixstraat 79, Jordaan ☎ 420 4075

☆ DE BUURVROUW ♭C7

The loud and smoky 'Woman Neighbour' – a scary vision of whom looms over the exit – embraces a casually alternative crowd with a taste for bourbon and both loud guitars and trippy beats. Still managing to slip in a pool table, its limited size guarantees frolicsome interaction.
St Pieterpoortsteeg 29, Old Centre ☎ 625 9654

☆ DE KOE ♭B9

A split-level bar with two distinct atmospheres. Downstairs is a great (and cheap) restaurant serving typically international café dishes. This gives way to the boozy 'neighbourhood bar' mayhem up above, where the unpretentiously dressy crowd make football stadium amounts of noise. Dead in the day, but a superb night out.
Marnixstraat 381, Jordaan ☎ 625 4482

☆ FINCH ♭E3

Completely forsaking a traditional wooden decor with a post-modern interior which would seem torn from the pages of *Wallpaper* magazine if it weren't for its intrinsically casual and non-rarefied air. Artist types come to drink and chill to loungey beats, and shots of a sultry, young Sophia Loren decorate their day menu of sandwiches and omelettes. All this makes it the perfect place to visit after rummaging around Monday's Noordermarkt.
Noordermarkt 5, Jordaan ☎ 626 2461

☆ HUYSCHKAEMER ♭F12

This bar has been at the vanguard of Utrechtsestraat's march up-market. Its winning combination of trendy food and beer is much emulated but never bettered by a plethora of newer bars. Popular both day and night, especially with a big gay crowd, it can get insanely busy around 5–6pm.
Utrechtsestraat 137, The Canals ☎ 627 0575

☆ LAND VAN WALEM ♭A11

Land van Walem makes the most of its fantastic location with a canalside terrace just made for balmy summer nights. The large postmodern interior attracts the fashionably dressed who indulge in an extensive champagne list and menu of breakfasts, sandwiches, quiches, and *carpaccio* (sliced raw beef).
Keizersgracht 449, The Canals ☎ 625 3544

☆ SCHUIM
♯D

Schuim is a long-standing arty bar with regular exhibitions by loc:
artists. It is populated by a largely intellectual, though unpretentiou
clientele who somehow turn it into an insane dance party on th
weekends. Schuim means 'foam', so scrub up for some good clean fun.
Spuistraat 189, Old Centre ☎ 638 9357

internet cafés

ASCII
♯E

Free internet service.
Jodenbreestraat 24, Old Centre

De Waag
♯D

This turreted, castle-like building is home to a yuppified bar-restaurant o
the same name and has the appearance of a pseudo-medieval banquetin
hall. Don't be put off by pretensions, though: the affluent and less-moneye
alike convene here (the latter especially for the free internet terminals).
Nieuwmarkt 4, Red Light District & Nieumarkt ☎ 422 7772

Freeworld
♯F.

Surf the net with a cappucino and a snack.
Nieuwendijk 30, Old Centre ☎ 620 0902

irish bars

Dubliners
♯F1

Tatty, tiny, and friendly, this is the most genuine Irish bar – the very first –
in Amsterdam. The only theme is getting very, very drunk. A close-kni
group of regulars (sketches of whom form a rogues' gallery on the walls)
it still manages to squeeze in a pool table and a 'truer' Irish pub experience
Dusartstraat 51, Dubliners ☎ 679 9743

Mulligans
♯A1:

The best place in the country if you like Irish folk music. The worst if you don't
Amstel 100, Old Centre ☎ 622 1330

O'Donnells
♯B13

An Irisher-than-Irish pub with its football field-sized patio that graces the
rather sterile Marie Heinekenplein. It is equally popular with local Dutch
residents and British ex-pats alike – resulting in some interesting scenes
when the football matches they regularly screen happen to be the
Netherlands vs England.
Marie Heinekenplein, De Pijp ☎ 676 7786

O'Reilly's *♭D6*
The place to watch British/Gaelic sports in the centre of town, O'Reilly's has real intimacy despite its size (it's massive).
Paleisstraat 103–105, Old Centre ☎ 624 9498

old world

☆ IN 'T AEPJEN *♭B7*
This bar oozes character from every beam of its 16th-century abode, and is popular with the more bourgeois of drinkers. Housed in one of Amsterdam's two remaining wooden buildings, the interior is a mish-mash of everything from old pharmacy shelves to 19th-century fairground bits and pieces.
Zeedijk 1, Red Light District & Nieuwmarkt ☎ 626 8401

☆ REYNDERS *♭C11*
White-aproned waiters serve in this most splendid 30s bar. Reynders has that quiet efficiency that typifies most people's perception of life 60 years ago. It's one of few bars on the Leidseplein worth visiting because the suburbanites who usually flock here all think it's 'old fashioned' and stay away.
Leidseplein 6, The Canals ☎ 623 4419

out of town

Dudok Café Brasserie
A self-conscious Dutch grand café where a post-work crowd congregates for drinks and dinner.
Meent 88, Rotterdam ☎ (010) 433 3102

Hotel New York
An art nouveau building that retains some original features. Feast on oysters or select more trad Dutch fare in the café-restaurant with its superb dockside view.
Koninginnenhoofd 1, Rotterdam ☎ (010) 439 0500

Huis Oudaen
Home-spun beers are brewed in the basement of this 14th-century house.
Oude Gracht 99, Utrect ☎ (030) 231 1864

proeflokaalen

☆ BROUWERIJ 'T IJ *♭ off map*
Worth the trek to culturally indulge in micro-brewed-in-a-windmill beer. While the inside offers a backdrop of bottles, most folks prefer to sit around the base of the De Gooyer windmill instead.
Funenkade 5, Oosterdok ☎ 622 8325

bars & cafés

bars & cafés

☆ DE ADMIRAAL
F6

Attracting those in need of an efficient post-work inebriator. Traditionally, proeflokaalen were standing room only as people would quickly sample and taste the myriad of different *jenevers* (Dutch gins) being distilled on location before making a takeaway investment. De Admiraal's take is somewhat different, with comfy couches encouraging drinkers to stay awhile.

Herengracht 319, The Canals ☎ 625 4334

De Ooievaar
B7

A 360-year-old building, once laundry and liquor store, is now an authentic *proeflokaal*. With a quintessential range of Amsterdam-distilled *jenever* (gin), it is guaranteed to leave you spinning and in good spirits.

Sint Olofpoort 1, Red Light District & Nieuwmarkt ☎ 420 8004

Lunchlokaal Wynand Fockink
C7

Extremely small but classic, this *proeflokaal* stocks a vast selection of bottles and barrels of all descriptions.

Pijlsteeg 31, Red Light District & Nieuwmarkt ☎ 639 2695

Oosterling
F12

You couldn't get much more trad Amsterdam than this. This old bar has one of the best selections of *jenevers* (Dutch gins) and whiskies in town.

Utrechtsestraat 140, The Canals ☎ 623 4140

☆ WIJNAND FOCKINK PROEFLOKAAL
C7

Wijnand Fockink is a classic *proeflokaal*. Stocked with bottles and barrels of a startlingly vast array of sticky liqueurs and *jenevers*, the idea is to walk in, drink up, and walk out – perhaps with a bottle in hand...

Pijlsteeg 31, Red Light District & Nieuwmarkt ☎ 639 2695

top terraces

Cobra Café
E11

The emphasis may be more on design than atmosphere. but the large terrace is a perfect spot to spend a warm summer night.

Hobbemastraat 18, Museum District & Vondelpark ☎ 470 0111

☆ CAFÉ 'T LOOSJE
D7

This café was a tramcar waiting room in the 50s and 60s. These days, the typically Dutch brown bar still draws a similar variety of clientele: from the old Amsterdammer to the young arty set. It is perpetually popular for the bustling atmosphere, Spanish-inspired food, monolithic beer selection, and cheap prices.

Nieuwmarkt 32–34, Red Light District & Nieuwmarkt ☎ 627 2635

☆ SOUNDGARDEN   ♭C5
This place rocks with a capital R. Defining the word grunge way before the genre existed, Soundgarden still caters to lovers of all that is loud and alternative. There is a restful waterside terrace out back where you can hear yourself think, if you happen to be still capable of thought. Indoors the focus is on hard drinking and even harder talking and tunes.
Marnixstraat 164–166, Jordaan ☎ 620 2853

☆ SPANJER & VAN TWIST   ♭A6
A modern café with a well-founded reputation for fresh and cheap sandwiches and vegetarian-friendly daily specials. The contemporary decor makes a change from the usual dark wood-panelled atmospheric handle on Jordaan drinking. They also have a great scenic terrace at canal level.
Leliegracht 60, The Canals ☎ 639 0109

☆ TIS FRIS   ♭E8
A people watcher's paradise, especially if you like watching the driftings of the many freaks (and tourists) who populate the Waterlooplein market area, Tis Fris also has outstanding, if pricey, sandwiches. One more thing: the name translates as 'it's refreshingly cool', and it's certainly a good place to chill out.
Sint Antoniesbreestraat 142, Old Centre ☎ 622 0472

☆ TRAMLIJN BEGEERTE   ♭B1
A brown café called 'A Streetcar Named Desire' has a bewildering array of sandwiches and a nice terrace from which to watch (you guessed it...) the trams – so daylight hours are the best time to pop in. Being a distance from the centre, it specializes in attracting an unpretentiously brash and talkative array of philosophizing locals.
Van Limburg Stirumplein 4, Haarlemmer & Westerpark ☎ 686 5027

☆ VERTIGO   ♭E9
The bar annex of the Nederlands Filmmuseum, Vertigo is housed in a grandiose former entertainment pavilion. It is Vondelpark's drinking haven for the more stylishly inclined and its main feature is its two terraces (one on the building's immense balcony and one on shaded ground level), which explains the name, because the fact the bar is in a basement doesn't.
Vondelpark, Museum District & Vondelpark ☎ 589 1400

☆ WILDSCHUT   ♭E13
Wildschut caters to a suited post-work crowd, but its location also makes it perfect for post-shopping refreshment. It is surrounded by prime examples of second-generation Amsterdam School architecture, best viewed from its spacious terrace, and sports a *Jugendstil* (art deco) interior.
Roelof Hartplein 1–3, Museum District & Vondelpark ☎ 676 8220

coffeeshops

Amsterdam's coffeeshops are the only places in the world where it's legit to get hash for cash, roll it up 'n' smoke it. But beware, once inside, gravitational suction sets in. Remember: you can always do what the locals do and take-away.

Bluebird
♭E8

Catching the Bluebird open can sometimes be problematic as the local constabulary pop in and shut it down on a regular basis. This coffeeshop, however, is renowned throughout the city for having one of the largest selection of hash and weed around.
Sint Antoniesbreestraat 71, Old Centre ☎ 622 5232

Cum Laude
♭E7

The interior decor, with its Yucca plants and white walls, creates an atmosphere of refined cool. At first glance this cofeeshop looks like a mini grand café but, although it is mainly devoid of giggle-fuelled silliness, it certainly does the business and it is definitely worth popping in for a 'coffee'.
Langebrugsteeg 7a, Old Centre ☎ 420 2132

Dampkring
♭B11

This coffeeshop is popular with Amsterdam's student population (like anywhere selling weed wouldn't be), with it's jungle interior and award-winning combustibles. Dampkring comes into its own in the summer, when the cool interior with its removable frontage makes it the perfect place to escape the heat. Their music policy has thankfully discarded the assumption that everyone wants Bob Marley all the time.
Handboogstraat 29, Old Centre ☎ 638 0705

De Overkant
♭B1

A neighbourhood coffeeshop at the end of tramline 10, De Overkant is on a relaxed and largely undiscovered square, and has a local, friendly ambience. The main selling point is the wide range of 'erb and the downright niceness of the place. If only the whole world could be like this... though most people here think it already is.
Van Limburg Stirumplein, Haarlemmer & Westerpark ☎ 686 8957

Easy Times
$C11$

This is one of the largest coffeeshops in town, and it even has a dance floor where you can perform your stoned monkey lope to the amusement of the regulars. The music here is dancehall but the place is free of Yardie stress despite (or because of) the presence of an airport-style metal detector. So it' may be a good idea to leave your gun at home.
Prinsengracht 476, The Canals ☎ 624 1572

Free City
$B5$

Remember the bar in *Total Recall?* Filmed here. At least it looks like it was. The woman with three breasts has yet to show, but her mates are here. Still, it's one of the friendliest places in town, especially at night.
Marnixstraat 253, Jordaan ☎ 625 0031

Free I
$A12$

Opposite hip-hop hang-out De Duivel, the punters here match up while the music swings between the *de rigueur* roots, reggae, and rap. The bamboo interior is bizarre, but the selection of weed (much of it appropriately African) is expansive.
Reguliersdwarsstraat 70, Old Centre ☎ 622 7727

Global Chillage
$A11$

Your own little piece of Goa. The regulars certainly seem to think it is. Dolphin noises, cushions on the floor, curious drapes – ridiculously cosmic but a welcome release from the hell of nearby Leidseplein.
Kerkstraat 51, The Canals ☎ 776 8373

Grasshopper
$B7$

For many, the Grasshopper is the first port of call after leaving Centraal Station. And you could do worse; they have a wide-ranging menu and none of the garish trappings that permeate the rest of the area.
Oudebrugsteeg 16, Old Centre ☎ 626 1529

Greenhouse
$ off map

The undisputed champ, Greenhouse is unparalleled merchandise-wise, boasting a mindblowing selection of smokables whilst remaining the only coffeeshop where you can get a beer and decent food. The little brother Greenhouse on the Waterlooplein has the same high standards, but is smaller and more accessible. It is also handy for the clothes market, but come here after shopping unless you like purple flares.
Tolstraat 91, De Pijp ☎ 673 7430
Waterlooplein 345, Old Centre ☎ 622 5499

Greenhouse Effect
♭B7

In amongst the brothels, pimps and pushers, Greenhouse Effect is the only place in this area to extract some charm from the omnipresent sleaze. This is one of the few coffeeshops that also dispenses alcohol, and its seedily exuberant atmosphere is reminiscent of a bawdy quayside tavern. Space shakes, cakes, and cookies combine with cool music to keep this compact coffeeshop crammed.

Warmoesstraat 53–55, Red Light District & Nieuwmarkt ☎ 623 7462

Kadinsky
♭F6

Kadinsky is almost unique amongst coffeeshops – it's clean and it makes optimum use of minimum space by relying on quality rather than quantity. Better than that; it's worlds away from the drug den atmosphere of most in this area, and universally helpful staff weigh the nordle out in front of you. And they have great chocolate chip cookies which – surprise surprise – they do a roaring trade in.

Rosmarijnsteeg 9, Old Centre ☎ 624 7023

Katsu
♭C14

Katsu is almost as great a Pijp institution as the nearby Albert Cuyp Markt – many of the diverse crowd of locals here are employed at the market. Half the clientele seem to live here, which makes the atmosphere friendly – it is reminiscent of the days of the pre-wine bar Pijp. This is the only place to have disturbed the Greenhouse's monopoly of the High Times Cup; one look at the exhaustive menu will tell you why.

1e Van der Helststraat 70, De Pijp ☎ 657 2617

The Other Side
♭B11

The Other Side is a gay coffeeshop which has an often mixed crowd. The music is quality house and they sell a wide range of smart/herbal accoutrements – the weed selection, however, is nothing special. It is worth knowing that the staff here treat tourists with less disdain than most other coffeeshops. This is a good bet for getting the lowdown on what's going on (gay) party-wise.

Reguliersdwaarsstraat 6, Old Centre ☎ 421 1014

Paradox
♭B5

A total Zen-like approach is favoured by this quiet coffeeshop, a tiny health food specialist whose doors slide wide open onto an ancient alley-like street and where English ex-pats hang out to read papers and indulge in fine smoke and unparalleled fruit shakes. The place itself is tiny and popular, never a good combination, but the atmosphere remains cordial, no matter how cramped the coffeeshop gets.

1e Bloemdwarsstraat 2, Jordaan ☎ 623 5639

Republiek $C2

Republiek is ostensibly like any other neighbourhood coffeeshop. What sets it apart is its extensive menu and lack of shadiness. In half the coffeeshops like this, folk skin up to check they haven't been sold a lump of cat poo. Here, people stick one together 'cos they want to stay a while.

2e Nassaustraat 1a, Haarlemmer & Westerpark ☎ 682 8431

Rusland $F7

Rusland is Dutch for Russia, hence the odd cyrillics stamped all over the walls. The coffeeshop is in keeping with the image of hipper bars in the area: spit and sawdust, noisy, and vaguely alternative, but by no means as boisterous.

Rusland 14–16, Old Centre ☎ 627 9468

Siberie $F3

Typical of Jordaan coffeeshops, Siberie reflects the tranquil nature of the area. Or everyone's been at it all day and can no longer master the power of speech. Either way, it's half gallery, half coffeeshop, and with a mean selection of board games, it is a low-decibel delight.

Brouwersgracht 11, Jordaan ☎ 623 5909

The Spirit $F2

The only coffeeshop in the Jordaan where the sleepy feel of the area is shaken off, The Spirit is noisy, smoky, and how a good coffeeshop should be. Hendrix-driven, a fair mix of locals and tourists, and a good weed menu, smoked with enthusiasm.

Westerstraat 121, Jordaan ☎ 625 4650

't Ballonetje $ off map

With plenty of broadsheets scattered around, 't Ballonetje is a convivial place to while away an afternoon, although it's not big on visceral thrills. Whether intellectual ramblings are preferable to those of the usual heads is debatable, but this would be the place to discuss it. And then forget you ever had the conversation at all.

Roetersstraat 12, Oost ☎ 622 8027

Tweede Kamer $F6

Small but perfectly formed, Tweede Kamer is something of an enigma. Centrally located and celebrated amongst Amsterdammers (Tweede Kamer is also the Dutch House of Commons), it has somehow escaped the notice of stoney Tony and his mates and remains a dark, wood-panelled oasis of relative calm.

Heisteeg 6, Old Centre ☎ 422 2236

clubs

Amsterdam is a house town. And a very hard house town at that. Outside this scene, funk and hip-hop dominate. Gabber, the hardest of hardcore, is talked about but seldom heard, save for the occasional 10,000-strong 'Hellraiser' parties at the Sporthal Zuid near the Olympic stadium.

Café Meander ⚲F6
A salsa evening which gets steamy and packed. Popular with students who dance what could be termed free-form, it is less stylish than many, but also more fun. The music switches from live acts to DJs spinning Latin tunes and The New Cool Collective play here regularly. ♻ Salsa on Sunday.
Voetboogstraat 3b, Old Centre ☎ 625 8430

Club Arena ⚲ off map
Arena is attached to a large backpackers' hostel, which makes its weekend dance club popular with the traveller fraternity. Fridays and Saturdays see Time Zones with everything from the 60s through the 90s, with groovy club sounds at Thursday's Pressure. It's plain good fun. ♻ Time Zones (Fri & Sat); Pressure (Thu).
's Gravesandestraat 51, Oost ☎ 694 7444

Cruise Inn ⚲ off map
Cruise Inn is home to Amsterdam 50s rocker contingent and they take it seriously. Showaddywaddy is a dirty word here, and the clothing is vintage rather than teddy boy. Classic rock 'n' roll abounds, although the local interpretation of classic can stray alarmingly from the norm. ♻ Sat.
Zeeburgerdijk 271, Oosterdok ☎ 692 7188

Dansen bij Jansen ⚲F6
The student club, Dansen is a booze-fuelled haven for daft dancing. As you would expect, it is big on exuberance but not on musical quality. Take it with a pinch of salt and you'll have a giggle. ♻ Thu–Sat. ♻ Sometimes you can only get in by showing student ID.
Handboogstraat 11, Old Centre ☎ 620 1779

Escape ⚲A12
Escape, a cavernous converted cinema, used to be tack personified, albeit with a good sound system. Chemistry, Amsterdam's biggest and most renowned house night, held here every Saturday, changed all that. It's lost some of its initial appeal but remains popular, and is even broadcast on

Dutch radio. Entrance hangs almost completely on the whim of the bouncers but it's usually worth the hassle if you get in. ♻ Chemistry (Sat); Mellow House (Sun). ❧ It's pretty commercial.
Rembrandtplein 11, Old Centre ☎ 622 1111

Exit ♱B11
Small, trendy club which favours deep house and trance. Although gay in style, Exit attracts a fairly mixed crowd. Its decor is postmodern, with a balcony overlooking the large dance floor. ♻ Transdancer (Fri); Experience Night (Sat).
Reguliersdwarsstraat 42, Old Centre ☎ 625 8788

Korsakoff ♱F5
Korsakoff is part of the alternative club scene (with live bands on Wednesdays). It has a punk vibe, although the music played contains a fair chunk of hip-hop and funk-metal. It's also a great place for late-night drinking as no end of people will ably demonstrate. ♻ Sat (Techno).
Lijnbaansgracht 161, Jordaan ☎ 625 7854

Maloe Melo ♱F5
A muscians hangout dubbed 'the home of the blues'. Their nightly free live music in the back room is just as likely to be of the rock, folk, or psycho-billy variety – with the additional chance that an international name might pop in for one of their many jam sessions.
Lijnbaansgracht 163, Jordaan ☎ 420 4592

Margaritas ♱A12
Margaritas is a cozy Caribbean club, where DJs showcase all things salsa and merengue. It's small but stylish with a crowd of often top dancers.
Reguliersdwarsstraat 108, Old Centre ☎ 625 7277

Mazzo ♱D5
Big on hard house and trance, something that few clubs can better. Another plus is the inexplicable friendliness of the bouncers, not that anyone complains. ♻ Com be Progressive (Thu); Sex, Love & Motion (Sat).
Rozengracht 114, Jordaan ☎ 626 7500

Melkweg ♱C11
This revamped milk factory is famed as a live venue, but it hosts some excellent club nights. Its Saturday Dance Arena is a cheap, cheerful alternative to the more exclusive clubs. The music is breakbeat oriented, with British labels Wall of Sound and Skint both running regular nights, along with Controverse All Stars every Thursday. ♻ Soundclash (Thu); Dance Arena (Sat). ❧ Monthly promoter nights often change dates – check press.
Lijnbaansgracht 234a, The Canals ☎ 531 8181

Paradiso
♯C11

When Paradiso rocks, it rocks hard. The 19th-century church, with its tiers of balconies, is ideally suited to big house parties. Best of the lot is Friday's (monthly) VIP club which, as well as being easy to get into (its capacity is 1000+), offers up quality hard house. It is also one of the premier live music venues in the city. ♻ Monthly Paradisco (Sat); monthly VIP Club (Fri).
Weteringschans 6–8, The Canals ☎ 623 7348

Sinners in Heaven
♯B12

Despite its reputation for a dodgy ol' crew of over-friendly men, Sinners in Heaven is enduringly popular with a fairly trendy bunch who get on down to R & B and hip-hop without getting too frenetic. Best bet is weekdays when it's less crowded. ♻ Thank God it's Friday (soul, R & B, garage). ♺ Overcrowded.
Wagenstraat 3–7, Old Centre ☎ 620 1375

Time
♯D6

Time has undergone a recent renaissance with the older club crowd, who mooch about to mellow house and hip-hop. More of a late night drinking spot, the joint ain't exactly jumping with the energy of youth, but you can at least hear yourself think. ♻ Riddem Bash – Fat Jamaican Beats (Tue); weekly Controverse All Stars gigs (Tue).
Nieuwezijds Voorburgwal 163, Old Centre ☎ (06) 2906 0665

Trance Buddha
♯D7

The place for Goa trance and tribal house, Trance Buddha is also a good bet for after-hours parties that go on well into the night. Dark and atmospheric, it is easy to get into but not always easy to leave after a long night. The downstairs chill-out area draws a 90s neo-hippy Goa crowd – it gets pretty sparse in winter when they go off to the Real McCoy. ♻ New Talent Night (Tue). ♺ It's crusty central.
Oudezijds Voorburgwal 216, Red Light District & Nieuwmarkt ☎ 422 8233

West Pacific @ Westergasfabriek
♯ off map

Perched on the edge of the sprawling Westergasfabriek complex, this club has been a place to be seen since it opened. Also a hip restaurant/bar serving great food early on, weekends see West Pacific in full-on club mode; but it remains laid-back, due mainly to the enduring popularity of the latino/mellow hip-hop beats that dominate here. ♻ Superbowl (Sun).
Haarlemmerweg 8–10, Haarlemmer & Westerpark ☎ 488 7778

Winston Kingdom $B7

On Sunday nights, the ever-trendy Winston Kingdom bar/venue transcends into two of the hottest club nights in town: Club Vegas is hosted by the ever-glamorous Ms Erin Tasmania and DJ Polack, who spins a mix of exotica, kitsch and easy-listening loungecore; whilst Cocktail 3000, with hostesses Coco Coquette and Jet Lag, is a forward-look to the next, next millennium and has dedicated a drink, Rosé, to the year 3000. The best place to end the weekend. ♿ Club Vegas (Sun); Cocktail 3000 (Sun). ♺ Sun only.

Winston Hotel, Warmoesstraat 123–129, Red Light District & Nieuwmarkt ☎ 623 1380

Zoo $B7

Another stalwart of the after-party scene, Zoo plays hard house to a crowd who remains impressively enthusiastic and seemingly impervious to the passing of time. Small and comfortable it's the ideal place to while away the hours. Irregular drum 'n' bass nights sometimes interrupt the usual programme.

Oudezijds Voorburgwal 3, Red Light District & Nieuwmarkt ☎ 638 1461

squat clubs

Many of Amsterdam's established squats run club nights to cater for the more eclectic, less affluent club-goer, providing an alternative edge to the mainstream scene. The most secure in town, **Vrankrijk**, is a throwback to the radicalism of 70s Amsterdam. Although not as alternative as some, it does have a fiercely anti-establishment aura, backed up by occasional nosebleed techno from local DJs. **De Trut** is ostensibly a gay and lesbian club (the management sometimes go so far as asking for your sexual preference at the door). The atmosphere is uplifting, as is the music, ranging from the squat-staple acid techno to housier beats. For a newer take on the squat scene, try **Kalenderpanden**, which books an audacious range of bands and produces some non-commercial, unglitzified dance evenings. But call before going as its future (or lack of) lies in the hands of the city authorities and developers. Live entertainment is also on offer at **ADM**, from post-punk robotic cabarets to live DJs. The only downside is working out how to get back into town from this way-out-west venue.

ADM $ off map

Hornweg 6–8, Havens West ☎ 411 0081

De Trut $A9

Bilderdijkstraat 165, Oude West ☎ 612 3524

Kalenderpanden   ♯ off map
Entrepotdok 93–98, Oost ☎ 460 6645

Vrankrijk   ♯D6
Spuistraat 216, Old Centre ☎ 625 324

sex clubs

The Red Light District is home to many sex bars. Most are a rip-off, with standard live sex shows by an undynamic cast. However, if you're determined to make the most of Amsterdam's sleazy reputation, **Casa Rosso** offers a 60-minute non-stop live show with various erotic acts in a theatre-like environment at ƒ75 (including drinks). **Yab Yum** claims to be the most exclusive men's club in the world. It is frequented by rich businessmen, which is no wonder with the ƒ150 entrance fee. For this you can drink all you want. For a more intimate encounter with one of the 'hostesses', it'll cost you ƒ500 an hour. **Why Not?** is the oldest gay sex club in Amsterdam. The strip and go-go shows are free, but one drink is compulsory. Watching a sex show will cost you ƒ44 and a private session with a boy in a room starts at ƒ250 for an hour.

Casa Rosso   ♯D7
Oudezijds Achterburgwal 106, Red Light District & Nieuwmarkt
☎ 627 8954

Yab Yum   ♯D6
Singel 295, The Canals ☎ 624 9503

Why Not?   ♯A7
Nieuwezijds Voorburgwal 28, Old Centre ☎ 627 4374

bloemendaal beach parties

Hitting the beach for a party is nothing new. But nowhere, not even in the sunshine state of California, does reality mirror the image so closely as an afternoon at Bloemendaal. Here, generously spaced, large beach bars pump out music from their terraces for the enjoyment of the previous night's club crowd. From May until late September, trains from Amsterdam to nearby Haarlem are full of clubbers making their weekly migration to the good vibrations. The music is mainly feel-good funk and the best of the bunch is a ramshackle affair called Woodstock, about five minutes walk from the bus stop, where the link between Bloemendaal and Haarlem offloads.

gay scene

With its laid-back, open-minded atmosphere, Amsterdam has one of the biggest and best gay scenes in Europe.

bars

April
B11

April attracts a newspaper-and-coffee crowd during the day, but fills up for happy hour (6–7pm). The premier pre-club venue for the gay crew, the sound system pumping house tends to drown out all but the most persistent of conversationalists. The revolving bar at the back keeps the young hip crowd moving and cruising.

Reguliersdwarstraat 37, Old Centre ☎ 625 9572

Backstage
F12

If you're a PeeWee Herman fan and around here during the day, don't miss dropping in to the thunderously camp Backstage for tea, sandwiches, and a constant stream of entertainment from the surviving Christmas Twin (a formerly famous American singing duo) proprietor.

Utrechtsedwars-straat 67, The Canals ☎ 622 3638

Getto
B7

For other gay excess, this area has the highest proportion of the city's leather bars. In the midst of them, heteros go homo at this trendy bar-restaurant, the place for inspired and innovative fun, with regular bingo (Thu) and karaoke tarot readings, DJs, Sunday brunch and fab cocktails (cocktail hour 5–7pm). The regular menu hops from nachos to kangeroo steak.

Warmoesstraat 51, Red Light District & Nieuwmarkt ☎ 421 5151

Havana
B11

Havana's name comes more from its understated Cuban-themed decor than any Latino rhythm or clientele. Drawing a fashion-conscious straight and gay crowd, it is particularly popular at weekends when DJs play speed garage.

Reguliersdwaarstraat 17, Old Centre ☎ 620 6788

Huyschkaemer
F12

Its reputation for personable service, worldly experimental café food, and a wackily designed split-level interior, has led to the broadening of its predominantly gay clientele with local hetero couples settling in for a romantic night out.

Utrechtsestraat 137, The Canals ☎ 627 0575

The Queen's Head
♯A8

Drag queen 'Dusty' runs this deliciously kitsch 50s bar – complete with carpeted tables. A wild crowd piles in for the weekly bingo nights and other off-beat floor shows.

Zeedijk 20, Red Lights District & Nieuwmarkt ☎ 420 2475

Saarein II
♯F5

The original Saarein emerged from the 70s feminist squatters' movement, but its sister bar is more trad than rad these days. The big difference is that (gay-friendly) men are now welcome, though it's still predominantly lesbian territory. Pool tables occupy the basement of this split-level brown bar, whilst upstairs is ideal for quiet conversation.

Elandstraat 119, Jordaan ☎ 623 4901

clubs

Cockring
♯B7

Very gay: so gay that women can't get in. It's also very popular, so much so that on high days and holidays many men can't get in either, with huge queues into the small hours. Inside, the music is predictably pumping and there is a darkroom for those who wish to expose themselves. Get the picture?

Warmoesstraat 96, Red Light District & Nieuwmarkt ☎ 623 9604

IT
♯B12

The hedonistic reputation of IT formed a substantial chunk of gay legend, but declined after the death of its owner/founder Manfred Langer. After being closed for most of the summer of '99 following a drug bust, it has now re-opened to welcome its glam – and often camp – regulars. Saturday is strictly gay, while the rest of the week is pretty mixed.

Amstelstraat 24, Old Centre ☎ 625 0111

De Trut
♯A9

Ostensibly a gay and lesbian club (the management sometimes go so far as asking for your sexual preference at the door). The atmosphere is uplifting, as is the music, ranging from the squat-staple acid techno to housier beats.

Bilderdijkstraat 165, Oude West ☎ 612 3524

Why Not?
♯A7

The oldest gay sex club in Amsterdam. The strip and go-go shows are free, but one drink is compulsory. Watching a sex show will cost ƒ44 and a private session with a boy in a room starts at ƒ250 for an hour.

Nieuwezijds Voorburgwal 28, Old Centre ☎ 627 4374

entertainment

From high-camp cinema to cutting-edge opera, Amsterdam is a veritable cultural cornucopia.

television & radio

Cable is the norm rather than the exception in Amsterdam. But despite around 30 channels to choose from, the emphasis is on quantity, not quality. The major commercial channels (RTL4, RTL5, SBS 6, Net 5, and Veronica) broadcast a plethora of American talk shows and sitcoms, plus some choice Brit hits. All English-language programmes are screened in English with Dutch subtitles. Twenty-four-hour music channels include the obligatory MTV, Dutch equivalent TMF (The Music Factory), and The Box (a phone-in video jukebox). The extreme EX is the only home channel devoted to sport, but no self-respecting sports bar is without Sky Sports. SBS 6 (commonly known as SBS Sex) has the odd explicit broadcast and some other channels have late-night movies. But for 100% sex, there's a hardcore porn channel (extra subscription only). Of the state channels (Nederlands 1, 2, and 3), 3 offers more cerebral and upbeat viewing (foreign flicks, art and music documentaries, etc). Thankfully, stalwarts BBC1 and BBC2 are just a button away.

Turn on, tune in and... well, probably turn off. With rare exceptions, Dutch radio stations are as appetizing as *stampot* (national dish of mashed potato and veg) – the majority have music that is all but lost in all talk, small talk, and call talk. Little excels above the standard fare of cheesy commercial pop, dished up by Radio 3 FM (91.5 FM), Radio 538 (107.9 FM), and Veronica FM (101.3 FM). Radio 5 (1008 AM) does, however, feature some fascinating documentaries, and Radio 3's Club Lek is an excellent contemporary music programme. Sadly, the best of the bunch, Kink FM (102.9 FM), is only available on cable. Pirate stations born from the squat movement get that famous Dutch tolerance treatment. There's the idiosyncratic Radio 100 (99.3 FM), which features anything from experimental sounds to Polish punk; the anarchistic chaos of Radio Patapoe (97.25 FM); and Radio de Vrije Keyzer (96.2 FM) (Tuesdays only).

the papers

Of the Dutch dailies, *Het Parool* is the choice of the savvy Amster-dammer, covering mostly local news, and has a good cultural weekend supplement, *PS*. The similarly moderate and popular *De Volkskrant* is more serious; *Trouw* is newsworthy and left-wing but with a strong religious bias; and *NRC Handelsblad* is rather stuffy. The biggest seller on the newsstands, however, remains the conservative *De Telegraaf*, popular for its sensationalist reporting (and financial news section). The functional *Financieel Dagblad* has a daily English page. Most newsstands, especially in the city centre, carry most of the English-language nationals. Otherwise head for the bookstores, of which Waterstone's is best for the English press.

listings mags & the free press

Two weekly Amsterdam freebies are *Amsterdams Stadsblad* and *De Echo*, good for cinema listings and local news. One of the only English-language listings guides (though not exactly hip) is the tourist board's *What's On in Amsterdam*: the articles are okay but day-by-day listings are uninspiring. For a different view, pick up the free, fortnightly *Shark*, which has an alternative take on Amsterdam, including *Queer Fish*, a centrefold with up-to-date info on the gay scene. Going underground is the free monthly flyer *Way Out: Alternative Uitlijst*; and the squatters' *Grachtenkrant* is a compilation of international press clippings, articles, and listings. Commercial freebies are the *Film Agenda, Pop Ladder*, and *Dance Agenda;* and the *Pop & Jazzlijst* is the best for concert info in Amsterdam (as well as out-of-town gigs). Although in Dutch, the free monthly *Uitkrant* has comprehensive listings plus articles on events. Pick up the freebies and flyers at the AUB Ticketshop, as well as in bars and cafés around town. For the more radical rags, head for the Fort Van Sjakoo bookshop (Jodenbreestraat 24, Old Centre).

websites

Info from *Time Out*'s Amsterdam guide, with a monthly agenda, is at **w** www.timeout.com; the City Council's site full of useful info is at **w** www.amsterdam.nl. A source for all entertainment activities is **w** www.theater.nl. Culture vultures should check out **w** www.aub.nl for info on museums and galleries. For alternative info, access Shark's website at: **w** www.xs4all.nl/~pipf or Amsterdam squatting info on **w** www.squatnet. In order to get an actual glimpse of the city check out **w** www.amsterdamlive.nl which has webcams set up at the city's major sites (like Centraal Station).

entertainment

music

Tickets at small venues can be bought at the door. Those for Melkweg, Paradiso, and ArenA can (and often need to) be bought in advance from the AUB Ticketshop. Some record shops, like Get Records, also sell tickets for Paradiso and Melkweg. You can book on-line at: **w** www.theater.nl ☺ There are more concerts at weekends, but you won't be bored on weeknights. Times of performances vary, so check with the venue. Most gigs at Melkweg and Paradiso start around 9pm for the support act, with the headliner on around 10.30pm.

☑ Prices range from ƒ10 for small acts to ƒ75 for biggies.

♠ Most venues are standing room only, except for the ArenA that has a seated area for cheaper tickets. Paradiso has a balcony with chairs.

❶ The Dutch music mag *OOR* carries informative music listings. Also keep an eye out for posters and flyers and regularly check the daily updated Paradiso website (**w** www.paradiso.nl). See listings mags.

cinema

Thu–Sat evenings are popular so book in advance. Call the Belbios-line ☎ (0900) 9363 for all cinemas or the Pathé-line ☎ (0900) 202 5350 for Pathé cinemas. Both are computer-operated and in Dutch,

so if you want an English-speaking operator ring the cinemas direct. To guarantee your reserved tickets buy and collect them 30 minutes before screening. Don't think there's anything wrong when halfway through the film the screen goes black; intervals are commonplace. ☺ Programmes run Thu–Wed with two evening screenings starting between 6.30–8pm and 9.15–10pm. Matinees start between 12.45–4pm. City, Kriterion, and The Movies have midnight screenings Fri–Sat.

♠ Seat reservation isn't possible, so arrive early.

☑ Tickets range from ƒ12.50 (daytime) to ƒ16 (evenings and weekends) in mainstream cinemas. Art-houses are cheaper (starting at ƒ11). There are often discount screenings on weekend mornings. Credit card bookings are rare, so use cash.

❶ The Belbios website has movie information and online bookings for most cinemas in the Netherlands (**w** www.belbios.nl). National newspapers review new films in their Wednesday editions. See also listings mags and free newspapers for film times.

theatre

Buy tickets directly from the theatres, or visit the AUB Ticket-shop and Amsterdam Tourist Board. For phone bookings try the AUB Uitlijn.

entertainment

◷ Most shows start at 8.15pm, with very few matinees. Most theatres are closed Jul–Aug.

♣ The larger venues have reserved seating, but the Nes theatres and the Bovenzaal have unnumbered seats, so arrive early for a good spot.

⊞ The big venues lead the pricing table, with the best seats costing ƒ38 at the Stadsschouwburg and ƒ65 at the Carré. Other Leidseplein theatres charge around ƒ25 whilst the smaller Nes venues are usually under ƒ18.

❶ *What's On in Amsterdam*, the *Uitkrant*, and the *Time Out* Amsterdam website have theatre listings. Try the useful, but conservative, *Roundabout*, available at a few bookshops, including the one located at Centraal Station. Also see **w** www.theater.nl

dance

Large venues have their own box offices where you can book by phone or queue for last-minute tickets. Tickets for most venues are available from the AUB Ticketshop and the Amsterdam Tourist Board, or by phone from the UitLijn.

◷ The dance season on both the formal ballet world and the independent circuit runs Sep–Jul. Most shows run through, but smaller companies may present an evening of different pieces with a short interval.

♣ At the Muziektheater, you can specify seats depending on availability, otherwise most Amsterdam theatres have a free-for-all seating policy.

⊞ Individual ballet tickets cost ƒ20–ƒ90, with ƒ15 off for unsold tickets for students 30 minutes before performance; expect to pay ƒ15–ƒ25 for independent dance.

❶ For a good overview of independent dance companies see **w** www.dansbeweegtje.nl. See newspapers and listings mags for details, particularly the *Uitkrant*. Also see **w** www.theater.nl

opera and classical music

Tickets for all venues are available from the AUB Ticketshop and the Amsterdam Tourist Board, or by phone from the UitLijn. Large venues have their own box offices where you can book by phone or queue for last-minute tickets. Tickets for smaller venues, such as churches, are available from the concert organizers but rarely at the venue itself, except just before a performance. Most opera performances play to full houses, and the concerts at the Concertgebouw often sell out months in advance, so if you want to be sure of tickets, book them in advance.

👕 Dress to impress or play it down. The Dutch have allowed formality to fly to the wind since the 70s.

☼ The popularity of summer festivals and tours means that major venues are open year-round, though the Beurs van Berlage is closed Jul–Aug. The opera and concert season runs Sep–Jun, but the summer 'break' at the Concertgebouw is filled with the popular Robeco Summer Concerts. Evening performances usually start at 8.15pm, although times vary.

🎫 Tickets are well-priced thanks to generous government subsidies. Individual opera tickets cost ƒ45–ƒ125; concert tickets, around ƒ25–ƒ70, but you can pay anything up to ƒ125 for a top-notch gig at the Concertgebouw. There are often discounts for students, CJP cardholders, and the over-65s. Tickets can be reserved for no extra cost at most venues.

❶ For up-to-date information visit **w** www.theater.nl or check out listings mags like the *Uitkrant*.

ticket offices

Amsterdam Uitburo (AUB)

Reserves tickets for classical concerts, opera, gigs, the theatre, and major events.

AUB Ticketshop

26 Leidseplein, The Canals 🚇 all
🎫 no surcharge (postage fee ƒ6)
◑ 10am–6pm daily (to 9pm Thu).

AUB Uitlijn (Ticketline)

☎ (0900) 0191 🚇 all
🎫 no surcharge (postage fee ƒ6)
◑ 9am–9pm daily.
❶ English-speaking operators.

AUB Website

www.aub.nl (in Dutch) and www.amsterdamarts.org (in English).

Amsterdam Tourist Board

Sells tickets for all major events and performances. The best place for info and tickets for the rest of the country's goings-on.

Ticketshops

Centraal Station (platform 2), Stationsplein 10, Old Centre 4040; Leidseplein 1, The Canals 🚇 all
🎫 surcharge payable
◑ 8am–9pm daily.
☎ (0900) 400 ❶ Information line only; English-speaking operators available (press 3 after the recorded message).

TIP

TIP, part of the Westergasfabriek, sells tickets to all major events.

Haarlemmerweg 8–10
☎ 681 3068 🚇 none
◑ 12–7pm Mon–Sat.

events

A seasonal guide to what's going on in Amsterdam ...

summer

Amsterdam Roots Festival
A melting pot of music and culture as performers (and cooks) from all over the world dish up and celebrate diversity.
Various venues including Melkweg ☎ 624 1777 ◑ 10 days in Jun.

Holland Festival
Despite its rather misleading title, this is an international festival of high-brow, quality performance of contemporary music and theatre.
Various venues ☎ 530 7111 ◑ Jun (not every year).

Echo Grachtenloop (Echo Canal Run)
Knobbly-knees and bodies-beautiful jog various distances around the canals. For those who get tired just watching, catch the less frenetic pace of Dutch singers performing outdoors on the Leidseplein.
Prinsengracht, Vijzelgracht & Leidseplein, The Canals ☎ 585 9222 ◑ mid-Jun.

KunstRAI Art Fair
The city's official annual art fair takes place in June when 160 galleries exhibit their best artists (mainly Dutch). Although a commercial event, galleries encourage browsing and welcome visitors, whether they intend to buy or not.
Various venues ☎ 549 1212 ◑ mid-Jun.

International Theaterschool Festival
Innovative, mime, dance, and theatre from the next generation of performers.
☎ 527 7613 ◑ 10 days end Jun.

Gerrit Rietveld Academie Degree Show ⌀ off map
Students graduate from Amsterdam's prestigious art academy.
Gerrit Rietveld Academie, Fred Roeskestraat 96, Zuid ☎ 571 1600 ◑ 6 days end Jun–beg Jul.

Over Het IJ Festival ⌀ off map
Large, avant-garde festival in a disused shipyard across the river IJ. Spectacular shows range from a multi-media performance about cyberbabe Lara Croft to performing Fiat cars.
NDSM-scheepswerf, Neveritaweg, Noord ☎ (0900) 9292 ◑ end Jun–beg Jul.

Vondelpark Open Air Theatre Festival

Catch some clowns or cabaret at this open air treat.
◑ *Jun–Aug.*

North Sea Jazz Festival

The best jazz festival outside the US, with 12,000 participants; 16 stages and around 17,000 visitors.
Den Haag ☎ (015) 215 7756 ◑ *1 weekend beg Jul.*

Julidans

A quality international contemporary dance festival.
☎ **624 2311** ◑ *10 days beg Jul.*

Robeco Summer Concerts
$D10

Fills the Concertgebouw with relaxed and enthusiastic concert goers, treated to world class orchestral and solo performances for a mere ƒ30.
Concertgebouwplein 2–6, Museum District & Vondelpark
☎ **(0900) 8012** ◑ *Jul–Aug.*

Kwakoe Festival

Soccer matches kick things off for Kwakoe, a huge multi-cultural festival held over different weekends (with varied themes).
Bijlmerpark, Bijlmermeer ☎ 690 1279 ◐ *6 weekends mid-Jul–mid-Aug.*

De Parade

Carnival style tents are set up at this great travelling theatre fair. Lots of fabulous fringe performances. A Winter Parade is at Westergasfabriek end of Dec. ❶ Catch the special festival boat from the Muziektheater.
Martin Luther King Park, Rivierenbuurt ☎ (033) 465 4577
◑ *17 days end Jul–beg Aug.*

Dance Valley

40,000 partygoers converge at the closest thing The Netherlands has to a valley for this huge outdoor dance music festival that closes with a laser show.
Spaarnwoude Recreation Area, Slotermeer ☎ 627 5555 ◑ *beg Aug.*

Amsterdam Pride

Amsterdam's gay pride march is unique. Although the parade along the canals is the highlight, there's plenty of fun for landlubbers with street parties, sports competitions, and cultural events. Lesbian and Gay Pride is held at the end of June (Pink Saturday) in a different Netherland town each year.
☎ **(0900) 0191** ◑ *1st weekend Aug.*

events

Hartjesdag (Day of Hearts)
A recently revived tradition in which both men and women dress up in drag, with the best cross-dresser crowned 'Queen of the Zeedijk'. Frocked-up festivities centre around the Zeedijk neighbourhood.
Zeedijk, Red Light District & Nieuwmarkt ☎ 625 8467 ◑ mid-Aug.

Grachtenfestival
The Prinsengracht concert, on a floating podium has grown into this weekend of events, with 70 chamber concerts in private houses and gardens.
Prinsengracht, The Canals ☎ 421 4542 ◑ 4 days mid-Aug.

Racism Beat It!
The Netherlands' largest free open-air festival with a multi-cultural myriad of bands and performances.
Spaarnwoude Recreation Area, Slotermeer ☎ 627 7766 ◑ Aug.

Uitmarkt
This preview of the forthcoming arts season sees diversities as wide as depraved cabaret, high-brow opera, and 'Holiday on Ice' doing their turns. Draw-backs are crowds and queues.
Museumplein & Leidseplein ◑ last weekend in Aug.

autumn

Bloemen Corso (Flower Parade)
Flowery floats wind their way through Amsterdam's streets after travelling from blooming Aalsmeer, the heart of the Dutch flower industry.
City route: Overtoom–Leidseplein–Leidsestraat–Spui–Nieuwezijds Voorburgwal–Dam ☎ (029) 732 5100 ◑ 1st Sat in Sep.

Chinese Parade
⊄C8
Dancing dragons and fireworks galore, appropriately based in the Chinese Quarter, represent February's Chinese New Year.
Nieuwmarkt ◑ Sep.

Open Monumentdag
Around 3000 historical monuments and gardens in the Netherlands (37 in Amsterdam) are opened to the public for one or two days every year.
☎ 522 4899 ◑ mid-Sep.

Jordaan Festival
⊄F5/E6
The high point for musical Jordaan: amateur crooners hit the open-air stage and through the sounds of accordions compose their airs to Amsterdam.
Elandsgracht, Jordaan ☎ 626 5587 ◑ mid-Sep.

Amsterdam Dance Event
Around 800 music biz bods (from DJs to record label reps) gather for this event. Public parties follow daytime conferences.
Felix Meritus; parties at Melkweg, Paradiso, Escape ☎ (0900) 0191
◗ *3 days in Oct.*

Sinterklaas Parade
St Nicolaas parades through the city on a white horse with his scary little helpers Zwarte Pieten (Black Peters) in tow.
Route: Prins Hendrikkade–Damrak–Dam–Raadhuisstraat–Rozengracht–Marnixstraat–Leidseplein ☎ 610 4904 ◗ *mid-Nov.*

High Times Festival
Stars and pipes as the Yanks invade the city en masse for this annual hash-bash, organized by New York-based *High Times* magazine. Coffeeshops compete for the Cannabis Cup.
Various venues including the Melkweg ☎ 624 1777 ◗ *4 days end Nov.*

International Documentary Film Festival
Focusing on documentaries from around the world, this festival comprises ten days of film screenings, lectures, and debates. The Leidseplein, where the majority are shown, is swamped with frenzied film fans, directors, and students.
Various venues including De Balie, Kleine Gartmanplant-soen 10, The Canals ☎ 553 5151 ◗ *10 days end Nov–beg Dec.*

winter

Pakejesavona
The Dutch used to celebrate Pakejesavona, or Presents' Day, more than Christmas Day, but now (sensibly) do both.
◗ *5 Dec.*

Amsterdam Ballongezelschap Party
♂C11
The Amsterdam Balloon Company, whose origins lie in the once squatted village of Ruigoord, organizes this annual party's avant-garde performances.
Paradiso, Weteringschans 6–8, The Canals ☎ 623 7348 ◗ *end Dec.*

New Year's Eve
Fireworks (the type illegal in many countries) go off all over Amsterdam in what's probably the craziest beginning to a new year in any city.
◗ *31 Dec.*

De Elfstedentocht (The Eleven Cities Tour)
Unique to The Netherlands, this event takes place only when the canals and lakes in the northern province of Friesland freeze over – which could be three years in a row, or once every 10 years. On a designated day, professional skaters and enthusiastic novices alike skate through 11 cities. It almost becomes a national holiday when it's on.
Begins & ends in Leeuwarden ☎ (058) 215 5020 ◑ *1 day in Jan or Feb.*

International Film Festival Rotterdam
The largest in the country and well worth an hour's trek. It features around 2000 feature films and 100 shorts.
☎ (010) 890 9000 ◑ *end Jan–beg Feb.*

Commemorative Service of the Dockworkers' Strike   *♯ off map*
An event to commemorate the actions of the brave dockworkers who, in 1941, during the German occupation, went on strike in protest against the treatment of Jews.
Dokwerker Statue, Jonas Daniël Meijerplein, Oost ◑ *25 Feb.*

spring

Stille Omgang (Silent Procession)
A night-time procession along the Heiligeweg (Holy Way) by Catholics celebrating the 1345 'Miracle of Amsterdam'.
Route: Spui–Kalversstraat–Nieuwendijk–Warmoesstraat–Nes
☎ (023) 524 6229 ◑ *1st Sun in Mar.*

Museum Weekend
One weekend a year (usually in April) around 200 of the mostly smaller museums in Amsterdam and the rest of the Netherlands offer free or reduced admission.
☎ (0900) 400 4040 ◑ *Apr.*

World Press Photo Exhibition   *♯A7*
The world's largest photo competition opens in the gothic Nieuwe Kerk before going on to 70 locations worldwide.
Nieuwe Kerk, Dam, Old Centre ☎ 676 6096 ◑ *6 weeks mid-Apr–end May.*

Koninginnedag (Queen's Day)
A national holiday, when the whole city becomes one big free party as a million people arrive for the wildest bash of the year. Everyday folk are allowed to sell anything and everything tax free.
◑ *30 Apr.*

Triple X Festival ♫ off map
Although the length of this cutting-edge multi-media festival depends on what subsidies it obtains each year, the quality of performance does not. Attractions include robot installations and mechanical performances.
Westergasfabriek, Westerpark ☎ 420 5316 ◑ *May.*

Legalize! Street Party
Party animals and activists unite in this, sometimes less-than-legal, street party to raise awareness of drug issues.
Amsterdam or The Hague ☎ (070) 380 8433 ◑ *beg May or beg Jun.*

Herdenkingsdag (Remembrance Day) ♫C7/A6
The city remembers victims of World War II with a service at 7.30pm on Dam Square, usually attended by Queen Beatrix. The gay community host their own memorial at the Homomonument.
National Monument, Dam, Old Centre & Homomonument, Westermarkt, The Canals ◑ *4 May.*

Bevrijdingsdag (Liberation Day)
Liberation in 1945 from German occupation is celebrated with festivities around town. Best bets are Dam Square (usually a pop concert followed by a dance party), the more chilled Vondelpark or the revamped Museumplein.
Various locations ◑ *5 May.*

National Cycling Day
National cycling day is officially celebrated with people taking to the 222 routes around the country on this one day.
☎ (0900) 400 4040 ◑ *2nd Sat in May.*

National Windmill Day
Just over half of the country's windmills and watermills turn their sails.
☎ 623 8703 ◑ *2nd Sat in May.*

Europerve Party ♫ off map
Fetishists of the world indulge: the name says it all!
Artis Zoo, Plantage Kerklaan 40, Oost ☎ 620 5603 ◑ *end May.*

Drum Rhythm Festival ♫ off map
Features rhythm and roots musicians.
Westergasfabriek ☎ 681 3068 ◑ *2 days end May.*

Open Ateliers
Local artists open their studios to the public.
☎ 626 4389 ◑ *May–Oct.*

sights, museums & galleries

Wander along the canals lined with grand mansions, duck down intriguing side streets, or head for the museums that boast some of the world's best art.

landmarks

Bartolotti Huis
B6

Curving with the bend of the canal, Bartolotti Huis is Dutch Renaissance architecture at its finest. Its blazing red-and-white façade bristles with masks, vases, and pillars. The house was built for Willem van der Heuvel, who called himself Guillelmo Bartolotti after an Italian relation who left him a fortune.
Herengracht 170–17, The Canals

Beurs van Berlage
B7

Designed by HP Berlage, this graceful monument to modernity was built as the stock exchange at the debut of the 20th century. Look closely and you'll see many of the ornamental details gently mock the traders' greedy pursuits. It now functions as a cultural centre.
Damrak 243, Old Centre

Blauwbrug
off map

The present-day bridge over the Amstel is a lesser version of Paris's Pont Alexandre III. But it was originally called Leeuwenbrug (Lion Bridge) after four lions carved on the structure. When the Calvinists took power in 1578, a Catholic faction gave the lions a lick of blue paint. And, though the paint soon peeled, the name 'Blue Bridge' stuck.
Amstel

Centraal Station
C4/D4

This neo-Renaissance fantasy, by PJH Cuypers, occupies a purpose-built island separating the city from the IJsselmeer (inland sea). The station's original first-class waiting room is now a grand café. Buskers from around the world gather to entertain the thousands who pass through daily.
Stationsplein, Old Centre

Cromhouthuizen
E6

Architect Philips Vingboons designed this row of canalside dream houses for Amsterdam's new money in 1662. He adorned them with circular 'bulls-eye' windows and stone fruit. Numbers 366–368 now house the Bible Museum.
Herengracht 364–370, The Canals

Dam
$C7

This is where the Amstel was originally dammed. On the west side is the stern Koninklijk Paleis, and in the centre the tall spire of the Nationaal Monument commemorates WWII victims. A somewhat grungy hang-out for the world-weary, the Dam is scheduled for a timely makeover.
Old Centre

De Dolphijn
$B6

Frans Bannigh Cocq, one of the richest men of his day, and the central figure in Rembrandt's *The Night Watch*, lived here from 1605 to 1655. A classic early 17th-century house, it was designed by Hendrick de Keyser.
Singel 140–142, The Canals

Goude Bocht
$B11

This section of the Herengracht, known as the Golden Bend, was the address for the bankers, merchants, and politicians of 18th-century Amsterdam. The prestigious series of façades (nos 475, 485, 493, and 527) are made of imported stone rather than native brick and adhere to a minimalist 'flat' style.
Herengracht, The Canals

Huis met de Hoofden
$B6

This refined Renaissance mansion gets its name ('House of Heads') from six busts that adorn the entrance. Officially, they depict six Roman gods and goddesses, but a more intriguing story tells of six robbers who were caught red-handed and beheaded on the spot by the housemaid – their crime and punishment then committed to stone.
Keizersgracht 123, The Canals

Klein-Trippenhuis
$F7

The narrowest house in Amsterdam sits at just 2.44m wide and is dwarfed by the surrounding canalhouses. Built for the coachman of the Tripp brothers, with leftover stone from their mansion opposite, it's as narrow as the mansion's front door, but its itty-bitty gable still manages to pack a pair of sphinxes.
Kloveniersburgwal 26, Red Light District & Nieuwmarkt

Leidseplein
$C11

In the 17th century, this square was an out-of-town parking lot for farmers and peasants to stash their wagons while they headed into town. It is now thronged by caricaturists and street performers by day, and is a neon whirl of theatres, terraced cafés, bars, and clubs by night.
The Canals

Magere Brug
♯ off map

There has been a white-painted drawbridge spanning the Amstel here since 1672. – the current bridge, however, doesn't live up to its title of 'Skinny Bridge'. Local legend says two sisters called Mager (meaning skinny) had the original pedestrian bridge built so they could visit each other. Photographers and kissing couples often loiter in the middle.
Amstel

Molen De Gooyer
♯ off map

Built in the early 18th century and moved to its present site 100 years later, this is the most central of Amsterdam's eight remaining windmills. When its corn-grinding days were over, the mill was converted into a public bath, and once that provision became obsolete, it became a brewery and bar.
Funenkade 5, Oosterdok

Munttoren
♯A12

Built on the remnants of a medieval city gate all but destroyed by fire in 1618, the Munttoren (Mint Tower) gets its name from a spell as Amsterdam's mint in the late 17th century. Its 16-bell carillon, was a 1699 addition by Francois Hemony, designer of the Oude Kerk's own set of chiming bells.
Muntplein, Old Centre

Muziektheater & Stadhuis
♯B12

Commonly known as the Stopera (Stadhuis and Opera), this two-in-one complex comprises the city hall and opera house. Built in 1987 against a barrage of opposition, critics have called it the 'set of dentures'. Inside, tall tubes of water levels are a reminder that you are standing beneath sea level.
Waterlooplein 22, Old Centre

newMetropolis
♯ off map

Renzo Piano, architect (along with Richard Rogers) of the Pompidou Centre, designed this copper-sheathed building to reflect the downward curves of the tunnel that passes under the harbour – a style that lends it the look of an ocean liner. The building houses the newMetropolis Science & Technology Center.
Oosterdok 2

Nieuwe Kerk
♯A7/C7

From Gothic beginnings, the Nieuwe Kerk reflects several centuries of intermittent fire damage, plunder, and occasional rounds of rebuilding. A tower, begun in 1646 with the intention of out-scaling the Oude Kerk, had to be abandoned when it became clear that it would also overshadow the neighbouring Stadhuis (now the Koninklijk Paleis).
Dam, Old Centre

Nieuwmarkt & De Waag
&D7

This beautiful market square, in the heart of tiny Chinatown, plays host to fairs, circuses, and a weekly organic food market. De Waag – the city's oldest surviving gatehouse, one time place of executions and, later, city weighing station – is today home to a glorious café.
Red Light District & Nieuwmarkt

Oude Kerk
&B7

This church started off as a wooden chapel in 1306, making it the city's oldest building. It was added to until 1571, and today its squat bulk sits ironically in the centre of the Red Light District, purveyor of all things sinful. Forever in residence is Rembrandt's wife Saskia, who is buried inside.
Oudekerksplein 1, Red Light District & Nieuwmarkt

Rembrandtplein
&A12

A butter market in the 17th century, this square still has a certain slippery quality. Comprising a plethora of tacky clubs, music bars, and fast-food joints, it's no wonder Rembrandt frowns down on the proceedings from his central pedestal.
Old Centre

Rijksmuseum & Museumplein
&E11

A 19th-century architectural extravaganza, the Rijksmuseum houses an impressive collection of Dutch art. Just behind is the city's biggest open space, the recently revamped Museumplein. You can now cool off in the pool, chill-out on the roof of the underground supermarket, or get the T-shirt at the shop.
Museum District & Vondelpark

Schreierstoren
&A8

Legend has it women waved teary farewells to their sailors here, hence the name Weepers' Tower. But historians now say the women weren't crying so much as shouting in frustration at declining economic conditions. Today the tower attracts a happier crowd to its maritime-themed café.
Prins Hendrikkade 94–95, Red Light District & Nieuwmarkt

Tuschinski Theater
&A12

Resembling an old Fritz Lang movie set, this 1921 cinema combines ostentatious art deco kitsch with eastern motifs. Dazzling geometrics, Persian carpets, peacocks, and fringed Chinese lanterns create a unique pastiche of fanciful styles.
Reguliersbreesstraat 26–28, Old Centre

sights, museums & galleries

Westerkerk *♫A6*
The city's tallest and most beautiful tower is 85m-tall, and is topped by an Imperial crown which the city added to its coat of arms in 1489. The tower and its bells mean as much to Amsterdammers as the Bow bells do to East Londoners, and a true Jordaaner must be born within earshot.
Westermarkt, The Canals

viewpoints

Beurs van Berlage *♫B7*
Damrak 243, Old Centre ☎ 626 5257 ◑ *11am–5pm Tue–Sun.*

Ciel Bleu Restaurant *♫ off map*
Ferdinand Bolstraat 333, De Pijp ☎ 678 7450 ◑ *12pm–1am daily.*

Kalvertoren *♫B11*
Singel 457, The Canals ☎ 427 3901 ◑ *10am–7pm daily (from 11am Mon; to 9pm Thu; to 6pm Sat; 12–7pm Sun).*

Metz & Co *♫A11*
Keizersgracht 455, The Canals ☎ 520 7020 ◑ *9.30am–6pm Mon–Sat (from 11am Mon; to 9pm Thu), 12–5pm Sun.*

newMetropolis Café *♫ off map*
Oosterdok 2 ☎ (0900) 919 1100 ◑ *10am–6pm Tue–Sun.*

Oude Kerk *♫B7*
Oudekerksplein 23, Red Light District & Nieuwmarkt ☎ 612 6856 ◑ *by appointment.*

Westerkerk *♫A6*
Prinsengracht 281, The Canals ☎ 624 7766 ◑ *Apr–Sep: 10am–5pm Mon–Sat; Oct–Mar: by appointment only.*

Zuidertoren *♫F7*
Zuiderkerkhof 72, Red Light District & Nieuwmarkt ☎ 612 6856 ◑ *Apr–Sep: 10am–5pm daily; Oct–Mar: by appointment.*

The big six

Amsterdams Historisch Museum *♫F6*
Located in the restored city orphanage, this museum presents varied portraits of the fortunes and lifestyles of Amsterdam folk, from aristocrats to ordinary housewives, from the 13th to the 21st century. Through an elaborate narrative of texts, paintings, maps, prints, models, and archaeological finds you can witness the city flourish through the years: from its 13th-century kernel as a fishing village, through its Golden

Age, to today's personal-freedom-driven Amsterdam. Informative and imaginative displays, many almost like art installations, give an excellent overview of the city and its history. After a visit here, Amsterdam makes a whole lot more sense. ✧ Explanations in Dutch and English. ✧ Take the free walk down the museum's Civic Guard Gallery where group portraits of 17th-century guards are hung. ✧ The Goliath Café in the old orphanage courtyard is a great place to relax. ✧ The museum organizes events like slide shows and thematic bike trips eg. architectural tours past key Amsterdam School buildings. ❶ For much of 2000, the museum will undergo a facelift, remaining open if a bit dusty. It will then launch a new exhibition: *Amsterdam and Its People.*
Kalverstraat 92, Old Centre ☎ 523 1822
◑ *10am–5pm Mon–Fri; 11am–5pm Sat–Sun.*

Joods Historisch Museum   ♬ *off map*
Step into this museum, a complex of four Ashkenazi synagogues, to learn about Mokum Alef – Yiddish for 'the best city of all', and the Jewish name for Amsterdam. The first Jews to arrive in the city, around 1600, were Sephardis, merchants from Spain and Portugal. Poorer Ashkenazim, from Eastern Europe and Germany, formed the next wave of immigrants. By the end of the 17th century, Mokum was the centre of the world to European Jews. When World War II broke out, ten per cent of Amsterdam's population was Jewish and around 100,000 died during the war. Despite the loss, the influence on local culture was immense. Exhibits give a brief history of Mokum and themed exhibitions cover subjects like Jewish life and identity. This is *the* place to begin or end an exploration of Amsterdam's Jewish Quarter.
✧ Work of Charlotte Salomon, an artist and diarist who recorded WWII before she was sent to a concentration camp.
Jonas Daniël Meijerplein 2–4, Oost ☎ 626 9945 ◑ *10am–5pm Mon–Fri.*

Nederlands Scheepvaartmuseum   ♬ *off map*
If exploration and floaty things are your bag then check out this most earnest of museums. Located in a former munitions storage facility, it houses one of the world's most important maritime collections, with original vessels ranging from small pleasure boats to full-on naval battle ships. Dusty antique model ships, tow barges as ornate as any Venetian gondola, and the beautiful royal sloop paint a picture of sailing past.

The Dutch have a seafaring history as long as your arm and their worldwide adventures are charted here, along with fully operational nautical equipment dating from 1946 that helps to illustrate the history of World War II from a Dutch perspective. In the 17th century, Amsterdam led the world in marine cartography, so there's also a great collection of centuries-old maps, which portray the world with all its fanciful borders and wild landmasses. And if you still haven't had enough of ships, nearby is the interesting and unmuseum-like Werf 't Kromhout (at Hoogte Kadijk 147), one of Amsterdam's oldest dockyards. Here, you'll get a better idea of just how a ship is assembled. ♿ Docked outside the Scheepvaartmuseum is the *Amsterdam*, a replica 18th-century Dutch East India Company ship, on which actors re-enact duties and explain life on board.

Kattenburgerplein 1, Oosterdok ☎ 523 2222 ◑ *10am–5pm Tue–Sun (plus Mon Jul–Sep).*

Rijksmuseum
⌗E11

The striking exterior of the Rijksmuseum was designed by architect PJH Cuypers and opened in 1885. As a provincial man, he was so inspired by Amsterdam's artistic scene that he embellished the outside with texts and sculptures depicting local luminaries. He also added Gothic gargoyles, stained-glass windows, and a crypt-like underpass.

Inside, the museum has the best collection of 17th-century Dutch art anywhere, and treasures as varied as Balenciaga cocktail dresses, dancing bronze Shivas, and cabinets inlaid with ray-fish skin. The highlight of the collection is Rembrandt's most famous work, *The Night Watch*. From here, move on to the glitz of Amsterdam's Golden Age, the museum's main attraction. This exhibition includes 19 other Rembrandts, from captivating early portraits to later, painterly pieces like The Jewish Bride. Jan Steen's entertaining visual narratives of merry families reveal one aspect of 17th-century Dutch domesticity, whilst Vermeer's sober, symbolic interiors represent another. Stately portraits by Frans Hals are displayed alongside dramas on the high seas and wintry skating scenes.

Paintings from other ages include largely religious works from the 15th and 16th centuries plus a substantial selection of New-Classical, Romantic, and Impressionist works. Look out for George Hendrik Breitner, whose intimate evocations of 19th-century Amsterdam street life are unsurpassed.

Aside from paintings, the museum has four other departments. The sculpture and decorative arts section includes some 45,000 items including intricate ivory diptychs from France, a stunning collection of 17th-century dolls' houses, delftware, silverware, and art nouveau textiles that once belonged to Madame Pompadour. A huge collection of Asiatic art incorporates treasures from the Netherlands' colonial past, comprising Chinese porcelain, Japanese lacquerwork, and Korean ceramics. The rather dull Dutch history department traces the country's development with depictions of battles, bursting dykes, and model ships. There's also a print room, but these works are only displayed in temporary exhibitions.

❶ 1| Use south wing entrance to avoid queues. 2| Often crowded.

Stadhouderskade 42, Museum District & Vondelpark ☎ 674 7000 ◑ *10am–5pm daily.*

Stedelijk Museum
ⓂB10

The always vigorous Stedelijk has a stunning permanent collection but only has room to show selected bits and pieces at any one time: Mondrian, Man Ray, Matisse, Gauguin, Kandinsky, De Kooning, Picasso, Appel, Van Gogh, Chagall... the star-studded list goes on and on. But just as interesting are the special risk-taking exhibitions, such as the *We're Like Two Inflatable Dolls in a Hooker's Bad Dream* show, which help give new context to past and present. On permanent display are Malevich's Suprematist paintings (an avant-garde movement exploring composition and shape), Rietveld's striking De Stijl furniture, and Karel Appel's (member of the experimental CoBrA movement) *Appelbar*, a room completely covered in his murals.

✧ Contemporary shows in the associated Stedelijk Museum Bureau.

❶ This 19th-century building is just not big enough for the breadth of its collection, so the Stedelijk is going to gain a new face and a new wing during much of 2000. The museum, however, remains open.

Paulus Potterstraat 13, Museum District & Vondelpark ☎ 573 2911 ◗ 11am–5pm daily.

Van Gogh Museum
ⓂB10

To marvel at the largest collection of Van Goghs in the world, join the hordes in the almost-ethereal 1973 Rietveld building. It has a new wing, designed by Japanese architect Kisho Kurokawa, which is soothing and sensual, and the place to see ever-changing exhibits. But the focus of the gallery is the more than 200 paintings, 500 sketches, and 700 letters by this most famous of painters. Most of the exhibits were collected by Van Gogh's brother Theo, one of the few who supported the artist in his life-time. Neglected and penniless for most of his life, Van Gogh only became famous after his death.

On the first floor there are paintings ranging from his subdued early style (*The Potato Eaters*, 1885) to that period of feverish brightness that has come to symbolize his insanity (*Wheatfield with Crows*, 1890). It's clear to see from these later works why Van Gogh is the painter who put 'pain' into the word 'paint'. The ground floor, meanwhile, houses a strong collection of Van Gogh's contemporaries, and many of the artists he admired, including Monet, Gauguin, and Seurat. ✧ Expect a line outside, although the new wing spreads out the hordes more thinly inside.

Paulus Potterstraat 7, Museum District & Vondelpark ☎ 570 5200 ◗ 10am–4pm daily.

contemporary art

Arti & Amicitiae
ⓂE7

An artists association with a very posh 'clubhouse'. It features all kinds of art, from computer-manipulated imagery to extraordinary fashion designs.

Rokin 112, Old Centre ☎ 623 2995 ◗ 12–6pm daily.

Stedelijk Museum Bureau ♭D5
A roomy exhibition space run by the Stedelijk Museum, also organizes lively, funky, and challenging shows. It is devoted to new work by young, local artists, including painting, sculpture, video, mixed media, and photography.
Rozenstraat 59, Jordaan ☎ 422 0471 ◐ 11am–5pm Tue–Sun.

Stichting de Appel ♭B11
Promotes young, up-and-coming local and foreign artists alike. Visiting exhibitions here might involve jumping on a trampoline, walking through a waterfall, or even getting thoroughly drunk on a piece of art. More often than not, this gallery gives you the chance to marvel at strange creations fabricated out of light and sound or even baby powder – the significance of which can sometimes go straight over your head.
Nieuwe Spiegelstraat 10, The Canals ☎ 625 5651 ◐ 12–5pm Tue–Sun.

famous houses

Anne Frankhuis ♭A6
Every day, thousands of people pass through the upstairs annex to see the famous hideaway of the Franks and the Van Daans. These two Jewish families hid for two years until 4 August 1944 when, tragically close to the end of the war, an informer revealed their hiding place (the reward was f7 per Jew, a princely sum at the time). The result? They were deported to concentration camps – Anne was first sent to Auschwitz, then Bergen-Belsen where she died a few weeks before liberation.

The 'Green Police', who took away the annex residents, left the hand-written pages of Anne's diary scattered on the floor. A secretary of the family business, Miep Gies, saved them for Anne's return. Anne's father Otto Frank, the only family survivor, eventually had them published, giving a unique and moving account of life in confinement during the war.

The house has been restored to appear as it did when Anne lived here (except for the annex furniture, which was removed by order of the Nazis). Her collection of magazine pictures – Greta Garbo, Ginger Rogers, Princesses Elizabeth and Margaret – are pinned to the wall. There are even pencil marks made by Otto Frank to track the growth of his daughters, and the map on which he plotted the progress of the Allied armies towards Amsterdam. It is well worth reading the diary before you visit; it will make the experience all the more profound. In the new wing, computers lead you on a multimedia journey through the Anne Frank House. Annually-changing exhibitions concentrate on current issues, like nationalism. ✆ The line to get in often winds right around the block.
Prinsengracht 263, The Canals ☎ 556 7100 ◐ 9am–7pm Mon–Sun (to 9pm Apr–Aug).

Museum Het Rembrandthuis ♂E8

Rembrandt's most famous painting, *The Night Watch*, is thought to have been painted in the inner courtyard of this house, although he usually worked in a room on the first floor. From 1639 to 1658 this was the great master's home and studio, where he spent his happiest and most prosperous years. During this period he immortalized the women in his life in great works of art: his beloved wife Saskia, his mistress Hendrickje Stoffels, and a 'shrew in between', Geertje Dirck, whom he had committed to an asylum in Gouda.

Rembrandt became the most fashionable painter in Amsterdam, with powerful patrons and a large following of apprentices, although the house was also the scene of Rembrandt's steep fall from grace. Everything in it was seized when he went bankrupt in 1658, including his fabulous collection of art, antiques, and rarities, including Japanese swords and Venetian glass. The house has been refurbished as far as possible with furniture and artefacts from Rembrandt's day. A new wing exhibits over 100 of his etchings, of which the best are *The Barrel Organ Player*, *The Rat-Catcher*, *The Blind Fiddler*, *Christ Healing the Sick*, as well as some self-portraits.

Jodenbreestraat 4–6, Old Centre ☎ 624 9468 ◑ 10am–5pm daily (from 1pm Sun).

great interiors

Bijbels Museum ♂E6

The Bible Museum displays religious exhibits including archaeological finds from Egypt and the Middle East, models of the Temple Mount, the Delft Bible, and the first complete Bible published in Dutch. But the real reason to visit is to see the stunning interior. The highlight is the ceiling in the main hall, which was painted in 1717 by Jacob de Wit and features mythological scenes of sexy gods and goddesses. And outside, the garden is equally impressive. The waters of the fountain part for visitors to walk through without wetting a toe, there is a Judas Tree not yet sturdy enough for a hanging, and there is an example of the same species of bulrush that tugged at Moses's nappies. ❶ The exhibition itself is pretty dull.

Herengracht 366, The Canals ☎ 624 2436 ◑ 10am–5pm daily (from 1pm Sun).

Kattenkabinet ♂B11

A mayor of Amsterdam once lived in this 17th-century house, but now it has been taken over by cats. The Kattenkabinet (literally 'Cat Cabinet') prides itself on being the only museum in the world wholly centred on the cat fetish. But the house itself is worth more of a look than the feline exhibits.

The galleries lead you through such delights as an elegant 19th-century ballroom. Cat lovers should also head over to the Poezenboot (cat boat), moored at Singel 40, where abandoned cats are given a floating home.
Herengracht 497, The Canals ☎ 626 5378 F 626 6764
◗ *10am–2pm Mon–Fri; 1–5pm Sat–Sun.*

Koninklijk Paleis   ♭C7

The striking Royal Palace was originally a city hall, built in the 17th century when Amsterdam was the trading hub of the world. The classicist façade reflects the city's mood of confidence at the time and is bristling with allegorical sculptures by Artus Quellien and François Hemony. The palace is best appreciated inside, standing in the cavernous *Burgerzaal* (Citizens' Hall). Based on the assembly halls of Rome, it has an orgy of marble gods and goddesses, and a mosaic of heaven and earth inlaid in the marble floor. The adjoining *Vierschaar* (tribunal) is where death sentences were pronounced in the 17th century. Crowds on the Dam were able to look on and hurl insults through the windows.

The hall became 'royal' when Napoleon made his brother Louis King of The Netherlands. Louis ordered Dutch cabinet-makers to fill the building with Empire furniture within a matter of weeks. Today, it is state property and only used by Dutch royals for special occasions. ❶ Sometimes closed for state functions.
Dam, Old Centre ☎ 624 8698 ◗ 11am–5.30pm Mon–Fri;
12.30–5pm Sat–Sun.

Museum Amstelkring   ♭B7

Except for the varnish on a couple of paintings, the house looks like its 17th-century owner has just left. Upstairs, the attic church – *Onze Lieve Heer op Zolder* (Our Dear Lord in the Attic) – is a time capsule of clandestine Catholic worship in the 17th and 18th centuries. Amsterdam may not have been part of the religious killing fields of Europe, but Catholicism was repressed and the churches were turned over to Protestant worship in 1578. Catholics were, however, allowed to hold services in back rooms, attics, and sheds, and by 1680 there were 30 of these 'hidden' churches. They remained in use until 1795 when the arrival of Napoleon brought religious freedom. The Sael (living room) is also worth checking out – it's one of the best preserved 17th-century rooms in the city – as is the stunning period kitchen.
Oudezijds Voorburgwal 40, Red Light District & Nieuwmarkt
☎ 624 6604 ◗ 10am–5pm daily (from 1pm Sun).

Museum van Loon   ♭C12

This 17th-century canalside mansion shows how the upper crust of Amsterdam society lived for several centuries. It has a kitchen with all period mod cons and a delightful garden. The rooms, including an imposing master bedroom, are all adorned with fine furniture, porcelain, and sculpture.

Owner Willem van Loon co-founded the Dutch East India Company in 1602 and presumably made a fortune in the slave market, as the van Loon coat of arms features three negro slaves. There is a most unusual painting by Molenaer (1610–68), a family portrait that depicts the van Loons in the four phases of human life, from mischievous childhood to pensive old age. A second masterpiece, equally laden with symbolism, is a group portrait of the wedding of Willem van Loon and Margaretha Bos in 1637. Some of the van Loon family still live in a small apartment in the building.
Keizersgracht 672, The Canals ☎ 624 5255 ◑ *11am–5pm Mon, Fri–Sun.*

Museum Willet-Holthuysen
♭B12

Visit the Museum Willet-Holthuysen and get a glimpse inside a wonderfully snooty 17th-century canalhouse and see how the wealthy entertained in those days. The house served as a showcase even when the Willets (a family of merchants and art collectors) held court here over musical and literary evenings, art viewings, and costume balls. And, with all the gilded details, crystal chandeliers, satin, and velvet, it is just as you would imagine a rich merchant's house to be. The symmetrically prim French 18th-century classical garden looks like a Lilliputian version of Versailles – if you squint.
Herengracht 605, The Canals ☎ 523 1870 ◑ *10am–5pm daily (from 11am Sat–Sun).*

Theatermuseum
♭B6

No-one should pass up the chance to see inside a Herengracht house, and this is one of the best. The Theatermuseum occupies no fewer than five of them, including the landmark Bartolotti Huis. Crane your neck beneath opulent ceilings painted by Isaac de Moucheron and Jacob de Wit, brush through marble hallways and caress the beautifully carved oak banister. The exhibits themselves include a good collection of theatrical memorabilia, costumes, and sets. ♿ The garden café has a view of the tower of Westerkerk, Amsterdam's tallest.
Herengracht 168, The Canals ☎ 551 3300 ◑ *11am–5pm Tue–Sun (from 1pm Sat–Sun).*

Woonbootmuseum
♭E6

People who fantasize about living on a boat will get a certain *frisson* out of the Hendrika Maria, a commercial sailing barge built in 1914 and now a museum. For a sense of what it was really like in the old days, imagine what it must have been like to have to squeeze a family of ten into the deckhouse where the skipper lived. Visitors can also climb inside the former cargo hold which has been converted into a comfortable living room full of ships' models, maritime photos, along with other maritime memorabilia.
Facing Elandsgracht (opposite Prinsengracht 296), The Canals ☎ 427 0750 ◑ *10am–5pm Tue–Sun.*

Amstelkerk
ℰC12

Dedicated in 1670, the Amstelkerk was built of wood, with the intention of building a massive brick church at a later date, but funds for the grand scheme were never raised. The interior was, however, remodelled in neo-Gothic style in the 19th century when a wealthy benefactor donated ƒ25,000. Today it's a church and concert venue, and sitting in its quaint cobbled square, you would never guess the brash signs of Rembrandt plein are just two blocks away.

Amstelveld 10, The Canals ☎ 520 0070 ◑ 9am–12.45pm; 1.30–5pm daily.

Begijnhof
ℰF6

The ancient courtyard of 'Beguines', though only a few metres from the crowded Kalverstraat, belongs to another world. 'Beguines' were unmarried women who didn't want to be shut in nunneries so formed communes instead, living in small houses with tiny gardens around a common courtyard and chapel. They were not allowed to keep dogs – or entertain men. Some are still occupied by single women today. Although most of the architecture is 18th-century, No 34 is much older (c 1475) and one of only two wooden houses left in central Amsterdam (timber was banned as a building material in 1452 after a catastrophic fire). The courtyard has two churches. The Engels (English) Church, is so-called as it gave refuge to Protestant dissenters fleeing England during the Reformation. Later these protestants upped to Leiden and in 1620 formed the core of the Pilgrim Fathers, who left for the Americas. A second 'secret' Catholic church was built between two of the houses in 1665, when Protestantism ruled.

Begijnhof 34, Old Centre ☎ 622 1918 ◑ 9.30am–4.30pm daily.

Nieuwe Kerk
ℰA7/C7

The Church of Our Lady, or Nieuwe Kerk (New Church), was built in 1408 as a branch church to the Oude Kerk. In reality, though, they were bitter rivals – the merchants who frequented the Nieuwe Kerk pitted themselves against the Catholic hierarchy installed in the Oude Kerk. A war of chapel building (36 to the Nieuwe Kerk versus 38 to the Oude Kerk) followed until 1578.

After a terrible fire in 1645, the Nieuwe Kerk had a makeover. Its key elements are the choir screen, the finely carved pulpit, and the elaborately gilded organ. Imposing tombs contain the remains of the admirals who helped to make the tiny Dutch Republic a world power. The building is no longer a church, but is still used for 'investing' Dutch monarchs, and is an 'international centre' with a café in the former choir stalls. It is used as an exhibition hall for such things as the World Press Photo Exhibition.

✿ You may have to pay for an exhibition to see the church.

Dam, Old Centre ☎ 626 8168 ◑ 10am–6pm Mon–Sun (to 10pm Thu).

sights, museums & galleries

Noorderkerk
A7/C7

The Noorderkerk (North Church), built between 1620–1623, is one of the few Amsterdam churches still used for prayer. Believers gather here every Sunday morning in what was the first church in the Netherlands designed specifically for Protestant worship. It was used as a model for all Protestant churches throughout the Republic because the design was so suitable for this style of worship, putting preacher and pulpit in the middle of the congregation. As a 24-year-old student preparing for the ministry, Vincent van Gogh was so moved by a sermon here, he placed his silver watch in the collection plate – the only thing of value he had in the world. ❶ On Saturdays, an open-air farmers' market surrounds the church on what used to be its graveyard.

Noordermarkt 48, Jordaan ☎ 626 6436 ◐ 11am–1pm Sat; 10am–12pm & 7–8.30pm Sun.

Oude Kerk
B7

The elegant spire of the 'Old Church', built in 1306, presides over the Red Light District and the druggy scene of 'Pill Bridge'. Ransacked by radical Calvinists while it was a Catholic establishment, the church still has intriguing fragments of its past. The wooden roof survived and much 15th-century painting is visible, some of which only came to light after a cleanup in 1955. In addition, several centuries of Amsterdam burgomasters (chief magistrates) look down from their stained-glass portraits onto the huge grey flagstones that cover the remains of poets and admirals. A gargantuan organ, mounted on square-columned marble, spans the entire west wall. Look for the name 'Saskia' in the floor under the smaller organ – Rembrandt's wife was buried here when she died in 1642, one year after giving birth to their only child. ♫ The tower carillon is played every Sat 4–5pm.

Ouderkerksplein 23, Red Light District & Nieuwmarkt ☎ 625 8284 ◐ summer: 11am–5pm daily (from 1pm Sun); winter: 1–5pm daily.

Portugees-Israëlitische Synagoge
E8

This was the largest synagogue in the world in 1675. Little has changed since then except that the 800 candles that once illuminated services here are now only lit on special days. It was built by the small but wealthy Sephardic community of Jews as a showpiece. The complex includes one of the most famous Jewish libraries. The Dokwerker statue in front of the synagogue commemorates the strike by dockworkers on 25 February 1941 to protest against the deportation of Amsterdam Jews.

Mr Visserplein 3, Old Centre ☎ 624 5351 ◐ Apr–Oct: 10am–4pm Sun–Fri; Nov–Mar: 10am–4pm Sun–Thu; 10am–5pm Fri.

Sint Nicolaaskerk   ♬A8

This grandiose, neo-baroque (1888) church, dedicated to the patron saint of seafarers and of Amsterdam, dominates the skyline of the old harbour. The lavish interior has an impressive coffered ceiling and dome, illuminated by light streaming through the stained glass. Despite much restoration work, it still suffers from neglect due to a lack of parishioners. The church is the endpoint of one of Catholic Amsterdam's most important festivals, the Stille Omgang. This silent procession commemorates the 'Miracle of Amsterdam', which dates from 1345 and centres on a miraculously indestructible (by digestive juices and fire, at least) communion wafer.
Prins Hendrikkade 73, Red Light District & Nieuwmarkt ☎ 624 8749 ◑ 1–4pm Mon–Sat.

Westerkerk   ♬A6

The West Church (1631) has the tallest tower in Amsterdam, and the largest nave of any Dutch Protestant church. It is almost bare except for a plaque which records that Rembrandt was buried in an unmarked pauper's grave. A series of ladders in the tower leads you past the great oak frame that holds the church's massive bells. Look east for a fantastic view.

In the square on the south side, a statue of Anne Frank (1977) by Mari Andriessen vaguely recalls Degas' bronze ballerinas. Look also for the three pink triangles jutting into the Keizersgracht. This is the Homonument (1987), a memorial to homosexual victims of the Nazis.
Prinsengracht 281, The Canals ☎ 624 7766 ◑ Apr–Sep: 11am–3pm; Mon–Fri (plus Jun–Sep: 11am–3pm Sat); mid Sep–Easter: 10.30am–1pm Sun.

Zuiderkerk   ♬F7

The magnificent Renaissance tower of the South Church (1611) is one of the glories of Amsterdam and the view from the spire is one of the most famous and beautiful. This was the city's first Protestant church following the Reformation, but today it serves as the City Council Urban Development Department and the former graveyard is covered with community housing. A small plaque commemorates the low point in its history when it became a morgue during the 'hunger winter' of 1944, a year when more people died in the neighbourhood than the authorities were able to bury. ♿ Non-acrophobes should scale the wooden ladders to the top of the tower.
Zuiderkerkhof 72, Red Light District & Nieuwmarkt ☎ 622 2962 ◑ 12–5pm Mon–Fri (to 8pm Thu).

one-offs

Kindermuseum   ♬ off map

As if the feathered masks, big drums, and colourful costumes of the Tropenmuseum weren't enough: visitors from ages six to twelve can shed their parents and join a group at the Kindermuseum (Children's

Museum). For an hour and a half they'll enter a village from another part of the world and could be painting with the Mayans, cooking with Bolivians, or dancing with Zulus (depending on the current programme). ❶ Language could be a problem – phone and check first.

Tropenmuseum, Linnaeusstraat 2, Oost ☎ 568 8215
◑ *10am–5pm daily (from 12pm Sat–Sun).*

Klimhal Amsterdam ⚡ off map

Kids can climb up to the 21m-high ceiling (with safety equipment provided) at the Klimhal Amsterdam. Even though instructors (some English-speaking) are available for bookings, every three kids should also be guided by an adult. Climbers should wear loose clothes and trainers.

Naritaweg 48, Sloterdijk ☎ 681 0121 ◑ *5–11pm Mon–Thu (from 2pm Wed); 11am–11pm Sat; 11am–7pm Sun.*

Nederlands Filmmuseum ⚡F9

When you walk into this 19th-century pavilion you know you're in a cinematic temple – an old film projector guards the staircase instead of a gargoyle. But that's pretty much the extent of the 'museum'. It's more conceptual than that – consisting mainly of the building itself and an archive open to the public. Its two stylish theatres serve as the museum 'display cases' for an amazing collection of rare, under-appreciated films which you may never see anywhere else. Each month offers an ambitious thematic retrospective and over 1000 films are shown annually. ♿ Café Vertigo, next door, is cozy indoors, and a sprawling centre of activity in the summer outdoors. ♿ The museum runs a public film library (69–71 Vondelstraat).

Vondelpark 3, Museum District & Vondelpark ☎ 589 1400 ◑ *10am–half hour after last film ends.*

newMetropolis Science & Technology Center ⚡off map

The green prow-like silhouette jutting into the historic harbour is Amsterdam's new Science and Technology Centre. Although it looks much like an ocean liner, architect Renzo Piano intended no such association. Inside, visitors have five options – interactions, technology, energy, science, and humanity – and 220 workstations to choose from. Blow bubbles big enough to stand in, make appalling stinks in the chemistry lab, or set up your own electricity network. Many displays appeal to children, whilst others are highly sophisticated. All involve interaction: with technology, the environment, or other visitors. Young children can dress up as doctors, geologists, ballerinas, or scientists and check out their new look on television screens. ♿ Amsterdam's most expensive museum.

Oosterdok 2, Oosterdok ☎ 531 3233 ◑ *10am–6pm Tue–Sun.*

Tropenmuseum $D3

One of the city's most stimulating museums in one of its most eclectic buildings. Under soaring arches and colonial-style pillars, between walls decorated with comic-strip scenes from Indonesian fables, eight permanent exhibitions and temporary theme shows familiarize visitors with daily life in the tropics. Your average anthropological museum then? Well, no, not quite. What sets the Tropenmuseum apart is its talent to transport, by experiencing the exhibits using all five senses and putting interactivity high on the agenda. Rest in a reconstructed Qatar café watching a 'local' soap opera, get touchy-feely with the dry dung walls of a mud hut, or sample the cacophony of a chaotic Calcutta street. Theme shows tend to focus on contemporary aspects of our collective cultural heritage. ✥ Check out the café for tropical taste treats and the shop for books, CDs, and all things decorative. ✥ Latin American fixed exhibition focusing on the former Dutch colonies of the Antilles, Suriname, and Aruba (from Jun 2000).

Linnaeusstraat 2, Oost ☎ 568 8215 ◑ 10am–5pm Mon–Fri; 12–7pm Sun.

Verzetsmuseum $ off map

The Resistance Museum faces the Artis Zoo and is in one of the prettiest neighbourhoods of Amsterdam. The current display drops you into a labyrinth of streets made of moveable walls and partitions designed to look like the streets and buildings of various urban nooks, each one offering a subject with precisely-documented information. The winding 'streets' create a meaningful sense of disorientation (where hide-and-seek is no game). They bear witness to the heart-rending spectrum of human reactions of a nation at war: from collaboration to heroic resistance, with many shades of survival under the Nazi boot. State-of-the-art narrative devices and electronic aids tell the fate of Dutch Jews and the myriad forms of Dutch resistance from personal subterfuge to organized strikes, illegal newspapers, and espionage. By the end you feel like you've been in an occupied city. Perfect companion to a visit to the Anne Frankhuis. ❶ Investigate personal interests and contemporary issues at the 'information island'.

Plantage Kerklaan 61, Oost ☎ 644 9797 ◑ 10am–5pm Tue–Sun (from 12 Sat–Sun).

on the wild side

Hash Marihuana Hemp Museum $E7

The Dutch have been smoking the stuff since the 17th century, the Pygmies since the 8th BC, even though a medieval sage warns us that 'Hemp seed, if it be taken out of measure, takes men's wits from them'. Documenting both the narcotic and medicinal properties of cannabis, as well as the demonic strength of hemp, the museum even has a letter from Bill Clinton, relics from The Fabulous Furry Freak Brothers, and a detailed explanation of why the shape of Danish and American joints differs so drastically. ❶ The museum sells seeds too.

Oudezijds Achterburgwal 231, Red Light District & Nieuwmarkt
☎ 623 5961 ◑ *11am–10pm daily.*

Heineken Brouwerij
♫A14

The site of the old brewery, which was closed in 1986, has now been reconstructed as the PR face of Heineken. There are several daily tours which take visitors through the shiny copper intestines of the former brewery. Part Heineken-hype, part brew history, the multimedia tour inevitably leads you, and the other thirsty 30, through the beer-making process, the fermenting tubs, past the copper brewing kettles and old beer baubles to that much fantasized top-floor bar overlooking Amsterdam. Here, visitors can drink as many beers as human physiology allows in an hour. Everyone agrees – it's definitely worth the money. ✂ The ƒ2 is donated to charities such as the Red Cross and the World Wildlife Fund. ✂ There are four tours a day in summer (which are overrun) but only two the rest of the year, so get there well in time.

Stadhouderskade 78, De Pijp ☎ 523 9666
◑ *tours start at 9.30am & 11am Mon–Fri (duration approx 2 hrs).*

Sexmuseum Amsterdam Venustempel
♫B7

The sex 'museum' (or 'Venus Temple') is quite simply a pornorama. School kids interrupt their gum chewing to giggle with embarrassment, while the tourists aim their digital cameras at well-hung mannequins that throw open dirty raincoats. And then they tiptoe into video booths, prick up their ears for phone sex, and crowd into a room devoted to 'extreme excrescences in the field of sexual intercourse'. There are a few oddities, like scrimshaw dildos, phallic Asian rice-pounders, and naughty 19th-century postcards. One of the exhibits offers a surprising revelation about anal sex: Americans supposedly invented it.

Damrak 18, Old Centre ☎ 622 8376 ◑ *10am–11pm daily.*

green scenes

Amstelpark
♫ off map

Amstelpark offers lots of great rides for kids: a small train (ƒ3.50 adults, ƒ2.50 0–10 yrs), a merry-go-round, a pony (ƒ2.50), or a go-kart. Otherwise, kids might like to try their skills at the climbing frames, or mini golf (ƒ6.50 adults, ƒ4.50 0–10 yrs); or head for the lake, where two seals are fed daily at midday.

Amstelpark, Buitenveldert ☎ 644 4216 ▢ 69, 169
◑ *8am–sunset (rides 10am–5pm daily).*

Amsterdamse Bos
♭ off map

The Amsterdamse Bos is a forest on the edge of the town. Built in the 30s as a job scheme for the unemployed, it is almost 10 sq km in size. It has since become Amsterdam's most important nature area, and, consequently, it's a huge favourite with locals as the list of activities is endless. The Bosmuseum, which is free, explains all about the local wildlife and the history of the forest. In summer, the man-made Bosbaan lake is used for boating and swimming, while kids can enjoy themselves in the paddling pool as well as the well-equipped play area. A must are the (Dutch) summer performances at the open air theatre, but remember your anti-mosquito lotion. Canoes can be hired (*f*10–*f*19/hour) at the Grote Vijver and motorized boats (*f*15–*f*45/hour) and bikes (*f*10/2 hours–*f*12.50/day) at the main entrance on Nijenrodeweg (child seats and children's bikes available). Animal-lovers shouldn't miss the goat farm (free entrance), where kids can feed kids! Then they might like to try goats' milk or its cheese and ice-cream products in the café next door.
Entrances: Van Nijenrodeweg; Amstelveensweg (Amstelveen)
☎ 643 1414 ◑ *24 hours daily (watersports & bikes 10.30am–7pm daily; goat farm 11am–5pm Wed–Mon).*

Artis Zoo
♭ off map

Founded 160 years ago, Artis Zoo is one of the loveliest and most spacious areas of the city. Today it houses around 8000 animals from all over the world, zoological and geological museums, a planetarium, and a recently re-vamped aquarium. The many 19th-century buildings, including an old library, are worth a look, and the children's farm is simply a must for the offspring. But beware of free-running animals nibbling your coat or bag. If you feel peckish yourself, head for the conservatory café that overlooks the flamingo pond. There are many animals, from giraffes to monkeys, many housed in grand 19th-century enclosures.
Plantage Kerklaan 38–40, Oost ☎ 523 3400 ◑ *winter: 9am–5pm daily; summer: 9am–6pm daily.*

Beatrixpark
♭ off map

Just behind the RAI Exhibition Centre, this park is perfect for those seeking tranquillity. Even though the RAI has annexed some parts for extensions over the years, it's still big and even on sunny weekends there are quiet spots to sunbathe or watch the swans and geese in the pond. For those more interested in flowers, the Victorian walled garden is worth a look-see and children will love the kids' play area.
Entrances: Diepenbrockstraat; Europaboulevard; Prinses Irenestraat (Rivierenbuurt) ◑ *24 hours daily.*

Hortus Botanicus *♺ off map*

Hortus Botanicus dates back to 1682 and is one of the oldest botanical gardens in the world. It was originally set up to provide doctors with medicinal herbs and there's still a large number of plants as well as several giant trees. The major attraction is, however, the glasshouse itself, which was built in 1993. It has three climate divisions: tropical, subtropical, and desert. The collection of rare cycads, of which a few are possibly over 300 years old, is world-famous. The gardens have the oldest pot plant in the world as well as the oldest coffee bush in Europe, which originally came from East Africa and provided cuttings for many coffee-growing parts of the world.

Entrance: Plantage Middenlaan 2a (Oost) ☎ 625 8411 ◑ 9am–5pm Mon–Fri; 11am–5pm Sat–Sun (closes at 4pm Nov–Apr).

Museumplein *♺A13*

The Museumplein was recently redesigned by Danish landscape architect Sven-Ingvar Andersson. It used to be a bland and draughty square with a four-lane road bisecting it that was greened over in the controversial ƒ175-million makeover. But Amsterdammers have now taken a real shine to the plein and use it like a park. Its major attraction is a triangular grassed-over sloping roof, a fun spot to relax after a visit to one of the nearby museums with a great view of the bladers performing their death-defying tricks and the slam dunks by the shirtless basketball players. Bring your ice skates here in winter as, when it freezes over, the pond is used as a skating rink. ❶ Views; lots of bike racks. ♺ Expensive café.

Museum District & Vondelpark ◑ 24 hours daily.

Oosterpark *♺ off map*

Situated in the east of Amsterdam, the Oosterpark is used mainly by the eclectic mix of inhabitants of this area. Although once a graveyard, its spooky history doesn't keep fun seekers away. In summer, the small paddling pool cools down toddlers and in winter the big pond is ideal for ice-skating. During the year various activities take place: free classical concerts, a charity Aids event Walk For Life, and the Oosterpark festival.

Entrances: Linnaeusstraat; Oosterpark; ☎ 608 0111 ◑ 24 hours daily.

Rijksmuseum Gardens *♺E11*

The small gardens surrounding the Rijksmuseum are as beautiful as the building itself and the pictures inside. If the queue for the museum is way too long – which happens frequently – stroll through these gardens instead.

Entrances: Jan Luijkenstraat, Hobbemakade (Museum District & Vondelpark) ☎ 674 7000 ◑ 10am–5pm daily.

sights, museums & galleries

Sarpathipark ♀C14/D14

Right in the middle of De Pijp lies this quiet haven of green, named after Samuel Sarpathi (1813–1866), credited with shaking Amsterdam out of a lethargic stupor it developed in the 19th century. It's a great spot to feed ducks or eat lunch after you've shopped at the nearby Albert Cuyp Markt. In the park, you soon forget that you are in one of the liveliest areas of Amsterdam. It's used mainly by locals and the gay community for night-time cruising. ❶ No skaters. ♋ No café or toilets.

Entrances: 1e van der Helststraat; 1e Sweelinckstraat; Ceintuurbaan; Sarpathipark (De Pijp) ◑ 24 hours daily.

Vondelpark ♀E9

Where else in Amsterdam can you see llamas and cows, hire skates, take part in a laughing session (8–9am every morning people laugh away their stress together), see concerts, watch films, play football, smoke a joint, cruise for gay sex, and get a tan all in the same place? The Vondelpark, named after the Dutch poet Joost van den Vondel (1587–1679), is Amsterdam's most popular park – it has become the place to see and be seen. It gets really busy when the sun comes out as families with kids, the cool and trendy, old hippies, and stoned bongo players all mingle together peacefully. The park is used day and night and the area near the rose garden is a favourite spot with gays.

♋ Too crowded with skaters at times.

Entrances: Stadhouderskade; Amstelveensweg (Museum District & Vondelpark) ◑ 24 hours daily.

Westerpark ♀3aA/3aB

This is Amsterdam's hippest centre for art and music. With its closed-off kids' playground, dog area, football pitch, and children's farm it is an ideal place to go after a visit to Westergasfabriek. It's also a stone's throw away from a newly built ecological residential area (houses are heated with used water, the by-product of an electrical power station, and no cars are allowed) and trendy restaurant Amsterdam, housed in a former water pump tower. The park is soon to have an amphitheatre, lily and sculpture garden.

Entrances: Nassauplein; Haarlemmerweg ◑ 24 hours daily.

outdoor pools

There are several outdoor swimming pools scattered around Amsterdam. As in any city, they are a favourite destination for families on sunny weekends so, to avoid the crowds, it's best to go during the week. All have a children's pool as well as recreational and sunbathing areas; some have lockers for your valuables. Each pool has its own, different hours for lane swimming –

so it's a good idea to phone before you set out. **Sloterparkbad** is the only swimming pool with natural water and it has a nude sunbathing area. You can also swim and sunbathe naked at the recreational areas

Het De Miranda Bad   �address off map
De Mirandalaan 9, Rivierenbuurt ☎ 642 8080
◑ 7–9am Mon–Fri, 9.30am–5pm Sat–Sun.

Flevoparkbad   ≈ off map
Zeeburgerdijk 630, Zeeburg ☎ 692 5030
◑ 10am–6pm daily.

Sloterparkbad   ≈ off map
Slotermeerlaan 2–4, Slotermeer ☎ 611 4565/613 3770
◑ 10am–5.30pm daily.

hofjes

Though hofjes are a fascinating part of Amsterdam's history, you'd miss them if you didn't know they were there. Hofjes (little courtyards) were built by churches and merchants to house widows, unmarried women, the elderly, and the poor. These small 17th- and 18th-century houses, with their lovely courtyards, are still home to single women and students, and are a quiet haven in this ever-crowded city. This may be because the entrances are hard to find and often lie behind non-descript wooden doors. The most famous is **Begijnhof**, although strictly speaking this is not a real hofje as it was built to house Beguines, a religious sisterhood. Most of the 47 hofjes in Amsterdam are closed to the public, though the Begijnhof and some in the Jordaan – **Andrieshofje**, **Cleas Cleashofje**, **Karthuizerhof**, **Lindehofje**, and **Suykerhofje** – are open to visitors 9am–6pm.

Andrieshofje   ⊘B5
Egelantiersgracht 107, Jordaan

Begijnhof   ⊘F6
entrance on Spui, Old Centre

Cleas Cleashofje   ⊘F2
Eerste Egelantiersdwarsstraat 3, Jordaan

Karthuizerhof   ⊘F4
Karthuizersstraat 171, Jordaan

Lindehofje   ⊘D2
Lindengracht 94, Jordaan

Suykerhofje
Lindengracht 149, Jordaan

C3

sights, museums & galleries

out of town

Castle De Haar
Was a 14th-century ruin until architect PJ Cuypers reconstructed it early this century. See the extravagant interior and the surrounding estate, including the transplanted village of Haarzuilens.
Kasteellaan 1, Haarzuilens, Utrect ☎ (030) 677 3804 **◑** *Castle: tour times vary through the year; Park: 10am–5pm daily (Nov–Jul).*

CoBrA Museum of Modern Art
For those interested in early 20th-century work. The thrust is post-World War II art, concentrated around the intractable and colourful CoBrA group. The name derives from the home cities of the artists (COpenhagen, BRussels, and Amsterdam) and their manifesto reads 'no to theories, yes to creativity'.
Sandbergplein 1–3, Amstelveen ☎ 547 5050 **◑** *11am–5pm Tue–Sun.*

Haags Gemeentemuseum
The work of early modernist architect Hendrik Berlage: Dutch-New Yorker Piet Mondrian is the star of the show.
Stadhouderslaan 41, Den Haag ☎ (070) 338 1111 **◑** *11am–5pm Tue–Sun.*

Koninklijke Porceleyne Fles
The Royal Delft Factory is the only survivor of the original 32 factories established in Delft in the 17th century.
Rotterdamseweg 196, Delft ☎ (015) 256 9214 **◑** *9am–5pm Mon–Sat (plus Apr–Oct: 9.30am–5.30pm Sun).*

Mauritshuis
One of the best galleries in the Netherlands, housing the Royal Picture Gallery as well as works by the Dutch Masters, Andy Warhol, and others.
Korte Vijverberg 8, Den Haag ☎ (070) 302 3435 **◑** *10am–5pm Tue–Sun (from 11am Sun).*

Museum Boijmans Van Beuningen
Holds Dali's famous *Spain*, Magritte's *Impressions d'Afrique*, examples of the visionary work of Hieronymus Bosch, and more.
Museumpark 11, Rotterdam ☎ (010) 441 9400 **◑** *10am–5pm Tue–Sun (from 11am Sun).*

Museum Catharijnecon-vent

Housed in a 15th-century convent, this museum has an exceptional collection of religious artefacts that includes illustrated bibles and secular manuscripts.
Nieuwegracht 63, Utrect ☎ (030) 231 7296 ◑ *10am–5pm Tue–Sun (from 11am Sat–Sun).*

Panorama Mesdag

The creation of a 19th-century artist who oversaw the painting of a massive view of Scheveningen in 1881. Climb the stairs to get closer to the painting and the eye is tricked by the clever perspective techniques.
Zeestraat 65, Den Haag ☎ (070) 310 6665 ◑ *10am–5pm daily (from 12pm Sun)*

Rijksmuseum van Oudheden

Brings together archaeological finds from near and far, with unique Egyptian mummies and the results of Dutch digs.
Rapenburg 28, Leiden ☎ (071) 516 3163 ◑ *10am–5pm Tue–Sun (from 12pm Sat–Sun).*

Stedelijk Museum De Lakenhal

Collections include a history of the city's cloth trade, antique furniture, and paintings by Dutch Masters Jan Steen and Rembrandt, as well as Lucas van Leyden's early masterpiece *The Last Judgement*.
Oude Singel 28–32 , Leiden ☎ (071) 516 5360 ◑ *10am–5pm Tue–Sun (from 12pm Sat–Sun).*

Stedelijk Museum Het Prinsenhof

This museum is where William of Orange lived until murdered in 1584. Also features local memorabilia and 16th- and 17th-century art.
St Agathaplein 1, Delft ☎ (015) 260 2358 ◑ *10am–5pm Tue–Sun (from 1pm Sun).*

Teylers Museum

Exhibits astronomical and medical equipment, as well as paintings from great Dutch and Italian masters like Rembrandt and Michelangelo.
Spaarne 16, Haarlem ☎ (023) 531 9010 ◑ *10am–5pm Tue–Sun (from 12pm Sun).*

Vredespaleis

The Peace Palace is the seat of the International Court of Justice. Scottish-American benefactor Andrew Carnegie commissioned the neo-Gothic building after the first International Peace Conference was held in Den Haag in 1899. Each room is themed to the country that sponsored it.
Carnegieplein 2, Den Haag ☎ (070) 302 4242 ◑ *guided tours: 10am, 11am, 2pm & 3pm Mon–Fri.*

body & soul

Spas and saunas are an everyday part of life in Amsterdam, so do the Dutch thing, kick back and take it easy with any, or many, of these sumptuous spoilings.

haircare

HIP
♯A13

If you're HIP, you're here. Hair Innovating People's new minimalist interior and creative approach incorporate new styles and superb product choice (Paul Mitchell and Fudge). Prices start at ƒ65 for men and ƒ75 for women, whilst a head of highlights ranges between ƒ100–ƒ190.
Hobbemastraat 5, Museum District & Vondelpark ☎ 664 4744
◑ *10am–6pm Mon–Sat (from 1pm Mon; to 9pm Thu).*

Lemonhead
♯B5

The place to get an ultra-cool haircut. The products used are the ever-funky Fudge range which is indeed sweet news for your locks. With by far the most convenient opening times in the city, Lemonhead stays open until 10–11pm (depending on whether the owner has a party to go to). Prices are ƒ60 for a wash, cut and blow-dry.
Nieuwe Leliestraat 29, The Canals ☎ 427 1940 ◑ *10am–10/11pm daily.*

Scissor Hands
♯C6

This place screams trendy, with varnished wooden floors, old-style barber chairs, funky light fittings, and glass cabinets full of lotions and potions. Whatever you fancy, Vincent and Dorien will do as you ask without charging a fortune. Prices start at ƒ65.
Hartenstraat 7, The Canals ☎ 422 2205 ◑ *10am–6pm Tue–Sat (to 9pm Thu).*

beauty treatments

Arianne Inden
♯A11

In just a few years, Arianne Inden has realized her dream with the creation of this mini empire of four salons located in the best parts of town. Using quality, own-brand products, she offers a good service at reasonable prices: facials start at ƒ45, a quick eyebrow pluck is a mere ƒ17.50, waxing ƒ15–ƒ60, and a massage ƒ85. This is a little piece of heaven on earth. Indulge.
Leidsestraat 40, The Canals ☎ 420 2332 ◑ *10am–6pm Mon–Sat (to 9pm Thu); 1–6pm Sun.*

Tilly's Nail Studio ♯D7

In a tiny studio on the lively Nieuwmarkt, you'll find Tilly's a hive of activity. Tilly herself was trained in the USA and has passed on her skills to the staff, making them the best in town. Prices are reasonable at ƒ105 for one colour and ƒ130 for two. Tilly also sells a fab range of own-brand polish including a heat-changing colourama that varies with the temperature of your hands.

Nieuwmarkt 22, Red Light District & Nieuwmarkt ☎ 622 9114
❶ *10am–6pm Tue–Sat (to 8pm Tue, to 4pm Sat).*

Victoria Active Club & Beauty Studio ♯C4

Once inside this blissful sanctuary, the hustle and bustle of city life falls from your shoulders. No membership is needed to use the gym, pool, or salon. So if it's a quick swim (ƒ5), a one-off fitness session with a personal trainer (ƒ37.50), a 20-minute sunbed session (ƒ20), a massage (ƒ85 per hour), or a beauty treatment (from ƒ45), you'll get a right royal service every time.

Damrak 1–5 (entrance via Hasselaerssteeg), Old Centre ☎ 623 2773
❶ *11.30am–11pm daily (7am–11pm Tue & Fri; 9am–6pm Sat–Sun).*

Yves Rocher ♯E7

Yves Rocher is one of the few gems on Kalverstraat. At first glance it looks like a beauty product shop, but in the back you'll find a salon offering everyday treatments at less than everyday prices (ƒ10–ƒ65). You'll be tempted by the colourful shelves full of products on your way out, and with prices as low as ƒ4.95 for aloe vera showergel, you know it won't break the bank.

Kalverstraat 23, Old Centre ☎ 625 6460 ❶ *9.30am–6pm Mon–Sat (from 1pm Mon; to 9pm Thu; to 5pm Sat); 12–5pm Sun.*

alternative therapies

Anna Marie van Zoelen ♯C3

Not only does this salon offer top quality service using wonderful products (like Aveda), but they do so in the most stunning surroundings: the clean lines, fresh colours, and an abundance of tropical plants make for a relaxing atmosphere. Foot reflexology (ƒ47.50), shiatsu massage (ƒ85), stress release (ƒ47.50), lymphatic drainage (ƒ95), and hot oil scalp massage (ƒ55) are all popular treatments and guaranteed to make you feel a million guilders.

Prinsenstraat 9, The Canals ☎ 624 8717 ❶ *10am–6pm Wed–Mon (to 9pm Thu).*

Centrum voor Integrale Geneeskunde ♦ off map

There are 13 different therapists to choose from at this thriving centre, including homeopathy, physiotherapy, shiatsu, hypnotherapy, yoga, acupuncture, and psycho-therapy. Appointments are necessary and can be made between 9am–5pm Mon–Fri. Prices vary depending on therapists.

Nieuwe Keizersgracht 58, Oost ☎ 638 1279 🄾 9am–5pm Mon–Fri (to 2pm Wed).

Chinese Medical Centre ♦A8

This is *the* place in Amsterdam for traditional Chinese therapy. Situated on the outskirts of Chinatown and Nieuwmarkt, some of the many offerings include acupuncture for ƒ80, Tuina massage (the stimulation of energy sources for optimal function and relaxation) for ƒ70, and a selection of natural Chinese herbal medicines and remedies. The founder, Dr Dong Zhi Lin, is very knowledgeable about the art of these age-old traditions.

Gelderskade 67–73, Red Light District & Nieuwmarkt ☎ 623 5060 🄾 9.30am–5.30pm Mon–Sat.

body art

Eyegasm ♦D11

Roxanne, owner of Eyegasm, was the first woman in Amsterdam to own a tattoo parlour and employ all female staff, and she certainly knows her art. This body art parlour, which specializes in one-off tattoos, is dead cool, and features resident DJs, super-friendly staff as well as state-of-the-art sterilisation equipment. Inking starts at ƒ100 and piercings at ƒ30.

Kerkstraat 113, The Canals ☎ 420 5841 🄾 11am–8pm Tue–Sun.

Housewives on Fire ♦B6

You can pop in without an appointment Thursday to Saturday from 11am–7pm or call in advance at all other times to temporarily adorn yourself with a work of art. Even the drabbest wallflower can blossom with the aid of in-house stylists doing the latest in hair colours, dread and extension work, henna tattoos, and second-skin club clothing. Housewives on Fire provides hair extensions at ƒ10 per piece (special effects ƒ150), crazy colours at ƒ90– ƒ125, and a chill-out area with in-house DJs and tunes for sale.

Spuistraat 130, Old Centre ☎ 422 1067/622 9818 🄾 9am–7pm Tue–Sat (to 9pm Thu); 12–5pm Sun; 12–6pm Mon.

A Bigger Splash
♫F5

Splash is not cheap at ƒ35 for a day's membership and ƒ365 (plus a ƒ100 registration fee) for 12 weeks, but once inside the facilities and equipment are the best in Amsterdam. The downside is that the patio doors are nearly always wide open allowing all and sundry to see you work out. Services include diet guidance, personal training, physio-fitness, sauna, and a steam room.

Looiersgracht 26–30, The Jordaan ☎ 624 8404 ◑ 7am–midnight daily.

Fitness Factory
♫F6

If you need to work off all those fries and mayo, this is the place. Complete with Turkish steam room, and separate male/female sauna, the Factory will whip you into shape in a jiffy. Daily access costs ƒ20 which, if you decide to join, is deductible from your first monthly fee (ƒ100 per month).

Nieuwezijds Voorburgwal 301, Old Centre ☎ 624 4441 ◑ 9am–10pm Mon–Fri; 10am–4pm Sat–Sun.

Garden Gym
♫E8

Work up a sweat at the Garden Gym, where the accent lies on aerobics, body-shape, and callanetics (9.30am–9.30pm daily). Prices are okay at ƒ120 for use of the (limited) fitness facilities, over 70 classes, a sauna, and shower facilities (ƒ87.50 between 9.30am–3.30pm). Also on offer are massages, physiotherapy, diet advice, and sunbeds. Female friendly.

Jodenbreestraat 158, Old Centre ☎ 626 8772 ◑ 9am–11pm Mon–Sat (from 12pm Tue & Thu); 10am–7pm Sun.

Jansens Gym
♫E7

Jansens is a hip and stylish place to be seen sweating in. Up-to-date on all the happening fitness fads, including spinning, turbo leisure, and body lift, you can pop in here for a one-off session for ƒ25. Otherwise an all-in, four-weekly membership will set you back ƒ130.

Rokin 109, Old Centre ☎ 626 9366 ◑ 10am–10.30pm Mon–Fri; 12–8pm Sat–Sun.

Squash City
♫A3

There are plenty of other things to do at this squash club, including fitness and dance classes (stress release, hip-hop, and funky groove). The 14 squash courts cost ƒ14 per person before 5pm on weekdays and ƒ18.50 at other times. Monthly membership is ƒ62.50 and if your skills aren't up to scratch, try a lesson at ƒ35.

Ketelmakerstraat 6, Westerdok ☎ 626 7883 (squash) ☎ 626 7596 (fitness & aerobics) ◑ 8.45am–midnight daily (to 9pm Sat–Sun).

body & soul

Fenomeen
off map

This is a squat sauna with chill-out room, garden, and Turkish steam room, as well as outside showers for the summer. There's tasty fare (whole foods and herbal teas) to see you through the day. Entrance is ƒ11 from 11am–6pm and ƒ13.50 from 6–11pm. A massage (ƒ130–ƒ140) may, if you're lucky, be done by a professional masseuse moonlighting for extra cash.
1e Schinkelstraat 14, Vondelpark ☎ 671 6780 ◑ 1–11pm daily.

Koan Float
F6

It's a fine art being able to relax, but one you will be able to learn quickly at Koan Float. You're left to float in salty water and a feeling of total relaxation washes over you. It works wonders on your body, mind, and overall sense of well-being. Floats are ƒ55–ƒ100 and massages ƒ65–ƒ115.
Herengracht 321, The Canals ☎ 555 0333 ◑ 9.30am–10pm Mon–Thu.

Oininio
C4

For enlightenment without drugs of any kind, visit this New Age department store, sauna and restaurant. Tranquil surroundings greet you the moment you step into this oasis. Walk up the stairs to find sea-salt foot soaks, a dry heat room, and an amazing Turkish steam room complete with a cascading water-wall. Step onto the roof terrace for fresh air and a fantastic view of the city or a swing in a hammock. Inside, enjoy a steaming yogi tea or nibble on tasty Muesli-nut cake. Sheer bliss and worth every penny: ƒ19 10am–12pm; ƒ23.50 12pm–5pm; ƒ29 until midnight. Facials cost ƒ62.50, massages ƒ90, and body treatments ƒ90. Call first as unstable finances leave the future of this legendary spa hanging in the balance.
**Prins Hendrikkade 20–21, Old Centre ☎ 553 9359
◑ 10am–midnight daily.**

Sauna Deco
B6

This sauna in a knockout art deco building is to die for. Built out of remnants of a 20s Paris department store, it has elaborate ironware and amazing stained glass windows. Enjoy the Turkish steam room, massage facilities, or grab a bite at the café. Words can't do justice to this place: you'll just have to see it for yourself. And, at only ƒ26.50, you'd be foolish not to.
**Herengracht 115, The Canals ☎ 623 8215 ◑ 11am–11pm Sun–Fri;
1–6pm Sat.**

games & activities

Whether from the dizzy heights of a helicopter or from the wicked local brews, explore the countless (other) ways to get that legendary Amsterdam high.

beer tasting

Tasting Amsterdam's finest local brews is an authentic Dutch experience (or at least an excuse for one). Take a free tour of the **Brouwerij't IJ** on Fridays (4pm) then sample the range of beers, from the smooth 5% Pilzen (Pils) to the lethal 9% Columbus. ❶ Avoid the sediment to avoid the hangover.
Brouwerij 't IJ   ♯ off map
Funenkade 7, Oosterdok ☎ 622 8325 ❶ 3pm–8pm Wed–Sun.

bingo

Amsterdam's gay bars definitely have the monopoly when it comes to bingo. Catch drag hostesses 'Legs Eleven' Jeanne P'arc at the **Getto** on Thursdays, or 'Two Fat Ladies' Dusty who packs 'em in at **The Queen's Head** on Tuesdays.
Getto   ♯B7
Warmoesstraat 51, Red Light District & Nieuwmarkt ☎ 421 5151 ❶ 10pm Thu.

The Queen's Head   ♯A8
Zeedijk 20, Red Light District & Nieuwmarkt ☎ 420 2475 ❶ Tue.

boating

There's no better way to view Amsterdam than from the water – especially if you are at the helm. If you're out to impress, rent one of **SESA**'s electric saloon launches, or a classic 20's craft from **Canal Classics**, complete with your own skipper.
Canal Classics (Canal Bus)   ♯E11
Stadhouderskade 42, Museum District & Vondelpark ☎ 623 9886
❶ Reservations 9am–6pm daily.

SESA   ♯C8
Nieuwmarkt, Red Light District & Nieuwmarkt ☎ 509 5050
❶ Apr–Oct: 10am–10pm daily.

games & activities

bungy jumping

Amsterdam may well have a thriving cannabis culture but this has got to be the ultimate high. At 75m, this crane, within vomiting distance of Centraal Station, guarantees the biggest rush and, rather reassuringly, is set over water.

Bungy Jump Centre Amsterdam ⌖off map
Oostelijke Handelskade 1, Oosterdok ☎ 419 6005
◑ *May & Oct: 12–9pm Thu–Sun; Jun–Sep: 12–9pm daily.*

casino

Don't take any chances before you get in: bring along ID, leave your sports shoes at home, and dress appropriately if you want to place your bets here. On Wednesdays, women not only have free entrance but get a free drink too – guaranteed to raise an eyebrow on even the most poker-faced of male customers.

Holland Casino ⌖C11
Max Euweplein 62, The Canals ☎ 521 1111 ◑ *1.30pm–3am daily.*

chess

Who said size didn't matter? For a larger cerebral challenge than a chess café can offer, test your skills on this huge outdoor board, located on a square named after the Netherlands' only world chess champion, Dr Max Euwe.

Max Euweplein ⌖C11
The Canals ☎ 553 0300 ◑ *summer: 9am–8.30pm daily; winter: 9am–6.30pm daily.*

fever pitch

So you think a trip to Amsterdam isn't complete without seeing the – arguably – best team in the world play? Well, forget it! Tickets for Ajax matches are only available if you have a season card. The good news, however, is that for Ajax matches that aren't sold out – although they are few – there are some tickets kept aside for tourists. To get them you have to fax the Ajax office (ꜰ 311 1480) from your home country and beg! If this fails, you can always go to one of the free Ajax training sessions held outside the ArenA (Arena Boulevard 29, Bijlermeer). Information on matches and training schedules can be found on their English website (ᴡ www.ajax.nl), which also tells you all about the Ajax museum and shop, or by calling ☎ 311 1444.

go-kart racing

A must for all thrill-seeking speed junkies. Take your pick of 200cc karts, quads, or stock cars at this, the largest go-kart centre in the world. For those too chicken to go the course, there's the race simulator, virtual 'CamCar' (a virtual reality Formula One game), or the fabulous themed restaurant, 'Pit Lane'.

Bleekemolen Indoor Kart & Speed Centre   ♫ off map
Herwijk 10, Geuzenveld ☎ 611 1120 ◑ *1pm–11pm daily (from 12pm Fri–Sat).*

helicopter tours

The price is high but so is this amazing aerial view over the network of canals and hidden gardens. Although the helipad is 40 minutes away by train, it takes just 20 minutes before you're circling the city. Helicopters can also be chartered from Schiphol but cost double.

Lelykopters   ♫ off map
Lelystad Airport, nr Schiphol ☎ (0342) 443 205
◑ *9am–6pm Mon–Fri; 10am–4pm Sat–Sun.*

horse riding

Brush up your riding skills with lessons or gallop through the wooded Amsterdamse Bos with either the **Amsterdamse Manege** or **Manege Nieuw Amstelland**. For the less equinely inclined, both stables have bars.

Amsterdamse Manege   ♫ off map
Nieuwe Kalfjeslaan 25, Amstelveen ☎ 643 1342
◑ *9am–10pm daily (to 7pm Sat–Sun).*

Manege Nieuw Amstelland   ♫ off map
Jan Tooropplantsoen 17, Zuid West ☎ 643 2468
◑ *9am–midnight daily (to 6pm Sat–Sun).*

ice skating

Every few years, Amsterdam's canals freeze over giving a rare opportunity for skating. If you get the urge, your best bet is to head down to the flea market on Waterlooplein for a cheap secondhand pair of skates. For guaranteed ice, the **Jaap Eden IJscomplex** has a large outdoor skating rink operating in winter.

Jaap Eden IJscomplex   ♫ off map
Radioweg 64, Watergraafs-meer ☎ 694 9894
◑ *Oct–mid-Mar: times vary.*

karaoke

A Japanese lounge environment is created at this trendy gay bar known for its monthly Club Fu night, hosted by drag queen Vera Springveer. DJs spin cool tracks between pop star wannabes strutting their stuff.

Getto ♯B7
Warmoesstraat 51, Red Light District & Nieuwmarkt ☎ 421 5151
◑ *1st Mon of the month.*

laser games

Explore group dynamics (and dissolve underlying tensions) in 20 minutes of pure, unadulterated beaming. With three floors of hidden challenges, this is the largest laser complex in Europe.

The Force ♯ *off map*
Oranje Vrijstaatkade 21c, Oost ☎ 663 5516
◑ *11am–midnight daily (to 1am Fri–Sat).*

pool

Four-floored pool mecca **Bavaria** (which also has seven snooker tables and one carambole table) is the largest in the Netherlands. For a more casual atmosphere head to **De Keu**, complete with cats and cool music.

Bavaria Poolcentre ♯E14
Van Ostadestraat 97, De Pijp ☎ 676 7903 ◑ *2pm–1am daily (to 2am Fri–Sat).*

De Keu ♯ *off map*
1e Helmersstraat 5, Zuid West ☎ 689 1449 ◑ *4pm–1am daily (to 3am Fri–Sat).*

rollerblading

Vondelpark offers the perfect place to pose and practise, avoiding all the pedestrians, pushchairs, bicycles, horse-riders, and hippies. And for the really adventurous, the weekly Friday Night Skate, a 15km skate through the city (weather permitting), leaves from outside the park's Film-museum returning to the Blauwe Theehuis about 2 hours later. The routes vary every week.

Rent A Skate ♯E9
Vondelpark (Amstelveensweg entrance) ☎ (06) 664 5091 ◑ *Mar–Nov: 11am–9.30pm Mon–Fri; 12–5pm Sat–Sun.*

sex bars

Whether it's the unlimited free drinks or the women doing unmentionable things with bananas, the **Bananen Bar** is an infamous slice of Amsterdam sleaze that perpetually makes for a popular stag night destination. Not quite mashed banana the way Mom makes it.

Bananen Bar ⊘D7
Oudezijds Achterburgwal 37, Red Light District & Nieuwmarkt
☎ 622 4670 ◑ *8pm–2am daily (to 3am Fri–Sat).*

the supper club

Treat yourself to a truly decadent dinner at Amsterdam's most beautiful restaurant. DJs and video jockeys entertain whilst you lounge around on mattresses and are waited on hand and foot: masseurs and tarot readers attend to your sensual and spiritual needs between courses.

The Supper Club ⊘C7
Jonge Roelensteeg 21, Old Centre ☎ 638 0513 ◑ *8pm–1am daily (to 3am Fri–Sat).*

tenpin bowling

Bowling is a laugh at any time but before hitting the clubs on Friday and Saturday nights, check out the 'Twilight Bowling' at the 18-laned **Knijn**.

Knijn ⊘ off map
Scheldeplein 3, Zuid ☎ 664 2211 ◑ *10am–1am Mon–Fri (to 1.30am Fri); noon–1.30am Sat; noon–midnight Sun.*

tuschinski theater

Impress your date with a seat in a box and a glass of champagne in one of the world's most beautiful cinemas, a 20s former variety theatre. At weekends, the music hall atmosphere is revived with acts – ranging from mime to tap dancing – taking place before the last screenings of the night.

Tuschinski ⊘A12
Reguliersbreesstraat 26–28, Old Centre ☎ (0900) 202 5350
◑ *10am–midnight daily.*

hotels

Amsterdam hotels are always in hot demand, so bag your bed early. They tend to be on the small side, but like the Dutch themselves, they're friendly, relaxed and unpretentious. If you want a room with a view ask when booking, as most central hotels have great vistas of the surrounding canals.

f–ff

Acacia
♭D2

Kind staff and a nostalgia for the past make this hotel/studio/houseboat combination simple, charming and, economically, a damned good idea. Family-owned, the three options (14-room hotel, two studios for three or four, and three houseboats for up to five) are painted in quaintly traditional old Jordaan colour combinations: Bordeaux red and old rose, bottle green, and yellow. There are perfectly adequate self-catering facilities in the studios and aboard the houseboats. It's not bang in the centre, but it's a good option for a quieter stay in Amsterdam.

Lindengracht 251, 1015kh (Jordaan) ☎ 622 1460 f 638 0748
e acacia.nl@WXS.nl ▯ 3, 18 ♠ 21 ▯ ▯ ▤ MC/V (singles & doubles: f145)

Amstel Botel
♭B8

This place looks a bit like floating council offices. The identical rooms are not huge, but they are quiet, comfortable, and all have TVs. Amstel Botel is a good deal and handy for Centraal Station. The sensation of floating is fun, and the Botel is docked on the wide River IJ. Be sure to ask for the great waterside view or you'll find yourself admiring the post office's main sorting depot.

Oosterdokskade 2–4, 1000ck (Oosterdok) ☎ 626 4247 f 627 6753 ▯ 7, 10
♠ 79 ▱ ◑ ▤ all (single: f131; double: f149)

Arena
♭ off map

Not so much a hostel as a way of life, this stylish youth culture centre has a great atmosphere, is good value, and provides funky sounds at its own nightclub. Situated in a listed orphanage, the Arena offers modern rooms, each with a shower or bath en suite. Some of the rooms are split-level, creating separate lounging and sleeping areas. Chill out with guests and locals at the café-restaurant Alfresco with its outdoor terrace and garden.

's-Gravesandestraat 51, 1092aa (Oost) ☎ 694 7444 f 663 2649
e info@hotelarena.nl w www.hotelarena.nl ▯ 6, 10 Ⓜ Weesperplein
♠ 115 ▱ ◑ ▯ ▯ ♿ ▤ AE/MC/V (double: f110–f160; dorm: f27.50)

De Harmonie $D12

The welcome here's pure gold. Young, Dublin-born Theresa Martin runs this small, clean-but-basic canalhouse like a large, warm, chaotic family home. The rooms are very plain, with lino flooring, but who cares? She welcomes groups, young travellers, or 'anyone who likes a laugh'. Theresa can show you the most fun spots, drink you under the table and still manage to bring you breakfast in bed the next morning.

Prinsengracht 816, 1017jl (The Canals) ☎ 625 0174 F 622 8021 🚊 13,14,17 🚊 18, 21, 22 ✦ 10 ☎ ☎ ✍ ▤ all (single: ƒ80; double: ƒ150–ƒ160)

Euphemia $E11

Quietly situated a short walk from Leidseplein, this former convent has a good atmosphere, even better prices, an institutional look... and its own ghost. In the breakfast room, plough your way through a huge breakfast in the morning, and in the evening, bring in your own supper and hang out with the other guests. Hot showers and large, clean, basic rooms – all with TVs. Euphemia is gay-friendly and pretty much everyone-else-friendly too.

Fokke Simonszstraat 1, 1017id (The Canals) ☎ 622 9045 F 622 9045 e euphemia-hotel@budgethotel.a2000.html w www.euphemiahotel.com 🚊 16, 24, 25 ✦ 30 ✍ 🅿 ⅋ ▤ all (single: ƒ90; double: ƒ130–ƒ160)

Flying Pig Palace $F9

Pig owners Ron and Willem will tell you: good accommodation, low prices, and a laid-back atmosphere make the Pig a palace. Situated near the Vondelpark, this large, spotless, popular hostel is run for backpackers and travelling folk by friendly kindred spirits. All rooms have a little shower room and WC, and guests are allowed free run of the kitchen. There's no curfew to spoil the party, and the Pig Palace's bar is open all night, with some of the cheapest prices in town. Meanwhile, in the heart of the Old Centre (Nieuwendijk 100), the Flying Pig Downtown is set in a spacious listed building. It has a late night coffeeshop right next door and a popular brasserie, restaurant, and garden. Alternatively, with the free kitchen facilities, you can cook your own meal.

Vossiusstraat 46, 1071aj (Museum District & Vondelpark) ☎ 421 0583 F 421 0802 e headoffice@flying pig.nl w www.flyingpig.nl 🚊 3, 12 ✦ 130 ☎ 🎧 ▤ AE/MC/V (singles & doubles: ƒ60–ƒ120; dorm: ƒ26–ƒ40)

Gaasper Camping Amsterdam $ off map

Decent camping doesn't get much cheaper than this. Southeast of greater Amsterdam, the city's newest campsite is fast becoming one of its most popular. Centraal Station can be easily reached using the metro, but you could be forgiven for never venturing to the city. Close by is the fun-filled Gaasperplas park, with a lake and a miscellany of reasonably priced watersports. Amsterdam? Who needs it?

Loosdrechtdreef 7, 1108az (Bijlermeer) ☎ 696 7326 F 696 9369
🅼 **Gaasperplas park** 🛏 🗔 🅿 ♿ ⊟ none (adult: ƒ6.50; child: ƒ3.50; caravan: ƒ9; tent: ƒ7)

Hemp Hotel
ℱ F12
From hemp hotels to hemp beer, this small, friendly, and cheap hotel offers it all. The themed bedrooms bring to life the cultures of India, Afghanistan, Tibet, and the Caribbean, with hand-carved furniture and window frames, colourful murals, and hemp futons. At the bar and restaurant, a relaxing variety of hemp lollies, ice cream, hemp seeds, and 11 kinds of hemp beers is available. What's more, breakfast (including fresh hemp rolls and muffins) is included in the price.

Frederiksplein 15, 1017xk (The Canals) ☎ 625 4425 F 471 5242
e greenfin@euronet.nl w www.hemp-hotel.com 🛏 4 ♦ 5 ⌂ ℘ 🗔 ⊟ MC/V (single: ƒ90; double: ƒ135)

Het Amsterdamse Bos
ℱ off map
Though it's a 30-minute bus ride to downtown Amsterdam (the service is every half hour), the woodland setting makes it worth the trip. And, if your legs are up to it, you could always opt for a testing but enjoyable trek by hired bike. The large park offers distractions of its own, such as horse riding and watersports, and prices include hot showers. There is a friendly bar and restaurant, and a decent shop. There are also huts which sleep up to four and have a stove, but bring your own kitchen utensils and a sleeping bag.

Klein Noorddijk 1, 1432cc (Aalsmeer) ☎ 641 6868 F 640 2378 🛏 171 🛏 ℘ 🗔
🅿 ⊟ MC/V (ƒ8.50; under 4s: free)

Hotel Brouwer
ℱ A7
In 1917, Gerrit-Jan Brouwer bought this small hotel on the lovely Singel, and today his grandson Willem-Hendrik with his Californian partner Colleen – is still running it with tender loving care. Scrubbed, sloping wooden floors and period Delft tiles provide authentic Calvinistic simplicity, unchanged by renovation. There are eight pretty little rooms with beds made up in crisp white bed linen of broderie anglaise – all have en suite bathrooms and canal views. A Dutch sprookje (fairytale) of a hotel, with fairytale prices too.

Singel 83, 1012ve (The Canals) ☎ 624 6358 F 520 6264
e akita@hotelbrouwer.a2000.nl w www.hotelbrouwer.nl 🛏 1, 2, 5, 13, 17
🛏 21 ♦ 8 ⌂ ♿ ⊟ none (single: ƒ77; double: ƒ154)

Hotel de Munck
F12

Set in this beautifully restored sea captain's house of the 17th-century East India Company, de Munck is a delightfully eccentric hotel. Friendly, laid-back owner Rob serves up a breakfast to the strains of Elvis on the period jukebox, in a dining room splattered with platters from the 60s. There's a pop twist in the rooms too, with 60s-style elements such as old clocks and pictures. Quiet, clean, and pleasantly kitsch.

Achtergracht 3, 1017wl (The Canals) ☎ 623 6283 **F** 620 6647 🛏 4 ✦ 16 ⌨ ✿
🅿 ▤ all (single: *f*95; double: *f*175)

Hotel Hestia
F9

Situated in a peaceful residential area at the edge of the Vondelpark, this simple, friendly hotel is just a stone's throw away from central Amsterdam. The white walls and perfectly polished floors of the lobby and breakfast room give a sense of orderliness, while the bedrooms lend a warmer touch to your stay. En suite facilities in every room, plus a lift and helpful staff, make it one to note for anyone with physical disabilities. There are also rooms for four or five people to share. Babysitting and limousine services on request.

Roemer Visscherstraat 7, 1054ev (Museum District & Vondelpark)
☎ 612 3710 **F** 685 1382 **e** manager@hestia.demon.nl 🛏 2, 3, 5, 12 ✦ 18 ⌨ ✿
✿ ♿ ▤ MC/DC/V (single: *f*150; double: *f*180–*f*235)

Hotel Washington
C13

Book at least two months in advance at this small, homely hotel, as its days as a best kept secret are long since past. Situated on a pleasant, quiet street near the Museumplein and Concertgebouw, over 80% of its guests are visiting musicians and artists. Clean, quiet, and discreet, this hotel is intelligently and sensitively managed, with a restrained, peaceful atmosphere – as long as five floors and no lift doesn't faze you.

Frans van Mierisstraat 10, 1071rs (Museum District & Vondelpark)
☎ 679 7453 **F** 673 4435 🛏 16 ✦ 17 ⌨24 ✿ ▤ AE/MC/V
(single: *f*110–*f*140; double: *f*200–*f*275)

House Boat
off map

Cute and well-cared for, this traditional Dutch houseboat is divided into two: a prettily decorated terraced studio for up to three (two sofa-beds and a single), and, with its own entrance, a small, modern double room, decorated in traditional Dutch farmhouse blue and green. Both units have an equipped kitchenette, a TV, video, CD player, and phone. The owners, Ilonk and Marcel, also have a smaller boat for two. It's not central, but is very economical.

IJsbaanpad 70a, 1076cw (Zuid) ☎ 664 6835 **F** 471 3359 🛏 6, 1
🚌 170, 172, 370 ✦ 3 ✿ ♿ ▤ none (singles & doubles: *f*110–*f*150)

International Budget Hostel ♭B9

Set in a converted warehouse in a leafy canal street, this is a quaint city hostel in one of the best locations in town. It is a buzz with young travellers. The canteen dishes up a great Big Breakfast, and is a good place for making new pals or relaxing with a joint. At ƒ2 a go, you can buy Amsterdam's cheapest beer here too. The two top floor doubles are cozy, and it's great to hire out both with friends. Rooms are high-ceilinged with large windows, but plain.

Leidsegracht 76, 1016cr (The Canals) ☎ 624 2784 F 626 1839
e IBH@budgethotel.a2000.html 🏠 7, 10 ♠ 14 ⌀ ⌀° ▯ ▤ AE/MC/V
(double: ƒ120–ƒ150; dorm: ƒ40)

Karen McCusker

Want to stay with friends? Karen and Paul would love to have you. A breakfast tray of home-baked treats, easy-going hospitality, and a sincere desire to please make a visit here a charming and personal affair. Situated two floors above a store in a bustling shopping street, this is urban Amsterdam. But painted beams, homey style, and the Vondelpark close by make it a romantic stay. The McCuskers are doin' it for love.

Call for details (Museum District & Vondelpark) ☎ 679 2753 F 670 4578
🏠 2 ♠ 3 ⌷ ▤ ▤ none (singles & doubles: ƒ77–ƒ144)

Marcel's B&B ♭A11

Renowned artist and graphic designer Marcel van Woerkom offers a friendly and very personal welcome in his immaculately renovated, self-designed apartments. There are five light, modern, and spacious rooms for two, three, or four people; some en suite; and a private patio garden. Marcel is part owner of De Uitkijk, the city's first avant-garde cinema, and so offers free tickets to guests (although not on weekends). He feels most at home with fellow creative types: artists, musicians, and media folk. One to book early.

Leidsestraat 87, 1017nx (The Canals) ☎ 622 9834 F 622 9834
e Info@marcelamsterdam.nl **w** www.marcelamsterdam.com 🏠 1, 2, 5 ♠ 5
⌀ ▤ none (single: ƒ125; double: ƒ200–ƒ300)

Mark's Bed & Breakfast ♭B1

Residing in a lively – and now trendy – working class neighbourhood, Mark's is anything but traditional. Rather confusingly, it is in fact Martin who runs Mark's, and he does so with plenty of TLC. It's the coziest, campest apartment in town, with tiger skin prints, a draped bed in the honeymoon double, a very sexy shower room, and burning hot hues everywhere. Gay or straight, male or female, Mark's is cheap and it's fun.

Van Beuningenstraat 80a, 1051xs (Oude West) ☎ 776 0056 F 681 5060
e m.noordam@flash.a2000.nl **w** www.geocities.com/collegepark/
plaza/3686 🏠 10 ▯ 18 ♠ 2 ⌷ ⌀ ▤ none (single: ƒ125; double: ƒ175)

NJHC City Hostel Vondelpark $F9

Good, very affordable family accommodation that welcomes – among others – guests with physical disabilities. The rooms are simply furnished, and all have en suite facilities. There are lifts and the entrances to rooms are wide enough for wheelchair access. The hostel is situated within five minutes' walk of a little peace (the park), a little culture (museums), and some lively nightlife (Leidseplein). The friendly Brasserie Backpackers is the place to acquaint yourself with fellow guests.

Zandpad 5, 1054ga (Museum District & Vondelpark) ☎ 589 8996
F 589 8955 e fit.vondelpark@NJHC.org 🏠 3, 12 ♦ 475 beds 🖵 🖉 🕤 ♿
🖃 **MC/V (single:** ƒ85; **double:** ƒ90; **dorms (members):** ƒ38;
dorms (non-members): ƒ43

Orlando $D12

Inspired by Virginia Woolf's Orlando, after which the hotel is named, Paul Lodder and Paul Westerman have created this very stylish home from home, where the hospitality is relaxed and friendly. Each room is individually styled with an eye for interesting furniture and contemporary art. The Orlando provides a warm welcome to Amsterdam. There are just five rooms here, so early booking is essential.

Prinsengracht 1099, 1017jh (The Canals) ☎ 638 6915 F 625 2123 🏠 4 ♦ 5 🖵
🖉 🖃 **all (single:** ƒ130–ƒ200; **double:** ƒ150–ƒ250)

Prinsenhof $D12

Situated in a good area, this basic but comfortable family hotel is one of the city's best budget stays. Attractive styling, with a clean, plain, and simple interior, and a fresh, plentiful continental breakfast served in a blue and white breakfast room. Monument status means old, steep stairways, but just think what it's doing for those butt muscles.

Prinsengracht 810, 1017jl (The Canals) ☎ 623 1772 F 638 3368
e info@hotlprinsenhof.com w www.hotelprisenhof.com 🏠 4 ♦ 10 🖵 🖉 🖉
🖵 🖃 **AE/MC/V (single:** ƒ85; **double:** ƒ125)

Shelter City $D7

Hot or cold breakfast you could live on and the best priced beds in Amsterdam – this sister hostel to the more pastoral Shelter Jordan (just for the 18–35 set) is a clean, safe oasis in the centre of the Red Light District. The bathrooms and showers have had a facelift and the dorms are now divided into smaller spaces for four to eight sharing.

Barndesteeg 21, 1016 (Red Light District & Nieuwmarkt) ☎ 625 3230
F 623 2282 e city@shelter.nl w www.shelter.nl Ⓜ Nieuwmarkt ♦ 7 🖵
◑ 7.30am–midnight daily (to 1am weekends). 🖃 **none (dorm:** ƒ23)

Shelter Jordan Christian Youth Hostel $D5

A major refurbishment has made this very clean (there's even a no-smoking policy), well-equipped hostel even better. Substantial hot or cold breakfasts are served in the friendly, cozy café. Male/female segregation abides (for 18–35s only), but there's some privacy with divided dorms for four, eight, twelve, or twenty. This non-evangelical Christian youth hostel is run on strict lines (there's a curfew at midnight weekdays, 1am weekends), but you won't find cheaper – unless you visit Shelter City, of course...

Bloemstraat 179, 1016la (Jordaan) ☎ 624 4717 F 627 6137
e jordan@shelter.nl w www.shelter.nl 🚋 13, 14, 17, 🚊 21 ✦ 8 🖵
◑ 7.30am–midnight daily (to 1am weekends). 🚭 none (dorm: f23)

Utopia $A7

To stay in this hotel you've got to be either seriously curious about, or seriously into, smoking illegal substances. In short, the Ritz it ain't. Above a coffeeshop selling alcohol and hash, Utopia is small and musty – and the windows stay securely shut. But the staff, guests, and customers are a very friendly bunch and the bar is pure Amsterdam. It's fun, atmospheric, buzzy, and as packed as a well-rolled joint.

Nieuwezijds Voorburgwal 132, 1012sh (Old Centre) ☎ 626 1295 F 622 7060
🚋 1, 2, 5, 13, 17 🚊 21 ✦ 10 🖵 📱 🚭 none (singles & doubles: f60)

Van Ostade Bike Hotel $E14

Comfy and clean, friendly and youthful; this is known as the 'bike hotel'. Situated in De Pijp, Amsterdam lies like a pearl at your (pedalled) feet when you hire two wheels from them, for a trifling f10. You'll receive maps on arrival showing all the best routes, and fellow-biker staff are there too, to offer knowledgeable advice. Rooms are light and airy, and children are welcome at this good but basic B&B. It's easy to find: the walls outside are decorated with... go on, guess.

Van Ostadestraat 123, 1072sv (De Pijp) ☎ 679 3452 F 671 5213 🚋 3, 4 ✦ 16 🖵
🅿 🚭 none (singles & doubles: f95–f150)

Vliegenbos $off map

Set in 25 hectares of woods in Amsterdam's northern district, Vliegenbos is just a six-minute bus ride to the city centre, yet close to beautiful waterlands as well. Hire one of their bikes and explore. Well-run and orderly, the site offers good facilities for people with physical disabilities, plus a general store, camp shop, bar, and restaurant. Hot showers are free and, if you prefer more shelter from the storm, a few basic hiker's huts are available, with bunk beds for four and elementary cooking facilities.

Meeuwenlaan 138, 1022am (Noord) ☎ 636 8855 F 632 2723 🚊 32 🛏 🌐 📱 🅿
♿ 🚭 none (adults: f13.75; child: f8.80; tent: f35)

The Winston ♯B7

If you're looking for cozy, keep walking. The Winston looks like an art school building and has the same buzz. Situated in Amsterdam's oldest street, it's within yelling distance of both the Dam and the Red Light District. Rooms are clean, light, and airy, but basic. Visit the exhibitions of The Dot Room and – yes! – The Toilet. You can submit your own work too. Music nightly and the grooviest rental bikes in town.

Warmoesstraat 125–129, 1012ja (Red Light District & Nieuwmarkt) ☎ 623 1380 **F** 639 2308 **e** winston@winston.nl **w** www.winston.nl ⌂ 4, 9, 16, 24, 25 ⬤ 66 ▭❋ ▯ ▤ all (single: ƒ120–130; double: ƒ148–ƒ185)

ƒƒ–ƒƒƒ

Ambassade Hotel ♯F6

Comprised of ten 17th-century gabled canalhouses, this mature hotel offers Amsterdam's swishest night in. The rooms are tastefully decorated and all have en suite facilities. The tranquil atmosphere makes it a favourite with the literati: Salman Rushdie, Günther Gras, Doris Lessing, and Umberto Eco all stay here when in town. So contemplate your novel and watch the boats go by from the splendid upstairs lounge or contemplate your navel in the hotel's flotation and massage centre. And always take the first meal of the day in the chandeliered breakfast room – you never know who you might meet.

Herengracht 341, 1016az (The Canals) ☎ 626 2333 **F** 624 5321 **e** info@ambassade-hotel **w** www.ambassade-hotel.nl ⌂ 1, 2, 5 ⬤ 59 ▱ ▱ ▱ᵒ 🅿 ▤ all (single: ƒ270; double: ƒ335)

Amsterdam House ♯B12

Aside from its rather featureless canalside rooms, Amsterdam House offers a peaceful and well-priced stay aboard its moored canalboats. Short, or long-term rentals are available for fully equipped, self-catering houseboats, which can accommodate between two and ten people. The boats are simple, modern and clean, and surprisingly spacious. There are more than adequate kitchen facilities, attractive sitting rooms, showers, and bedrooms, with linen and towels included. Most boats are moored along the Amstel in pleasant, central locations.

Amstel 176, 1017ae (Old Centre) ☎ 626 2577 **F** 626 2987 **e** info@amsterdamhouse.nl **w** www.amsterdamhouse.com ⌂ 9, 14 ⬤ 16 ▱ ▤ all (singles & doubles: ƒ195–ƒ295)

Amsterdam Wiechmann ♯E6

The Dutch would describe this hotel as gezellig: convivial and cozy, and just a little bit cute. Here you'll find down-to-earth Amsterdam hospitality from friendly owner and erstwhile music club owner, Ted Boddy. In a Texas accent, Dutchman Ted will tell you stories of when Mark Knopfler, the Eagles, and the Sex Pistols came to stay. And Emmylou Harris liked it so much she gave them her gold record for the single Elite Hotel. Pretty location, homely antiques, clean, comfortable, and traditional. Enjoy the canal view from the huge windows of the street level breakfast place.

Prinsengracht 328–32, 1016hx (The Canals) ☎ 626 3321 F 626 8962 ⌂ 1, 2, 5 ♦ 40 ⌷ ⌽ ▭ none (single: ƒ110–ƒ150; double: ƒ200–ƒ250)

Atlas Hotel   ♫A10

Charming, peaceful and welcoming, the Atlas offers modern comfort in a rather splendid, art nouveau building. Although it's conveniently sited for the social hubbub of the city centre, homely Atlas offers every reason to stay indoors, with its friendly lounge/bar/restaurant where, morning and evening, guests gather to talk, eat, and drink. Fine, well-designed rooms and 24-hour service mean you might be forgiven for never making it downstairs.

Van Eeghenstraat 64, 1071gk (Museum District & Vondelpark) ☎ 676 6336 F 671 7633 ⌂ 2 ♦ 23 ⌷ ⓐ ⌽ 🛈 ▭ MC/DC/V (single: ƒ210; double: ƒ240)

Black Tulip Hotel   ♫A8

This upmarket hotel caters only for male gays into S&M, and combines luxury with lust. Situated near Warmoesstraat, home to greased-up leather queens and leather bars, all rooms are equipped with a sling and bondage hooks. In addition each room has different S&M facilities, such as a metal cage or a bondage chair, which can make checking out a tad difficult... For those travelling light, boots and other S&M items, such as a strait-jacket or body bag, can be rented and kinky videos are also available.

Geldersekade 16, 1012bh (Red Light District & Nieuwmarkt) ☎ 427 0933 F 624 4281 W www.blacktulip.nl ⌂ 22, 32, 33, 34, 35, 39 ♦ 9 ⌷ ⌽ ♿ ▭ all (single: ƒ195; double: ƒ265–ƒ350)

Botel – La Casalo   ♫ off map

This is Amsterdam's smallest hotel – a converted houseboat with four guest rooms and a lounge/breakfast room. Each of the rooms has its own theme, be it the traditional Dutch style of the Amsterdam Room, complete with its own Rembrandt (could that be an original?), or the wild prints and ethnic art of the African Room. Alternatively, you might plump for the delightfully louche Cancan Room, or the mosquito-netted 'Latin Quarter'. Breakfast in your room or in the owner's traditional Dutch lounge, with its large teak table and TV.

Amsteldijk 862, 1079ln (Rivierenbuurt) ☎ 642 3680 F 644 7409 ⌂ 4 ♦ 4 ⌷ ⌽ ▭ all (single: ƒ220–ƒ260; double: ƒ235–ƒ275)

Canal House Hotel ♫A6

This family-owned hotel is a treasure. It is, in fact, two canal-side houses set in a quiet neighbourhood just round the corner from the Anne Frankhuis. Most of the rooms feel like you're in a 17th-century time warp (but with all the modern comforts of course). The bedrooms are piled high with antiques, and beds are made up with cotton sheets and patchwork quilts. The garden – though inaccessible to guests – provides a fine view from the breakfast salon.

Keizersgracht 148, 1015cx (The Canals) ☎ 622 5182 F 624 1317 w www.canalhouse.nl 🛏 13, 14, 17 🚋 21 🌼 26 ◻⬝🌮 ⌀ ⬝ ⎕ ⊟ MC/DC/V (single: ƒ265–ƒ345; double: ƒ285–ƒ345)

Hotel de Filosoof ♫ off map

Solve the world's problems – or your own – in the cozy Victorian bar. For no other reason than because it's interesting and fun, every modern room is decorated to a philosophical or classical theme, allowing you to seek enlightenment in the airy Zen room, or provide your own erotica in the virgin-white Eros bridal room. Situated next to Vondelpark, the large (for Amsterdam) garden is an oasis of calm.

Anna van den Vondelstraat 6, 1054gz (Museum District & Vondelpark) ☎ 683 3013 F 685 3750 e Filosoof@xs4all.nl w www.xs4all.nl 🛏 1, 6 🌼 25 ◻ ⬝ ⎕ ⊟ all (single: ƒ165; double: ƒ195)

Hotel New York ♫F3

Justifiably a favourite with the fashionable, it is one of Bette Midler's top European hotels, and fashion designer Franco Moschino stayed here too. Set in a beautiful location right on Herengracht, the New York comprises three modernised 17th-century herenhuizen (townhouses). It is run with care by Fernando Dik and Mizebasic, and is clean and unfussy. It is popular with straights as well as gays, and is a hotel so nice they should have named it twice.

Herengracht 13, 1015ba (The Canals) ☎ 624 3066 F 620 3230 🛏 18, 22 🌼 17 ◻ ⬝ ⎕ ⌀ ⊟ all (single: ƒ150; double: ƒ200–ƒ250)

Seven Bridges ♫C12

Situated near the Seven Bridges, this is a small, stylish hotel. An uncompromising view on quality and a good eye for antiques has resulted in nine rooms with wonderful furniture, sumptuous soft furnishings, and hand-painted tiles in the en suite bathrooms. Film director Werner Fassbinder had the good sense to stay here in his time. And no dining room means bed and breakfast in the nicest, most literal way.

Reguliersgracht 31, 1017lk (The Canals) ☎ 623 1329 🛏 4 🌼 9 ◻ ⬝ ⊟ AE/MC/V (single: ƒ200–ƒ300; double: ƒ220–ƒ360)

hotels

Toren
♭A6

A comfortable and well-turned out hotel. The bar is cozy and intimate, and once provided the set for an *EastEnders* story line. All 'superior' rooms have a whirlpool, and those in the bridal suites can naturally accommodate two for bath-time frolics. Rooms are individually decorated, and well-equipped.

Keizersgracht 164, 1015cz (The Canals) ☎ 622 6352 F 626 9705 e hotel. toren@tip.nl w www.toren.nl 🛏 13, 14, 17 🚊 21 ♦ 40 ▤ some rooms only ✐ ✐̸ ▯ 🅿 🗗 all (single: ƒ200; double: ƒ265)

The Waterfront
♭E6

Under the ownership of William de Ham, this hotel has undergone a complete refurbishment. Now it's fresh, sweet, and simple, with a scaled-down Dutch-colonial/country style – the whole design scheme creates an elegant, orderly environment. It's cheapish, small, clean, and staffed by William and his friendly American assistant.

Singel 458, 1017aw (The Canals) ☎ 421 6621 F 421 6621 e hotel@ waterfront.demon.nl 🛏 1, 2, 5 ♦ 11 🚊❷❹ 🗗 all (single: ƒ150; double: ƒ195)

ƒƒƒ

Estherea
♭F6

Look forward to warm and unpretentious hospitality in this attractive family hotel. Smart decor, deep carpets, and fresh bedrooms promise a pleasant and comfortable stay. Take a window seat in the breakfast room and enjoy a typical canal street view, or opt for the friendly conversation in the bar.

Singel 305, 1012wj (The Canals) ☎ 624 5146 F 623 9001 e estherea@xs4all.nl w www.estherea.nl 🛏 1, 2, 5 ♦ 70 ✐ ✐̸ ▯ 🗗 all (single: ƒ370; double: ƒ475)

Golden Tulip Schiller Hotel
♭B12

This hotel is named after hotelier/artist Frits Schiller, whose work appears throughout the building. The foyer decor is vibrant, while the brasserie is full of art deco flourishes. More smart than homely, the rooms are a riot of colour, with all mod cons and very comfortable beds. Its proximity to the cultural heart of town makes it a well-known hang-out for artists and literary types.

Rembrandtplein 26–36, 1017cv (Old Centre) ☎ 554 0777 F 624 0098 e sales@gtschiller.goldentulip.nl w www.goldentulip.nl 🛏 4, 9, 14 ♦ 92 ▤ ✐ ✐̸ ✐̸̸ ▯ ♨ 🗗 all (single: ƒ360; double: ƒ345–ƒ440)

Hotel-Brasserie Bodega 'Port van Cleve
♭B6

The Bodega 'Port van Cleve is a reliably good stay and is very central, overlooking the Royal Palace and right next to Magna Plaza shopping mall. It's smart, it's clean, and it's well-run, with a chic marbled lobby and reception area. Rooms are quiet and individually styled, combining good furniture, luxurious fabrics, and a peaceful atmosphere. Enjoy a pleasant, low-key service from the staff.

Nieuwezijds Voorburgwal 176–180, 10125j (Old Centre) ☎ 624 4860 ✆ 622 0240 **e** dieportvancleveamsterdam@wxs.nl **w** www.dieportvan cleve.com 🏠 1, 2, 5, 13, 17 🚉 21 ♦ 120 ⌂ ▯ 🖿 all (single: ƒ315; double: ƒ445)

ƒƒƒƒ

Amstel InterContinental Amsterdam   *ⓣ off map*

This is almost certainly the grandest of the city's hotels. Amid the stately rooms, there is a quiet and restful ambience, where the polished marble, crystal, and rich mahogany whisper of life's greatest luxuries. Restaurant La Rive is a fine match for the surroundings, while more down-to-earth tucker is served at the brasserie. The Tsar of Russia, Princess Di, Audrey Hepburn, and Madonna have all kipped in the spacious, well-appointed rooms, but these days it looks towards the business community.

Professor Tulpplein 1, 1018gc (Oost) ☎ 622 6060 ✆ 622 5808 **e** amstel@ interconti.com **w** www.interconti.com 🏠 6, 7, 10 ♦ 79 🖿❷ ↔ ✎ ✐ ✐° ▯ 🅿 🖿 all (singles & doubles: ƒ895)

Blakes Amsterdam   *ⓣE6*

Blakes Amsterdam is the first out-of-England expression of Anouska Hempel's concept of the 'fashionable small hotel'. All the rooms are individually designed, inspired by Dutch and Indonesian themes. The hotel complex, centred around two sheltered courtyards, was originally a poorhouse, but all traces of austerity have been exiled. The hotel is a haven of serenity, and the friendly staff help soften any sharp edges of perfection.

Keizersgracht 384, 1016gb (The Canals) ☎ 530 2010 ✆ 530 2030 **e** hotel@blakes.nl **w** www.slh.com 🏠 1, 2, 5 ♦ 26 🖿❷ ✎ ✐ ✐° ▯ 🖿 all (single:ƒ500–ƒ625; double: ƒ600–ƒ1000)

The Grand   *ⓣC7*

The Grand has a history that stretches back over 500 years. In its time, it has served as a convent, an inn for royalty, the location for the Admiralty, and as the City Hall. The breadth of its history is reflected to some extent in the present hotel, largely restored to its 17th-century splendour, but with art nouveau and art deco touches. Each room is individually designed and offers views onto the canals, the secluded garden, or the courtyard. World-renowned chef Albert Roux oversees the smart Café Roux.

Oudezijds Voorburgwal 197, 1012ex (Old Centre) ☎ 555 3111 ✆ 555 3222 **e** hotel@thegrand.nl **w** www.thegrand.nl 🏠 4, 9, 16, 24, 25 ♦ 182 🖿❷ ↔ 🌊 ✎ ✐ ✐° ▯ 🅿 ♿ 🖿 all (single: ƒ730; double: ƒ765)

Grand Hotel Krasnapolsky
⚡C7

The Kras is grand and monumental – the largest and best known hotel in Amsterdam. You can enjoy breakfast or lunch amidst the palms of the splendid Winter Garden or opt for the lounge if you prefer to watch Amsterdammers go about their business on the square. The stylish rooms offer an oasis of calm. The staff are attentive, and the porters are a mine of information on stories of the rich and famous who have stayed here.

Dam 9, 1012js (Old Centre) ☎ 554 9111 **F** 622 8607
e book@krasnapolsky.nl **w** www.krasnapolsky.nl 🚊 4, 9, 14, 16, 24, 25
🛏 376 🗐 🄬 ↤→ 🖉 🖉 🕸 🖵 🅿 🖂 all (single: ƒ570–ƒ615; double: ƒ650–ƒ695)

Hotel de L'Europe
⚡E7

This is a prestigious joint, but is reassuringly warm and unstuffy, dovetailing original late 19th-century splendour with the comforts of the modern world. Rooms are spacious, gracious, and bright. The restaurant is noted for its haute cuisine, but take care not to be upstaged by waiters in full evening regalia. The two-storey penthouse is fabulous, but choose the honeymoon suite for a chance to revel in your own whirlpool.

Nieuwe Doelenstraat 2–8, 1012cp (Old Centre) ☎ 531 1777 **F** 551 1778
e hotel@leurope.nl **w** www.Leurope.nl 🚊 4, 9, 14,16, 24, 25 🛏 100 🗐 🄬 ↤→
🌊 🖉 🖉 🕸 🖵 🅿 🖧 🖂 all (single: ƒ575; double: ƒ655– ƒ755)

Hotel Pulitzer
⚡C6

James Stewart, Catherine Deneuve, and Isabella Rossellini have all been attracted to this beautiful hotel. Twenty-four 17th-century canalside houses unite around an Italianate courtyard and provide an array of individually styled rooms – from the cosy and beamed to the more lavish and capacious. Paintings from the hotel's own collection are hung in the rooms, and the Pulitzer also has its own gallery. In the dining room, the Brunch Frans Hals by Thierry de Cromières reflects the hotel's penchant for mixing wit and style.

Prinsengracht 315–31, 1016gz (The Canals) ☎ 523 5235 **F** 627 6753
e sales@sheraton.com 🚊 13, 14, 17 🚊 21 🛏 226 🗐 🄬 ↤→ 🖉 🖉 🕸 🖵 🅿 🖧 🖂 all
(single: ƒ695–ƒ760; double: ƒ770–ƒ840)

Seven One Seven
⚡A11

Exclusive and discreet, there's no hotel sign on the door of this luxurious private guesthouse which offers total privacy to a select clientele. Designed by Kees van der Valk, it demonstrates a splendid, robustly masculine style, with a witty attention to detail. Henk de Lugt heads an attentive staff, while an all-in price for breakfast, traditional afternoon tea, and drinks makes for a relaxed, natural hospitality. Not the place for baggy shorts and T-shirts: a strong sense of comme il faut safeguards high standards here.

Prinsengracht 717, 1017jw (The Canals) ☎ 427 0717 **F** 423 0717 🚊 16, 24, 25
🛏 7 suites 🖵 🗐 🄬 🖉 🖉 🕸 🖂 all (singles & doubles: ƒ575–ƒ1000)

practical information

Admission charges

Charges for museums and sights vary, but are generally f5 to f15, although a few are free or as much as f24. If you're visiting several museums buy a *museumjaarkaart*, an annual museum card for just f45. It saves money on museum entrance fees even if you just visit a few, offering free or reduced admission to around 400 museums throughout the Netherlands (19 in Amsterdam). It is available from the Amsterdam Tourist Board and all major museums. For more information call ☎ (0900) 404 9010 **W** www.museumjaarkaart.nl. The Amsterdam Tourist Board and 40 affiliated hotels sell a packet of 31 coupons giving free and reduced admission to museums, boat trips, and diamond factory tours. For more information call ☎ (0900) 400 4040 f36.

Banks

The ABN AMRO, ING Bank, Postbank, and Rabobank are the four major operators. Opening hours are generally 9am–5pm Mon–Fri. The Postbank is open until 6pm daily (8pm Thu) and 10am–1.30pm Sat. Bank holidays mean closed doors and long queues at ATMs. 24-hour cash dispensers are at all major branches. In general, banks charge less commission on money exchange, but have worse exchange rates. The most central banks are:

ABN AMRO Dam 2 ☎ 523 2000
ING Bank Damrak 80–81 ☎ 550 3100
Postbank Singel 250 ☎ 556 3311
Rabobank Dam 16 ☎ 495 0950

For international money transfers, your best bet is **Western Union** ☎ 0800 0506, or pop into the GWK (Centraal Station ☎ 627 2731, Schiphol Plaza ☎ 653 5121).

bars & cafés

Types: cafés fall into two main types – those for drinking and those for eating (called *eetcafés*), but there is an overlap. Both bars and cafés serve coffee, soft drinks, and alcohol (a mixture of imported and local brews). Brown cafés are drinking spots with wood panelling, tobacco-stained walls, and are typically in the Jordaan. Grand cafés are large, opulent places, some of which are now trendy bars. *Proeflokalen* traditionally are 'tasting' houses for *jenever* (Dutch gin).

Opening times: generally 8pm–1am weekdays and until 2–3am Fri–Sat.

Late opening: all over the city you'll find bars and cafés with extended hours.

Ordering: don't expect to be served first, even when first in the queue: cry *meneer* and *ober* (mister and waiter) if all else fails. Many have table service so you can pay in one go at the end.

Children: are allowed in bars when with an adult. Alcohol is legally sold to those over 18 years (although ID is rarely asked for).

Smoking: only some bars and cafés allow dope smoking, but if nicotine's your habit, feel free.

Food: bars usually offer simple snacks although more upmarket ones have full menus. The fare is decent but is not going to win a Michelin star.

practical information

bureaux de change

An abundance of offices can be found in the city centre, offering better rates of exchange than most banks, but watch out for hidden charges and check the advertised rate is the buying not the selling one. Expect to pay 3% commission on traveller's cheques' exchanges, with a minimum charge of ƒ5. Exchange rates are non-negotiable – business is business. The most trustworthy and competitive places are: **Thomas Cook** who offer instant money transfer to anywhere in the world within 10 minutes, as well as the usual exchange services:
Dam 23–25 ☎ 625 0922 ◐ *9am–6pm daily*; Damrak 1–5 ☎ 620 3236 ◐ *8am–8pm daily*; Leidseplein 31a ☎ 626 7000 ◐ *8.45am–6.15pm daily*. **GWK** are good if you landed without a guilder to your name: Centraal Station ☎ 527 2371 ◐ *24 hours daily*; Schiphol Plaza ☎ 653 5121 ◐ *24 hours daily*. **Pott's** offers the most competitive rates in the city: Damrak 95 ☎ 626 3658 ◐ *8am–8pm daily*.

children

The Dutch don't welcome kids with open arms so if you take them to bars, cafés, and restaurants expect frowned looks from other customers. You'll be hard pushed to find a kids' menu, highchair, or play area and only invaliden toilets tend to have shelves for changing babies nappies.
Transport: children under 4 travel free and older ones get cheap fares.
Museums: most offer reduced entry for children.
Child minders: the larger hotels have child minding services, or you can try the **Babysit Centre de Amsterdamse** ☎ 697 2320 or the 24hr **Oppas Centrale** ☎ (036) 534 5436.

Activities: pop into the AUB for information on what to do with the kids.
Hotels: ask individual hotels if they have family or child rates, also check on childrens facilities (play areas, babysitting, etc).

conversions

Clothing	Women's			
European	36	40	44	46
US	6	10	14	16
British	8	12	16	18
Shoes	**Women's**			
European	37	38	39	40
US	5	6	7	8
British	4	5	6	7

Clothing	Men's			
European	46	50	54	56
US	36	40	44	46
British	36	40	44	46
Shoes	**Men's**			
European	40	42	43	44
US	7	8	9	10
British	6	7	8	9

courier services

International services:
DHL ☎ (0800) 0552 ◐ *24 hours daily*;
TNT ☎ (0900) 899 1111;
UPS ☎ (0800) 099 1300.
National services within the Netherlands:
Holland Parcel Express ☎ (0800) 023 3220
Speedy Couriers ☎ 494 0770

credit & debit cards

Cash dispensers (ATMs) are prolific in Amsterdam, although they empty at breakneck speed on national holidays and Sundays. The only debit card system accepted is PIN (only for those with Dutch bank accounts). But you can get cash from ATMs using most credit cards. Major credit cards are widely accepted, although they are not

referred method of payment and if
a make a purchase under ƒ50 you'll
bably be charged a fee for the
vilege. The most widely accepted
ds are MasterCard (EuroCard) and
a. Cash advances on credit cards
ur charges. Note that most
ermarkets do not accept credit
ds. For lost or stolen cards contact:
erican Express ☎ 504 8504;
sterCard/EuroCard ☎ (030) 283 5555
a ☎ (06) 022 4176

rency

Netherlands' currency is the
lder (made up of 100 cents),
resented by the prefix ƒ, fl, or NLG.
ns are 5c (stuiver), 10c (dubbeltje),
(kwartje), ƒ1 (piek), ƒ2.50
ksdaalder), and ƒ5. The bank notes
found in denominations of ƒ10, ƒ25,
, ƒ100, ƒ250, and ƒ1000, the last of
ich no shops will accept. Prices are
given in euros. The guilder will be
laced in 2002 when the euro
omes the only legal tender.

stoms & quarantine

sterdam customs (douane) has a
ods to declare' lane and a 'no goods
leclare' lane. There are no
arantine laws, but the import of
langered species is prohibited, as
meat, flowers, and plants
stoms ☎ 586 7511).

ntists

ou need immediate help, call the
ntal Helpline (Tandarts Bemidelings
eau) ☎ (0900) 821 230, for the
me and number of the nearest
ntist [→insurance].

abled visitors

one or visit the **AUB** or **Amsterdam**
urist Board for information on
abled access to hotels, museums,

and restaurants. Certain areas, like the
Jordaan, have cobbled streets that
make life uncomfortable for those in
wheelchairs. Public transport is
problematic for disabled visitors.

driving
There's no doubt about it: driving in
Amsterdam is a hazard and parking
costly, so leave the car at home and
walk or use public transport.

drugs
Although weed/cannabis is widely
available and openly smoked, it is in
fact illegal. Smoking is 'allowed' in
coffeeshops, at home, and in the park,
but do it with discretion and always
respect no smoking signs. Weed breaks
down into two types: skunk is cross-
bred and super strong (grown under
UV lights); bush is milder and more
natural. Shops have sprung up selling
all manner of legal narcotics and
ready-rolled joints. Hard drugs are
another matter: the police will be
tough on anyone found in possession.

duty free
Duty free goods are still available to
non-EU nationals within the usual
limits: 200 cigarettes, 50 cigars, 250g of
tobacco, 1 litre of spirits or 2 litres of
wine. Most airports have huge savings
on cosmetics, perfume, and other items
for EU nationals as well, who have no
limits when entering the Netherlands.
If you are unsure of the restrictions call
customs (☎ 586 7511).

electricity
The Netherlands uses 220V (on 2-
pronged plugs), so British appliances
can only be used with an adapter. US
(and other 110V) appliances will also
need a transformer.

practical information

email & internet

Major hotels, libraries, and a sea of internet cafés ensure global communication. For quick access try one of the city's internet terminals (resembling payphones) dotted across town, the free terminals at **De Waag**, or the main branch of the public library (Prinsengracht 587, The Canals), which has 25 terminals for free use (half-hour limit).

embassies & consulates

American Embassy Museumplein 19 (Amsterdam) ☎ 664 4661/674 0321
Australian Embassy Carnegielaan 4 (The Hague) ☎ (070) 310 8200
British Consulate Koningslaan 44 (Amsterdam) ☎ 676 4343/675 8121
Canadian Embassy Sophialaan 7 (The Hague) ☎ (070) 311 1600
Embassy of Eire Dr Kuyperstraat 9 (The Hague) ☎ (070) 363 0993
New Zealand Embassy
Carnegielaan 10 (The Hague)
☎ (070) 346 9324

emergencies

For emergency police, fire brigade, and ambulance services ☎ 112.
For emergency medical attention, make your way to one of the following major hospitals:
Boven IJ Statenjacht St 1 ☎ 634 6346
Onze Lieve Vrouw 1e Oosterpark St 279 ☎ 599 9111
Slotervaart Louwesweg 6 ☎ 512 4113

help & advice lines

AA ☎ 625 6057 for alcohol related problems.
Aids ☎ (0800) 022 2220.
Legal Advice ☎ 444 6333.
SOS ☎ 675 7575 (similar to the Samaritans).

hotels

Peak season, Apr–Sep (and Dec), sees nearly all hotels full with prices at the highest. Queen's Day (Apr 30th) and New Year's Eve are busy too, so book i advance. There are often cheap deals you leave it late in the day. Try the **Amsterdam Tourist Board** (Damrak 7 ☎ 520 7000) and **Amsterdam Last Minute Reservation** (Wysmullerst 9 ☎ 408 1600) for late availability and bargains. For student try the **ASVA-OBAS agency** (☎ 623 8052).
Charges: prices vary considerably, so sh around. Hotel prices usually include 6% VAT, but watch out for the additional 5" visitors' tax. Cheaper hotels tend to giv all inclusive rates. If breakfast is includ you'll be served cheese, ham, a croissar and a boiled egg. Avoid using the phor in your room as charges are higher tha pay-phones.
Tipping: it is common to tip staff in luxury hotels, but not in smaller establishments.
Check-out time is usually 11am.

immigration

If you're intending to stay longer tha three months, report to the **Vreemdelingen Politie** (☎ 559 6300) with your passport, birth certificate, health insurance, employment and housing contracts, bank details, and two passport photos. If you are stayin permanently and working, you shoul also report to the **Bevolkings register** (census) (☎ 608 0109) and obtain a *sofi* (tax) number (☎ 687 7777).

insurance

Comprehensive medical insurance is recommended for all visitors, especia non-EU citizens. Keep receipts as you'

y first and claim later. EU nationals
ould acquire an E110, E111, or E112
rm as well [→medical matters].

ft luggage

-hour access lockers are available at
hiphol Airport and Centraal Station.
ote that once you've re-opened a locker
u'll have to pay again to continue
ing it. They cost between ƒ4 and ƒ8 per
hours, depending on the size.

st property

port all lost items to the police
559 9111) to substantiate insurance
aims. A lost passport should also
reported to your embassy or
nsulate as soon as possible. If you lose
ything on your travels, contact the
VB (public transport authority) ☎ 551
11 or Schiphol Airport ☎ (0900) 0141.

aps

e A–Z Stratengids Amsterdam is a
luable companion as are Amsterdam
sy City and Amsterdam in One 1999.
e Slechte on Kalverstraat offers these
discount prices. The Amsterdam
urist Board also has city maps on sale.

easurements

a rule, metric measures are used.

etric : imperial	imperial : metric
nm = 0.04 inch	inch = 2.5 cm
:m = 0.4 inch	1 foot = 30 cm
n = 3.3 ft	1 mile = 1.6 km
:m = 0.6 mile	1 ounce = 28 g
= 0.04 oz	1 pound = 454 g
:g = 2.2 pounds	1 pint = 0.6 l
= 0.17 gallons	1 gallon = 4.5 l

edical matters

r emergency treatment
→emergencies]. If it's not, go to the
ut-patient department of one of the

hospitals listed [→emergencies] or
you can call the doctor's line (with
English-speaking operators ☎ 503
2042) for advice. If you need to look for
a dokter (GP) call the Ziekenfondsraad
(health-care advice line ☎ 347 5555)
who will also advise on payment
procedures and E111 [→insurance]. For
abortion and contraception advice call
the Rutgerstichting (family planning
clinic) (Overtoom 233 ☎ 616 6222).

medicine & chemists

A drogisterij (chemist) sells everything
from toothpaste to tampons and
operates normal shop hours. All non-
prescription drugs are kept behind
the counter – you even have to ask for
aspirin. Apotheken (pharmacies) sell
medication only on receipt of a
prescription (on which the charges
vary depending on the items) and are
open ◑ 9am–5pm Mon–Fri. There is a
24hr chemist open somewhere in the
city at all times – check the local
paper de Telegraaf.

office & business services

Multi Copy (Weesperstraat 65
☎ 624 6208) and Printerette
(Spuistraat 91–93 ☎ 625 1744,
Spuistraat 128 ☎ 627 2425) offer faxing,
computer terminals, colour copying,
and binding. For someone else to do
the work, contact the Euro Business
Centre (Keizersgracht 62–64 ☎ 520
7500) for a 24hr service of bilingual
secretaries, voicemail services, and
office space. Mail-boxes can be opened
at the Mini Office (Singel 417 ☎ 625
8455). For stationery call into the main
post office (Singel 250 ☎ 556 3311) or
drop into department store HEMA
(Kalvertoren ☎ 422 8988) [→email
& internet].

practical information

opticians
Pearle opticians have the largest number of stores in the city and do free eye tests. The most central is at Singel 457 ☎ 623 6429. **Hans Anders** is also a good bet with eight stores around the city, offering competitive prices and a quick reliable service. The nearest to the centre is at Ferdinand Bolstraat 118 ☎ 664 1879.

photography
Capi (Schiphol Plaza ☎ 446 6310) offers a one-hour developing service, and they're open ◑ *7am–10pm* (you'll find them at Arrivals), as do **Super Photo** (Max Euweplein 60 ☎ 420 2870). The cheapest option is the **Albert Heijn** supermarkets: the most central is on Nieuwezijds Voorburgwal. If your camera needs fixing, try **NCR** (Lijnbaansgracht 162 ☎ 626 2790).

police
Call the police headquarters (☎ 559 9111) for the nearest station. Only use ☎ 112 in emergencies.

postal services
Post offices: the main post office, or **Hoofd Postkantoor**, is at Singel 250. Another handy one is next to Centraal Station at Oosterdokskade 3–5. Take a ticket and wait your turn.
Opening hours: 9am–5pm Mon–Fri (the Singel branch also opens 9am–1pm Sat).
Stamps: letters and cards within the Netherlands cost 80c; ƒ1 for the rest of Europe. The Singel branch has a stamp machine so you can avoid the queues. Put post for outside the city in the box marked overigebestemmingen.
Poste Restante: the Singel branch accepts mail for collection, but take ID.
Postal line: ☎ (0800) 0417 for information.

prostitution
The Netherlands lifted a ban on brothels in October 99, allowing prostitutes to work from licensed premises. The new laws on prostitutic also means that brothels, sex clubs, and 'windows' have to meet local authority standards. Around 5000 female prostitutes work the Red Light District. Rent-boys hang out around Centraal Station, but they often practise unsafe sex, so avoid. There are some major *faux pas* to the business: haggling, lack of personal hygiene, aggressive behaviour, and taking photos of the women.

public holidays
New Year's Day; Good Friday; Easter Sunday & Monday; Queen's Day (April 30th); Remembrance Day (May 4th); Liberation Day (May 5th once every fiv years); Ascension Day; Whit Sunday & Monday; Christmas Day; Boxing Day.

religion
For general enquiries about places of worship and service times, contact: Catholic ☎ 622 1918; Jewish ☎ 642 356: Muslim ☎ 698 2526; Orthodox ☎ 646 0046; Reform ☎ 624 9665.

restaurants & eetcafés
An eetcafé is a café that serves snacks a lunchtime, and full meals in the evening
Reservations: it's advisable to make a reservation in restaurants, but in eetcafés you can usually just turn up and sit down.
Opening times: usually until 9.30pm i eetcafés and 10.30pm in restaurants.
Payments: all major credit cards are widely accepted, but there are some surprising exceptions so check before ordering. Traveller's cheques need changing first.

...oking: no smoking sections are ...tually unheard of and the Dutch ...n't have a problem with smoking ...restaurants.

...fety

...sterdam is well policed, but like ...ery major city, it's not always safe to ...lk/cycle around in the small hours. It ...particularly important to be wary ...ound Centraal Station. Pickpockets are ...e, so keep an eye on your belongings ...en on busy streets and on the trams.

...opping

...ening times: generally 12–6pm Mon, ...m–6pm Tue–Sat with late-night ...til 9pm Thu. Sunday (12–5pm) ...opping is only in some stores. ...permarkets open longer hours. ...yment: can be made with credit ...rds and cash. Cheques are rarely ...ed and traveller's cheques are best ...shed in advance. ...turns: should be made within 7–14 ...ys. You must produce a receipt to ...change goods and to receive cash or ...edit notes. Sale goods are usually ...n-refundable. ...uarantees: are available on larger ...ods and equipment, but vary between ...ores and items – make sure you have ...oof of purchase and the guarantee ...lidated before leaving the store. ...les: are twice yearly; early winter ...id-Jan) and late summer (end ...ly–beg Aug). ...port: some stores offer VAT discounts ... purchases over ƒ300 for non-EU ...tionals. VAT is never refunded at ...ne of purchase [→VAT].

...oking

...eryone lights up everywhere in ...nsterdam – in bars, cafés, ...staurants, even cinemas and theatres

during the intervals (but not during performances). There are crowded smoking carriages on trains, but all trams, buses, metro trains and taxis are no-smoking [→drugs].

students

For cheap travel call **Budget Air** (☎ 626 5227) and **Eurobus** (☎ 560 8787). ISIC cards can be bought at the **NBBS** (Weteringschans 28 ☎ 260 5071), who act as a service point for **Usit Campus**, and **Budget Air**. **The Cartes Jeunes Personnes (CJP)** costs ƒ20 per year and can also get the under 27s discounts.

telephoning

Sounds: repeated beeps mean the line is engaged and a high-pitched continuous tone means the number is unobtainable. **Calling the Netherlands:** From the UK ☎ 0031; from the USA ☎ 011 31; from **Australia** ☎ 0011 31; from **Ireland** ☎ 0031. To call Amsterdam dial the inter- national code plus 20 then the number. **Calling from the Netherlands:** dial the international code and minus the first zero from the regional code: **UK** ☎ 0044; US ☎ 001; **Australia** ☎ 0061; **Ireland** ☎ 00353. **Freephone:** all free numbers begin 0800. **Enquiries & the operator:** for numbers within the Netherlands ☎ 118 – a Dutch recorded message will ask for the name, address, and city of the person you wish to reach. international directory enquiries ☎ (0900) 8418. The operator can be called ☎ (0800) 0410 for local and national queries. **Phone directories:** the official book is the *Koninklijke PTT Netherland*, there's also the *Goade Gids* (or Yellow Pages). **Rates and charges:** ƒ0.06 per minute peak, ƒ0.03 off-peak weekdays and ƒ0.02 on weekends and public holidays.

Phone boxes: most are phonecard operated. Cards come in units of ƒ10, ƒ25, and ƒ50 and are available from post offices and newsagents. Phone boxes have a minimum charge of ƒ0.5. **Phone centres:** Leidsestraat, the Rokin, and Damrak have loads of telephone centres with very competitive prices and are usually cheaper than phone boxes for dialling abroad. **Mobile phones:** it's often cheaper to buy a prepay mobile than to rent one as some networks sell them for as little as ƒ99. If you do only want to rent, you'll need a credit card for the ƒ2000 deposit. Prices are around ƒ39 per day, ƒ129 per week, and ƒ295 per month excluding VAT and insurance. Call ptt Telecom (☎ 653 0999) for information.

time

The Netherlands is on Central European Time, one hour ahead of GMT. Clocks go forward one hour in spring and back one hour in the autumn, on the same dates as GMT. Call the speaking clock in Dutch ☎ (0900) 8002.

tipping

Tipping is commonplace in bars, cafés, restaurants, hairdressers, and taxis. If you liked the service leave 10% in restaurants and cabs (or round up to the nearest ƒ5 or ƒ10). Leave ƒ5–ƒ10 for other services on top of the standard service charge already added to your bill.

toilets

Public toilets are few so pop into a nearby hotel or café, the latter of which will charge a ƒ0.5 fee, which is also applied in many clubs, bars, and restaurants, even if you're a patron.

tourist information

The **Amsterdam Tourist Board** ☎ (0900) 400 4040, provides information on tickets, hotels, excursion, and car hire, as well as stocking brochures, maps, listings, and museum cards. The **AUB** (☎ 621 1211) has information about what's on and ticket agency facilities.

tours:
boat tours

Amsterdam Canal Cruises
Stadhouderskade, De Pijp
☎ 626 5636 ▣ ƒ15–ƒ47.50 ◑ all year.
Canal Bikes
Leidseplein, Rijksmuseum & Anne Frankhuis ☎ 626 5574
▣ ƒ12.50 per person (2 persons) or ƒ10 per person (3–4 persons), per hour, plu ƒ50 deposit ◑ summer: 10am–10pm daily; winter: 10am–6pm daily.
Canal Boats
Kloveniersburgwal, Red Light District & Nieuwmarkt ☎ 422 7007
▣ ƒ65 per boat (6 persons) per hour (ƒ300 deposit) ◑ Apr–Aug: 10am–10.30pr daily; Sep–Oct: 10am–6.30pm daily.
Historic Ferries
☎ 460 5454 ▣ ƒ600/hr
Two historic ferries are for hire.
Museumboot
☎ 622 2181 ▣ ƒ22.50–ƒ27.50
◑ 10am–5pm daily.
Every 30–45 mins at key tourist spots.
Water Taxis
Stationsplein 8, Old Centre
☎ 622 2181 ▣ ƒ125 per boat for 30 min (8–12 persons) ◑ 8am–8pm daily.

bike tours

Yellow Bike
Nieuwezijds Kolk 29, Old Centre
☎ 620 6940 ▣ City Tour: ƒ32.50; Waterland Tour: ƒ42.50 ◑ 9.30am & 1pm daily (3 hour tour).

e City Tour rides past Amsterdam's
ain sights. The Waterland Tour goes
rther afield.

am tours

storic Tram
673 7538 ⊞ f6.60 ◑ Easter–Oct:
m–5pm Sun, every half hour.

y tours

st of Holland
mrak 34, Old Centre
623 1539 ⊞ f13–f125
urs by bus and boat.

lland International
ns Hendrikkade 33a, Old Centre
622 7788 ⊞ f15–f150
alking, bus, and canal boat tours.

dbergh Excursions
mrak 62, Old Centre
622 2766 ⊞ f28.50–f67.50
alking, bus, and canal boat tours.

Artifex
rengracht 342, The Canals
620 8112 ⊞ f385
t historians lead group tours.

alking tours

nsterdam Walking Tours
640 9072 ⊞ f195 (for up to 20
ople) ◑ times vary.
alking tours of the city centre and
wish quarter.

ee in Mokum
rtenstraat 18, The Canals
625 1390 ⊞ f5 ◑ 11am Tue–Sat.
nsterdammers with a passion for the
y lead groups on neighbourhood tours.

avel agents
st minute flights: KLM Call & Go
☎ 567 4587)
eap flights: Budget Air (☎ 626 5227)
fers extra discounts for those under
and ISIC card holders; EasyJet
☎ 568 4880) has low fares to some
ropean destinations.

For the whole kit 'n' caboodle:
NBBS (Rokin 38 ☎ 624 0989,
Weteringschans 28 ☎ 260 5071), who
also act as a Usit Campus service point.

traveller's cheques
The US dollar and pound sterling are
the most widely accepted. It's the
safest way to carry money abroad.
You'll need your passport for ID when
cashing them. [→bureaux de change]
[→banks]

VAT (Value Added Tax)
Goods in shops are taxed at 17.5%,
(books and children's clothes are 6%).
VAT can be reclaimed by non-EU
residents, but it's a long process,
needing a certified VAT form, receipt of
purchase, a visit to the VAT desk at
Schiphol, ID proving you are non-EU,
and unopened goods.

visas & entry requirements
A valid passport is required for entry
into the Netherlands. No visas are
needed for visitors from EU countries,
the USA, Australia, New Zealand, and
Canada for stays of up to three
months. If you are from elsewhere,
apply for a visa from your country of
origin. Stays of over three months
require a visa, which should be
obtained from a Dutch Embassy before
departure. Non-EU citizens require
proof of onward travel. No vaccinations
are required [→immigration].

weather
In general, the weather is rainy and
windy, although extremes of hot and
cold are possible. Pack for all seasons,
whatever time of year it is. Watch the
news or check local press for weather
information. For daily forecasts, see
w www.travelocity.com/weather

transport

arriving & departing

The Dutch take great pride in their punctual transport system. And so they should. No matter how you enter the country – by plane, boat, train, or coach – you're guaranteed to arrive at the right place at the right time.

by air: schiphol airport

Five metres below sea level and 18km (11 miles) from the centre of the city, Amsterdam Schiphol Airport is one of the world's most efficient airports. Annually around 37 million people breeze through its single terminal.

1st floor: departures
ground floor: arrivals

☎ **useful numbers**
Enquiries: (0900) 0141
(flights, transport, parking, hotels)
Airport police: 603 8111
Lost property: 601 2325
Left luggage: 601 2443
First aid: 601 2528
Medical emergencies: 601 2527
IHD (International Help for the Disabled): 316 1417
✆ **Mercure:** 617 9005
✆ **Sheraton:** 316 4300
✆ **Hilton:** 710 4000
w www.schiphol.nl

transport options: Schiphol–city centre

Ⅲ trains
20–30 min to/from Centraal Station.
☽ 24 hours daily, approx every 10 min from 5.41–12.48am and every hour on the hour from 1–5am.

💶 f6.50 (single). NB: *strippenkart* can't be used
♻ Quick and easy – straight into the heart of Amsterdam.
♻ Cheapest option.
♻ The train station is underground in the airport complex and within walking distance of both arrivals and departures.
♺ There are no luggage trolleys at Centraal Station.
♺ Trains are not accessible to wheelchairs – call in advance for assistance
☎ (030) 230 5566
☎ (0900) 9292

🚌 **KLM hotel shuttle**
20–45 min to/from hotel, depending on location.
☽ Route A daily times: every 30 mins from 7am–6pm, and hourly from 6–10pm.
☽ Route B daily times: every 30 min from 6.45am–6pm, and hourly from 6–10pm.
💶 f17.50 (single)
Route A runs along: Prinsengracht, Dam, Nieuwezijds Voorburgwal, Prins Hendrikkade, Vijzelstraat, and drops off at selected hotels.
Route B runs along: De Boelelaan, Europaboulevard, Ferdinand Bolstraat, Apollolaan, Beethovenstraat, Dijsselhofplantsoen, De Lairessestraat, Stadhouderskade, PC Hooftstraat, Koninginneweg.
♻ Door-to-door service.
♻ Don't have to be staying at any of the hotel destinations or fly KLM to use the service.

- Cheaper than a taxi.
- No service 10pm–6.45am.
- No wheelchair provision.
- Purchase tickets from the KLM
otel Shuttle desk in the main hall
f the airport.
☎ 649 5651

taxis
0–30 min journey.
24 hours daily.
💰 f55–f60
- Most convenient – there are always
lenty at the taxi rank outside the
rrivals Hall.
- Full wheelchair access if foldable.
- Quite expensive.

limos & cars
0–30 min journey.
24 hours daily.
💰 f100–f210 (executive
ars), f120–f210 (limos),
450 (stretch limo).
- Travel in style.
- Most expensive option.
- Check ahead for disabled access
TS is the best).
- Make reservations at least 24 hours
1 advance.
- Prices vary widely between
ompanies: check if prices include
ax and if there are hidden costs.
- Don't forget to give them your
ight details.

msterdamse Limousine Service:
☎ (0800) 235 5466

S Limousine Services:
☎ 673 7888

TS Excellent Transfer Services:
☎ 659 5333

by ferry

There are three main ferry routes from
the UK to Holland:

ferry essentials

UK–Rotterdam:
▶ P&O operates to/from Hull once a day
(14 hrs, £40 + per passenger, £161 + per car).
▶ P&O runs a bus service both to/from
Rotterdam (37km from the port) and
Centraal Station in Amsterdam. Buy
bus tickets with your ferry ticket.

UK–Hoek van Holland:
▶ Boat-train service: Stena-line
operates a service from London to
Amsterdam Centraal Station twice
daily (8 hrs 45 min, £79 return).
▶ There are also ferries to/from
Harwich twice daily (4 hrs 30 min,
£36 + per passenger, £125 + per car).

UK–IJmuiden-Amsterdam:
▶ DFDS Seaways operates a nightly
service every other day to/from
Newcastle (16 hrs, £68 + per car,
£59 + per passenger).

☎ useful numbers
P&O North Sea Ferries:
(01482) 377 177 (UK); 448 7171 (NL)
Stenaline UK: (0870) 570 7070 (UK);
900 8123 (NL)
DFDS Seaways: (0990) 333 000 (UK);
(0255) 534 546 (NL)
❶ In spring 2000 Amsterdam will have
a passenger terminal on the Oostelijke
for cruise ships from around the world.

by rail

Centraal Station has excellent services
running from destinations all over the
Netherlands and Europe, right into the
heart of Amsterdam.

transport

centraal station

▶ Open 24-hours daily.
▶ Ticket counters have yellow *Loket* signs.
▶ Platform 2 houses the toilets and an Amsterdam Tourist Board office.
▶ The GVB Public Transport Office is outside on Stationsplein for ticket buying and transport information.
▶ The rear exit leads to the free ferries to Amsterdam-Noord and other destinations.

national train essentials

▶ Children under 3 travel free and 4–11 year olds get 40% off.
▶ A one-day *dagkaart* allows unlimited train travel in the Netherlands for *f*73.50.
▶ Yellow, automatic ticket dispensing machines, labelled *Treinkaartjes*, help avoid queues at busy stations. Choose your destination, type in the code from the alphabetical list, choose first or second class, and then single or return.
▶ *Sneltrainen* are fast trains, whilst *stoptreinen* are slower, stopping at many stations.
▶ Train-taxis serve around 100 train stations in the Netherlands (but not Amsterdam) and take you to your final destination (within the town's boundaries) for less than the cost of a regular taxi. Tickets can be bought along with your train ticket and cost *f*7 when purchased at a station.
▶ Every train station in the Netherlands has bike-locking facilities and some have a *Rijwielshop* where you can have your bike repaired or rent one. To take a bicycle on a train, get a ticket: *f*10–*f*15 (single), *f*17.50–*f*25 (return).
▶ There are special compartments for bikes on trains.

international trains

▶ HSS Express runs from London to Amsterdam via Hoek van Holland .
▶ The high-speed THALYS gets to Paris in 4 hrs 15 min.
▶ Eurostar runs from London, via Brussels, to Amsterdam.

☎ **useful numbers**
General info: 557 8400 (NL)
NS: (0900) 9292 for national services (NL); (0900) 9296 for international services (NL) w www.ns.nl
Eurostar: (0990) 186 186 (UK)

by coach

Eurolines is the only major operator around Europe. Coaches arrive at Amstel Station where there are transport links into the centre of Amsterdam.

transport options: Amstel Station–city centre

⏽ train

8 min to/from Centraal Station.
🕐 5.42–0.48am, approx every 5–15 min.
💳 *f*3 (2 strips of *strippenkart*).
♿ It's just one stop to Amsterdam Centraal Station.
♿ Use *strippenkaart*.
♿ Less convenient than the metro for disabled travellers.

🚋 tram 12

30 min to/from Sloterdijk Station, 10–15 min to museumplein/Vondelpark.
💳 *f*4.50 to Sloterdijk (or 3 strips of *strippenkaart*), *f*3 to centre (or 2 strips of a *strippenkaart*).
🕐 6–0.03am, every 10–20 min.
♿ No disabled access.

🚇 **metro**

🕐 0 min to/from Centraal Station.

🕐 5.50–0.20am, every 5 min.

🎫 ƒ3 (2 *strippenkaart* strips).

❶ You can't pay in cash, only in *strippenkaart*.

🚕 **taxi**

❶ There are always plenty of taxis at the rank outside.

coach essentials

▶ Coach travel plays second fiddle to trains within the Netherlands as it is slower.

▶ Not all buses are marked Eurolines as various operators work different routes.

▶ **Ticketshops:**

Rokin 10 ❶ 9.30am–5.30pm Mon–Fri; 11am–5pm Sat.

Julianplein 5 ❶ 8am–10pm daily.

▶ Eurolines runs direct routes from major destinations to Amsterdam:

London: £44 + (9 hours 15 min)
Paris: £ + (8 hrs)
Brussels: £14 + (4 hrs 30 min)
Berlin: £30 + (9 hrs 30 min)

☎ **useful numbers**

Eurolines: (0990) 143 219 (UK); 560 8788 (NL).

getting around

It's easy to walk around town, but transport options are plentiful too.

general information

🎫 **travelcards & tickets**

There is one main type of ticket for all public transport. *Strippenkaart* (strip card) can be used on trams, buses, the

metro, and some overland trains. The city is divided into 11 zones – zone one encompasses the whole city centre. Every journey uses one more strip than the number of zones passed through. For example, a one-zone trip uses two strips, a two-zone trip three strips, and so on. Either stamp the ticket yourself at an automatic stamping machine (yellow boxes on trams and at metro stations) or the driver/conductor will do it when you get on. Once stamped, your ticket is valid for a set time (one hour in zones 1–3), during which time you can hop on and off any form of public transport. Passes of various time-lengths are also available.

▶ Two one-day tickets give one day's unlimited travel in the Netherlands on buses, trams, and the metro.

▶ Two or more people can use the same *strippenkaart* if travelling together – just stamp the number of strips for each person.

▶ On-the-spot fines of ƒ60 are imposed for travelling without a valid ticket.

Ticket type

2-strip, 1-zone single ƒ3
available from: Driver/conductor, GVB Ticket Office, Amsterdam Tourist Board, Some post offices and shops, Automatic dispensers

3-strip, 2-zone single ƒ4.50
available from: Driver/conductor, GVB Ticket Office, Amsterdam Tourist Board, Some post offices and shops, Automatic dispensers

8-strip ƒ12
available from: Driver/conductor, GVB Ticket Office, Amsterdam Tourist Board, Some post offices and shops, Automatic dispensers

15-strip ƒ12
available from: GVB Ticket Office,
Amsterdam Tourist Board, Some post
offices and shops

45-strip ƒ35.25
available from: GVB Ticket Office,
Amsterdam Tourist Board, Some post
offices and shops

1-hour unlimited tram/bus/metro
travel ƒ4.50
available from: Driver/conductor, GVB
Ticket Office, Amsterdam Tourist Board,
Some post offices and shops,
Automatic dispensers

1-day unlimited tram/bus/metro
travel ƒ12
available from: Driver/conductor, GVB
Ticket Office, Amsterdam Tourist Board,
Some post offices and shops,
Automatic dispensers

All Amsterdam Pass (one day's
unlimited travel on all public
transport) ƒ29.50
available from: Canalbus mornings,
GVB Ticket Office

Circle Amsterdam (every stop on Circle
tram line) ƒ12
available from: GVB Ticket Office,
Amsterdam Tourist Board

Weekly pass ƒ18
available from: GVB Ticket Office, Some
post offices and shops

♿ disabled travellers

Trams are generally not accessible to
wheelchairs. Even new ones that have a
lowered floor around the middle door
have a gap of around 20cm between the
tram floor and ground. Some buses have
steps which can be automatically

lowered but these are few. The metro is
fully accessible for wheelchairs and all
stations have lifts to the platforms. There
is a taxi service for wheelchair users,
Garskamp Personen Vervoer (Garskamp
People's Transport), but prices are ƒ35–ƒ85
for journeys within Amsterdam and
higher at night. Book one day in advance:
the phone lines are open 7–12.30am.

8 kids

Children under 4 travel free on public
transport and there are reduced fares
for 4–11s.

maps & leaflets

The GVB (Public Transport Company),
opposite Centraal Station, produces
free maps and leaflets in various
languages. Information is also available
from the Amsterdam Tourist Board.

☎ useful numbers

Public Transport Information: (0900)
9292 for all of the Netherlands.
Hold at the recorded message for an
English-speaking operator.
Lost Property: 460 5858
Garskamp People's Transport: 663 3943

walking

Some say the only way to really see
Amsterdam is on foot. Fortunately, the
centre is surprisingly small. It takes just
20 minutes to walk from Centraal
Station to Leidseplein. But a good map
is essential as many of the smaller
roads and canal streets look similar.

cars & bikes

Amsterdam is not a car-friendly city.
Parking is costly and dodging traffic in the
narrow streets can be hard. But renting a
car to go out of the city is a great idea.

rules of the road

▶ Drive on the right.
▶ Seat-belts are compulsory.
▶ Traffic lights go directly from red (stop) to green (go).
▶ Speed limits are: 50 km ph in cities, 70 km ph outside, and 100 km ph on motorways.

car rental

Budget: Overtoom 121 & Van Ostadestraat 234
☎ 612 6066/662 6614 ❶ Min age 19.
Hertz: Overtoom 333 ☎ 612 2441 ❶ Min age 25.
Ouke Baas: Van Ostadestraat 366 ☎ 679 4842 ❶ Min age 21.

motorbike rental

▶ Helmets are required for anything over 50cc.
KAV: Johan Huizingalaan 91
☎ 614 1435 ⌧ f100–f250 ❶ Min age 23
Moped Rental Service: Marnixstraat 208–210 ☎ 422 0266 ⌧ f35–f80
❶ Min age 16

petrol

24-hour Benzinestations are at: Marnixstraat 250 and Sarphatistraat 225.

parking

Meters run 9am–11pm daily and cost f5 per hour. If you get clamped, the Dienst Stadstoezicht will put a yellow sticker on your windscreen. 24-hour car parks cost f2.50–f4 per hour and f40–f50 for 24 hours.
ANWB Parking: Prins Hendrikkade 20a
☎ 638 5330
Europarking: Marnixstraat 250 ☎ 623 6694 ❶ Not 24-hour.
De Kolk Parking: Nieuwezijds Voorburgwal 12 ☎ 427 1449

transport

🚋 trams

The extensive tram network consists of 17 routes, making it the most popular and user-friendly form of cross-town public transport. Route numbers and final destinations are displayed at the front of trams. Tram stops themselves are indicated by yellow signs with the name of the stop, tram numbers served by it, and their destinations. Most stops have diagrams of the tram routes and some of the major ones have a digital clock indicating when the next tram is due. Generally speaking, tram stops are every 500m.
🕐 6am–midnight Mon–Fri,
6.30am–midnight Sat,
7.30am–midnight Sun. Generally speaking, trams on central routes run every 7–8 mins.
▶ Only some are wheelchair accessible.
▶ Drivers generally announce tram stops. They are usually sufficiently fluent in English, so ask them if you need help.
▶ Press a red button to get off at the next stop.
▶ Get on trams at the rear where the conductor will stamp your ticket, or use the automatic stamping machine yourself.
▶ Watch out for pickpockets (especially if it's crowded).
▶ Don't forget to re-stamp your ticket if travelling longer than your time limit allows.
▶ Circle Tram 20: the simplest way to get around the centre and see all the major sites and shopping areas. Trams run to 30 different stops every 10 mins daily between 9am–6pm and in both directions.

🚌 buses

More than 30 bus lines serve Amsterdam and tend to be used for heading out of the centre. However, the night buses that run along central tram routes are invaluable. Bus stops are easily identifiable by a yellow sign listing the numbers of buses, along with their destinations.
⊙ 24 hours daily.
Special local 'night buses' run every 30 min (numbered 71–79) ⊙ 1.30–5.30am Mon–Fri, 1.30–6.30am Sat–Sun.
▶ Buses and trams that run on the same route share stops.
▶ All night buses run to and from Centraal Station.
▶ Most buses are not wheelchair accessible.
▶ Buses only stop when hailed or when a passenger has pressed one of the red buttons on board, and there is no stopping between bus stops.
▶ Night buses are marked with an 'N' before the number and the signs at bus stops are outlined in black.
▶ On night buses you must also buy an extra ƒ2.50 supplementary fare ticket, regardless of whether you are using a *strippenkaart* or buying a single ticket from the driver.

Ⓜ metro

The metro is far from extensive, consisting of just four colour-coded lines, three of which run to and from Centraal Station, and a fourth which runs along the periphery of the city. It is used for journeys out to the suburbs of the city. The useful stops it serves, such as Nieuwmarkt and Waterlooplein, are often quicker to walk from Centraal Station than to go underground and wait for a train.
⊙ 6–12.15am Mon–Fri, 6.30–12.15am Sat, 7.30–12.15am Sun, every 7–8 mins.

▶ Good wheelchair access: carriages with extra space for wheelchairs are located in the centre of trains and marked by a blue circle sticker.
▶ Useful to get to/from Amstel Train/Coach Station.
▶ Trains have their number and destination at the front and there are signs on the platforms.
▶ An internal speaker on the train announces stops.
▶ Stamp your ticket at an automatic ticket stamping machine, located near the stairs/escalators to platforms.
▶ The four routes are simply colour-coded: yellow no. 54 (to Gein), red no. 53 (to Gaasperplas), green no. 50 (to Poortwachter), and orange no. 51 (to Gein-Isolatorweg).
▶ Metro trains display their number along with the final destination on the front of them.

other transport options

🚲 bicycles

The typically Dutch way of getting around the city also happens to be the most convenient: complete access, short journey times, and plenty of cycle lanes. If you'd rather someone else did the navigating, join a guided bike tour either in the centre or further afield.
⊙ 24 hours daily.
🚲 Bike hire: ƒ9.50–ƒ12.50 per day, and from ƒ38–ƒ60 per week.

☎ **Bike hire:**
Bike City
Bloemgracht 68–70 (closed Dec/Jan)
☎ 626 3721
Holland Rent-a-Bike
Damrak 247 ☎ 622 3207
MacBike
Mr Visserplein 2/Marnixstraat 220
☎ 620 0985/626 6964

Take-A-Bike
Centraal Station, Stationsplein 12
☎ 624 8391
▶ MacBike produces a useful free pamphlet and map for cyclists.
▶ All bike rental firms require a deposit and proof of ID.
▶ Most are Dutch bicycles (with back-pedalling braking). Regular handbrake or mountain bikes cost more.
▶ Cycle on the right, keeping to bike lanes.
▶ Bike theft is huge in Amsterdam, so lock to a grounded object or a rack.
▶ Make sure you don't get your wheels caught in tram lines (slippery when wet).

≈ canalbuses
Eco-friendly canalbuses, running on compressed natural gas, motor the canals on three routes. The Green and Red lines run similar routes by the Rijksmuseum, Leidseplein, Waterlooplein, Rembrandthuis, and Anne Frankhuis. The Blue line runs to the east of the city taking in Artis Zoo, Nederlands Scheepvaartmuseum, newMetropolis, and the Tropenmuseum.
◐ **Green line:** 10am–5.45pm every 40–50 min.
Red line: 10.15am–4.30pm every hour-and-a-half (with extra services at weekends).
Blue line: 9.50am–5.05pm every 30 min.
Canal Bus: ☎ 623 9886
▶ Tickets are valid until noon the following day and include travel on night buses.
▶ Tickets include a coupon of around ƒ300 worth of discounts at museums, restaurants, and shops.
▶ On board commentaries in seven different languages.
▶ Wheelchair access is only possible for those who can walk a couple of steps.

⇔ taxis & water taxis
Ordering a taxi in Amsterdam is simple: there's just one number to call. When you phone up you'll hear a recorded message telling you (in Dutch) the average wait for a taxi at this time. Wait for an English-speaking operator and be ready with the address of your current location. A taxi should arrive within minutes. A more extravagant option is taking a water taxi – they can pick up and drop you off anywhere on a canal.
◐ **Car taxis:** 24 hours daily.
Water taxis: reservations from 8am–8pm daily (taxis can be booked until midnight at the daily rate: after midnight it's double rate).
▣ Car taxis: start at ƒ5.80 and rise ƒ2.85 per km (a 24-hour rate). In slow traffic, meters automatically tick away at ƒ1 per minute. For larger fares, most taxi drivers accept credit cards.
Water taxis: ƒ125–ƒ250 per boat (depending upon number of persons) for 30 mins.
☎ **Taxicentrale:** ☎ (0900) 677 777
Water taxi: ☎ 622 2181

Car taxis:
▶ Full wheelchair access for foldable chairs.
▶ Can be hard to get beyond an engaged tone at weekends.
▶ Few female taxi drivers.
▶ Taxi ranks: Centraal Station, Dam, Haarlemmerplein, Leidseplein, Nieuwmarkt, Rembrandtplein, and Westermarkt.
▶ Taxis can be hailed: if empty, the sign on top will be lit.

Water taxis:
▶ Advance bookings are recommended for water taxis.

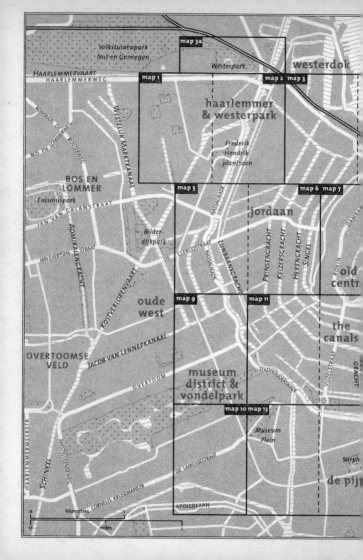

Volkstuinenpark
Nut en Genoegen

map 3a

Westerpark

westerdok

HAARLEMMERVAART
HAARLEMMERWEG

map 1

map 2 **map 3**

**haarlemmer
& westerpark**

Frederik
Hendrik
plantsoen

ADMIRAAL DE RUIJTERWEG

WESTELIJK MARKTKANAAL

BOS EN LOMMER

BOS EN
LOMMER

Erasmuspark

JAN VAN GALANSTRAAT

ADMIRALENGRACHT

JAN EVERTSEN STRAAT

map 5

Bilder-
dijkpark

jordaan

NASSAUKADE

DE CLERCQSTRAAT

NASSAUKADE

LIJNBAANSGRACHT

PRINSENGRACHT

KEIZERSGRACHT

HERENGRACHT

SINGEL

DAMRA

map 6 **map 7**

 KOSTVERLORENVAART

**oude
west**

POKIN

**old
centr**

OVERTOOMSE
VELD

JACOB VAN LENNEPKANAAL

OVERTOOM

map 9

map 11

STADHOUDERSKADE

**museum
district &
vondelpark**

**the
canals**

VIJZELSTRAAT

GRACHT

HAARLEMMERMEERSTE

SCHINKEL

AMSTELVEENSWG

CORNELIS KRUSEMANSTR

map 10 **map 13**

Museum
Plein

DE LAIRESSESTRAAT

APOLLOLAAN

Sarph

de pijp

kilometres

miles

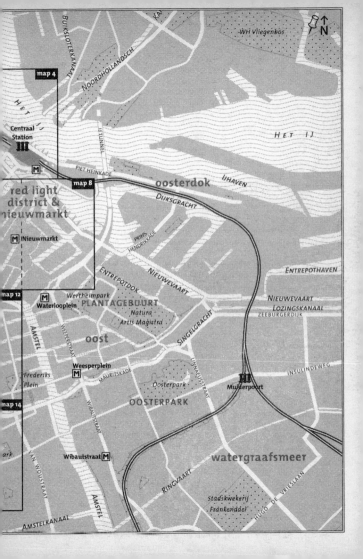

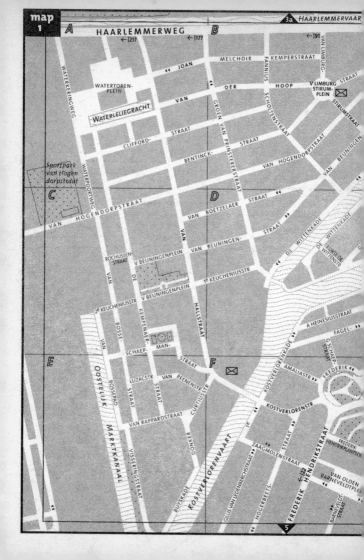

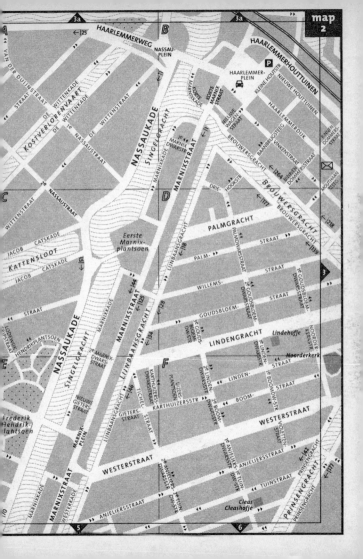

map 2

A

B

3a

3a

HAARLEMMERWEG

← 25

NASSAU-
PLEIN

HAARLEMMERHOUTTUINEN

P

HAARLEMMER-
PLEIN

KLEINE HOUTST

NIEUWE HOUTTUINEN

VAN DER DUINSTRAAT

STRAAT

DE WITTENKADE

KOSTVERLORENVAART

DE WITTENKADE

1e NASSAUSTRAAT

JOUTE
MARNIX
STRAAT

MARNIXKADE

NIEUWE
WAGEN-
STRAAT

HAARLEMMERDIJK

RAADHUISSTEG

VINKENSTRAAT

BINNEN
DOMMERS
STRAAT

NASSAUKADE

SINGELGRACHT

MARNIXKADE

MARNIXSTRAAT

MARNIX
DWARSSTR

BROUWERSGRACHT

BUITEN
DOMMERSSTR

DRIE HOOGSTR

BROUWERSGRACHT

BROUWERSGRACHT

←144

←118

2e NASSAUSTRAAT

WITTENSTRAAT

C

D

PALMGRACHT

JACOB CATSKADE

Eerste
Marnix-
plantsoen

LIJNBAANSGRACHT

PALMDWAESTRAAT

PALM-

STRAAT

←139

KATTENSLOOT

JACOB CATSKADE

←151

1e GOUDSBLOEM-
DWARSSTRAAT

3

STRAAT

←144

MARNIXKADE

MARNIXSTRAAT

←103

WILLEMS-

STRAAT

NASSAUKADE

SINGELGRACHT

←34

1e GOUDSBLOEM-
DWARSSTRAAT

GOUDSBLOEM-

STRAAT

LODEWIJK
TRIPSTRAAT

STRAAT

1e MARNIX-
DWARSSTR

LIJNBAANSGRACHT

2e GOUDS-
BLOEM
DW.STR

LINDENGRACHT

Lindehofje

HENDRIKPLANTSOEN

←146

2e LINDEN
DWARSSTR

1e LINDEN
DWARSSTR

NOORDER
KERKSTR

Noorderkerk

E

F

NIEUWE
GIETERS-
STRAAT

KARTHUIZERS-
STRAAT

UIZERS
PLANTSN

LINDEN-

STRAAT

2e BOOM
DWARSSTR

1e BOOMDWARSSTRAAT

MARNIX
PLEIN

LIJNBAANSGRACHT

KARTHUIZERS
STRAAT

TICHELSTRAAT

KARTHUIZERSSTR

BOOM-

STRAAT

Frederik
Hendrik-
plantsoen

1e ANJELIERSDWARSSTR

WESTERSTRAAT

VIOLETTEN
STRAAT

←142

MARNIXKADE

WESTERSTRAAT

ANJELIERSSTRAAT

2e ANJELIERS
DW.STR

PRINSENGRACHT

TUINSTRAAT

←117

MARNIXSTRAAT

WESTERSTRAAT

ANJELIERSSTRAAT

2e TUIN
DW.STR

1e TUIN
DW.STR

PRINSENGRACHT

PRINSENGRACHT

Cleas
Cleashofje

110

5

6

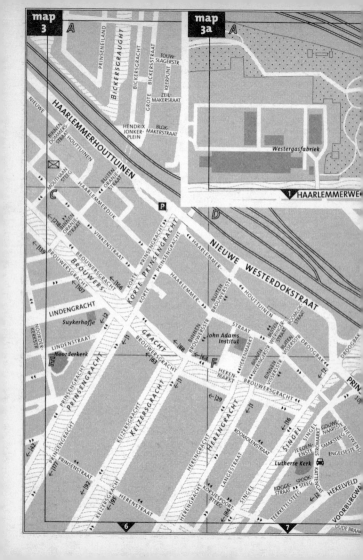

map
3

A

A

PRINSENEILAND

BICKERSGRAUGHT

BICKERSSTRAAT

GROTE BICKERSSTRAAT

TOUW-SLAGERSSTR

KEERPUNT

ZEIL-MAKERSSTRAAT

NIEUWE

BINNEN DOMMERS STRAAT

HAARLEMMERHOUTTUINEN

HAARLEMMERHOUTTUINEN

HENDRIX JONKER-PLEIN

BLOK-MAKERSTRAAT

Westergasfabriek

MOUTUINEN STEEG

BUITEN ORANJE STRAAT

HAARLEMMERDIJK

C

C

1 HAARLEMMERWE

BINNEN ORANJE STRAAT

PRINSEN

VINKENSTRAAT

BROUWERSGRACHT

KORTE PRINSENGRACHT

KORTE PRINSENGRACHT

HAARLEMMER

D

P

HAARLEMMER-

NIEUWE WESTERDOKSTRAAT

←139

BROUWERS

←166

BUITEN BROUWERSSTR

HOUTTUINEN

STRAAT

BINNEN WIERINGER

ROMEIN

←107

GRACHT

BINNEN WIERINGER STR

VISSERSSTR

DROOGBAK

LINDENGRACHT

Suykerhofje

←2

BROUWERSGRACHT

BINNEN BROUWERSSTR

John Adams Instituut

←188

←168

BINNEN WIERINGER

VISSERSSTR

DROOGBAK

NOORDER-KERKSTR

LINDENSTRAAT

Noorderkerk

PRINSENGRACHT

←1

←163

HEREN-MARKT

BROUWERSGRACHT

←12

PRIN

E

F

←129

KEIZERSGRACHT

SINGEL

PRINSENGRACHT

HERENGRACHT

HERENGRACHT

←116

JEROEN-ENSTE

SINGEL

GOUWE

SMAKSTEEG

NIEUWEZ

NAAKSTE

PRINSENSTRAAT

KEIZERSGRACHT

ROOMOLENSTRAAT

STROMARKT

ENGELSESTE

←192

←42

←117

LANGESTRAAT

Lutherse Kerk

←183

KEIZERSGRACHT

HERENGRACHT

HERENSTRAAT

HERENGRACHT

SINGEL

KOGGE-STRAAT

SPOOK-STEEG

TEERKETELSTEEG

KOKSESPOOR STEEG

HEKELVELD

VOORBURGW

OUDE BRAA

6

7

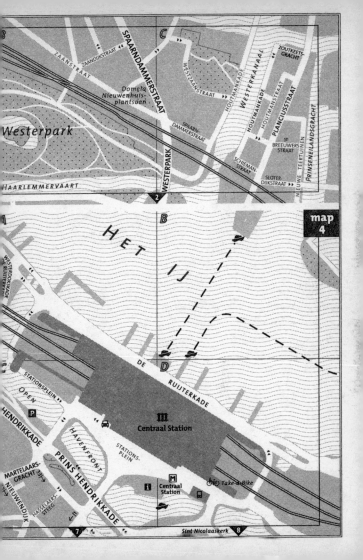

map
4

Westerpark

SPAARNDAMMERSTRAAT

ZAANDIJKSTRAAT

ZAANSTRAAT

Domela
Nieuwenhuis-
plantsoen

WESTZAANSTRAAT

HOUTMANKADE

WESTERKANAAL

HOUTMANKADE

ZOUTKEETS-
GRACHT

PLANCIUSSTRAAT

HOUTMANSTRAAT

1e TEERTUINEN

1e BREEUWERS-
STRAAT

PRINSENEILANDSGRACHT

SPAARN-
DAMMERSTRAAT

WESTERPARK

SCHIEMAN-
STRAAT

SLOTER-
DIJKSTRAAT

NIEUWE TEERTUINEN

HAARLEMMERVAART

B

HET IJ

WESTERDOKSKADE

W. RUIJTERPAD

DE RUIJTERKADE

D

STATIONSPLEIN

OPEN

HENDRIKKADE

HAVENFRONT

PRINS HENDRIKKADE

MARTELAARS-
GRACHT

NIEUWENDIJK

HASSELAARS-
STEEG

Centraal Station

STATIONS-
PLEIN

Centraal
Station

Take a Bike

Sint Nicolaaskerk

7

8

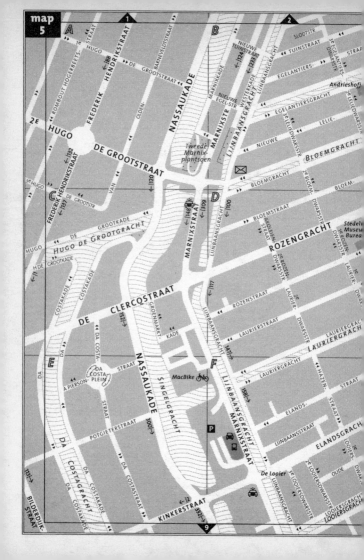

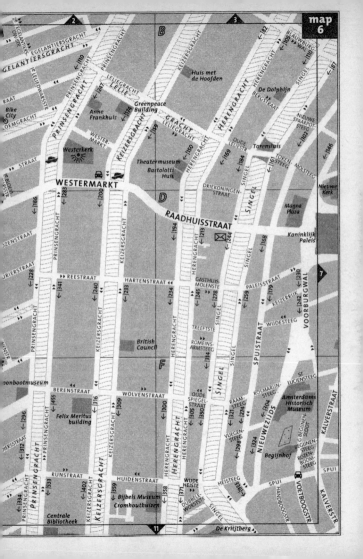

map
6

2   **3**

EGELANTIERSSTR

EGELANTIERSGRACHT

GELANTIERSGRACHT

PRINSENGRACHT

KEIZERSGRACHT

LELIEGRACHT

LELIE

Huis met
de Hoofden

De Dolphijn

BERGSTRAAT

HERENGRACHT

SINGEL

BLAUWBURG

WAL

Greenpeace
Building

RAAT

Bike
City

LOEMGRACHT

PRINSENGRACHT

ROZENBOOMGRACHT

Anne
Frankhuis

WESTER-
MARKT

KEIZERSGRACHT

GRACHT

LELIEGRACHT

HERENGRACHT

OUDE
LELIE

Torensluis

NIEUWE
SPAARPOT-
STEEG

TOREN-
MOLST EEG

Westerkerk

STRAAT

Theatermuseum
Bartolotti
Huis

HERENGRACHT

SINGEL

SINGEL

Nieuwe
Kerk

WESTERMARKT

KEIZERSGRACHT

DRIEKONINGEN-
STRAAT

D

RAADHUISSTRAAT

HERENGRACHT

Magna
Plaza

Koninklijk
Paleis

JZENSTRAAT

PRINSENGRACHT

KEIZERSGRACHT

HERENGRACHT

SINGEL

PALEISSTRAAT

KEIZERRIJK

VOORBURGWAL

7

REESTRAAT

HARTENSTRAAT

GASTHUIS-
MOLENSTE

SINGEL

SPUISTRAAT

WIJDESTEEG

RIERSTRAAT

PRINSENGRACHT

KEIZERSGRACHT

HERENGRACHT

TREEFTSTE

SINGEL

ROSMARIJN-
STEEG

ST
LUCIENSTEEG

British
Council

HERENGRACHT

ROMEINS-
ARMSTEEG

SINGEL

F

Amsterdams
Historisch
Museum

oonbootmuseum

BERENSTRAAT

WOLVENSTRAAT

RAAM-
STEEG

NIEUWEZIJDS

KALVERSTRAAT

Felix Meritus
building

KEIZERSGRACHT

HERENGRACHT

OUDE
SPIEGEL
STRAAT

HERENGRACHT

SINGEL

VLUEGEN-
STEEG

BEGIJNEN
STEEG

BEGIJNEN
STEEG
ROZEN-
BOOM-
STEEG

IERSSTRAAT

PRINSENGRACHT

RUNSTRAAT

HUIDENSTRAAT

WIJDE
HEISTE

HEISTEEG

Begijnhof

SPUI

SPUISTRAAT

PRINSENGRACHT

KEIZERSGRACHT

Bijbels Museum
Cromhouthuizen

HERENGRACHT

DUBBELE
WORTELST

SINGEL

HANDBOOGSTR

SPUI

KALVERSTRAAT

VOETBOOGSTR

Centrale
Bibliotheek

11

De Krijtberg

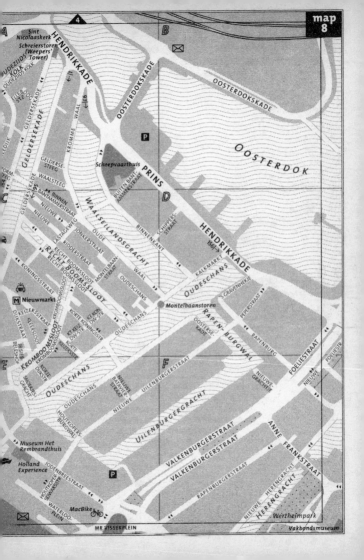

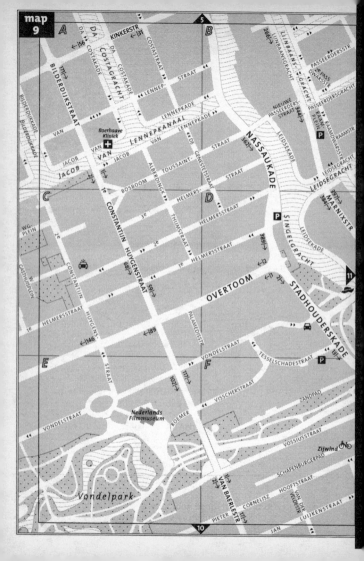

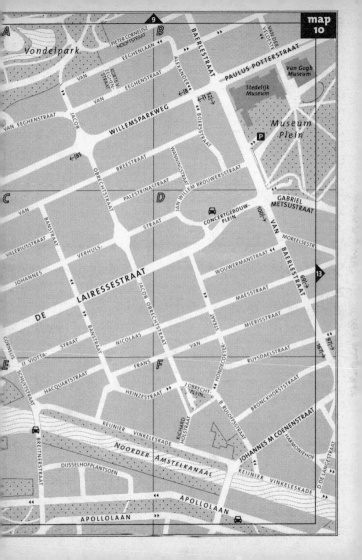

map
10

A

Vondelpark.

PIETER CORNELISZ HOOFTSTRAAT

VAN EEGHENLAAN

B

BAERLESTRAAT

VANDER VELDSTRAAT

PAULUS POTTERSTRAAT

Van Gogh Museum

KOENEN EGHEN STRAAT

VAN EEGHENSTRAAT

ALEXANDER BOERSSTRAAT

Stedelijk Museum

VAN EEGHENSTRAAT

←18

52↓
←11

JACOB

WILLEMSPARKWEG

BOERSSTRAAT

P

Museum Plein

VAN EEGHENSTRAAT

←185

BREESTRAAT

OBRECHTSTRAAT

PALESTRINASTRAAT

WANNINGSTRAAT

JAN WILLEM BROUWERSTRAAT

C

VAN

D

GABRIEL METSUSTRAAT

CONCERTGEBOUW-PLEIN

100↑

BANSTRAAT

VALERIUSSTRAAT

VERHULS-

STRAAT

MOREELSESTR

VAN BAERLESTRAAT

WOUWERMANSTRAAT

←69↓

13

JOHANNES

DE LAIRESSESTRAAT

JACOB OBRECHTSTRAAT

MAESSTRAAT

STRAAT

MIERISSTRAAT

CORNELIUS

IJ VIOTTA

STRAAT

BANSTRAAT

NICOLAAS

VAN

HONDECOETER

RUYSDAELSTRAAT

←161↓

E

SCHUYTSTRAAT

FRANS

F

J OBRECHT PLEIN.

STRAAT

BRONCKHORSTSTRAAT

HACQUARTSTRAAT

HEINZESTRAAT

RICHARD HOLSTRAAT

B RULOFFSTRAAT

HARMONIEHOF

JOHANNES M COENENSTRAAT

D DE LANGESTRAAT

BREITNERSTRAAT

REIJNIER VINKELESKADE

NOORDER AMSTELKANAAL

DIJSSELHOFPLANTSOEN

REIJNIER VINKELESKADE

APOLLOLAAN

APOLLOLAAN

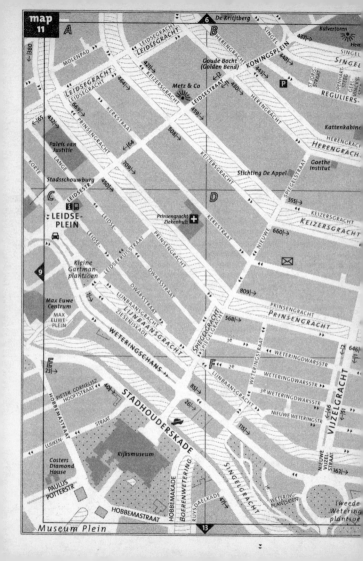

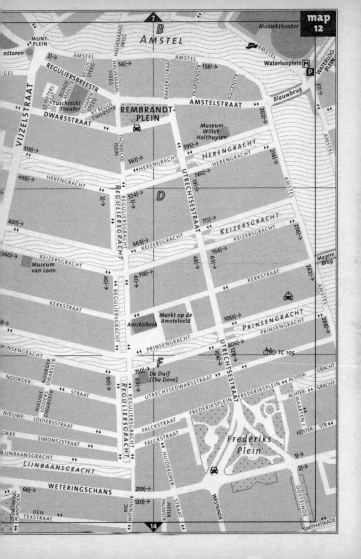

map
12

Muziektheater

7

B

AMSTEL

MUNT-
PLEIN

nttoren

2|→

AMSTEL

REGULIERSBREESTR

GEL

HALVEMAAN STEEG

BAKKERSSTEEG

AMSTEL

546|→

HALVEMAANSTEEG

138|→

PAARDENSTR

VIJZELSTRAAT

DWARSSTRAAT

Tuschinski
Theater

ST PIETERS
HALSTEEG

RUNDE MSTEEG

SCHAPENSTEEG

HET REGUL
DWARSSTR

REMBRANDT-
PLEIN

AMSTELSTRAAT

Waterlooplein

WATERLOO-
PLEIN

Blauwbrug

31|→

202|→

519|→

THORBECKE-
PLEIN

561|→

HERENGRACHT

Museum
Willet-
Holthuysen

595|→

HERENGRACHT

244|→

AMSTEL

498|→

HERENGRACHT

REGULIERSGRACHT

2|→

534|→
1|→

REGULIERSGRACHT

560|→
19|→

UTRECHTSESTRAAT

713|→

KEIZERSGRACHT

HERENGRACHT

256|→

601|→

663|→

KEIZERSGRACHT

766|→
63|→

KEIZERSGRACHT

262|→

AMSTEL

Magere
Brug

560|→

Museum
van Loon

401|→

411|→ 718|→

48|→

REGULIERSGRACHT

KERKSTRAAT

KERKSTRAAT

Amstelkerk

Markt op de
Amstelveld

1055|→

PRINSENGRACHT

PRINSENGRACHT

298|→

AMSTEL

PRINSENGRACHT

PRINSENGRACHT

REGULIERSGRACHT

UTRECHTSESTRAAT

806|→

104|→

TC 105

F

750|→

De Duif
(The Dove)

90|→
69|→

REGULIERSGRACHT

UTRECHTSEDWARSSTRAAT

FREDERIKSPLEIN

ACHTER-

GRACHT

NOORDER-

NOORDER
DWARSSTR

STRAAT

FREDERIKSPLEIN

ACHTER-

GRACHT

NIEUWE

NIEUWE LOOIERSDWARSSTRAAT

FALCKSTRAAT

MAARTEN

KOSTER- STR

OKKE

SIMONSZSTRAAT

FALCKSTRAAT

HUIDEKOPER

Frederiks
Plein

LIJNBAANSGRACHT

LIJNBAANSGRACHT

WETERINGSCHANS

259|→

PIETER
PAUWSTR

WESTEINDE

1|→

2|→

OOSTEINDE

66|→

2E WETERING
PLANTSOEN

DEN
TEXSTRAAT

120|→

WITSENSTR

SARPHATIKADE

14

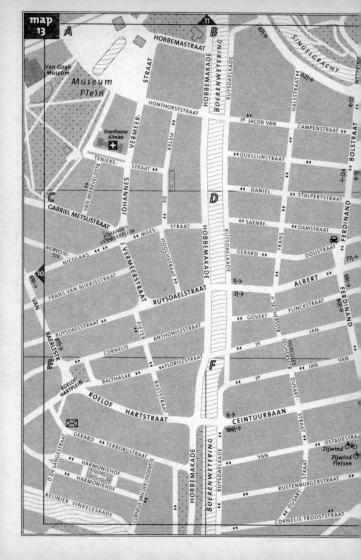

map
13

A

HOBBEMASTRAAT

B

11

SINGELGRACHT

47↗

WETERI →2

Van Gogh
Museum

Museum
Plein

HOBBEMAKADE

BOERENWETERING

RUYSDAELKADE

HALSSTRAAT

62↗

BOLSTRAAT →3

HONTHORSTSTRAAT

1e JACOB VAN

CAMPENSTRAAT

Boerhaave
Kliniek

VERMEER

STRAAT

PIETER

QUELLIJNSTRAAT

←24

←5

TENIERS

STRAAT →

DANIEL

STALPERTSTRAAT

FERDINAND

C

GABRIEL METSUSTRAAT

VAN MIEREVELDSTR

JOHANNES

DE

D

SAENRE-

FRANS

DAMSTRAAT

DOUSTRAAT

71↗

JOHANNES
VERMEERPLEIN

MAES

STRAAT

HOBBEMAKADE

RUYSDAELKADE

GERARD →

MOREELSE
STR

NICOLAAS

VERMEERSTRAAT

HOOGHSTRAAT

ALBERT →

68↗

10

FRANS VAN MIERISSTRAAT

RUYSDAELSTRAAT

1↗

2↗

VAN

GOVERT

FLINCKSTRAAT

FERDINAND

←65

906↗

RUYSDAELSTRAAT

97↗

PIETER

ANTHONISZSTRAAT

2e

SECHERSSTR

JAN

BAERLESTR

CORNELIS

FLORISZSTRAAT

1e

SECHERSSTR

E

ROELOF
HARTPLEIN

BALTHASAR

FLORISZSTRAAT

F

JAN

VAN

DUSART

ROELOF HARTSTRAAT

1↗

CEINTUURBAAN

186↗

GERARD →

TERBORGSTRAAT

VAN

OSTADESTR

HARMONIEHOF

HOBBEMAKADE

BOERENWETERING

RUYSDAELKADE

STRAAT

Zijwind
Zijwind
Fletsen

HARMONIEHOF

RUSTENBURGERSTRAAT

REIJNIER VINKELESKADE

CORNELIS VAN DER LINDENSTR

D DE LANGESTRAAT

DUSART

STRAAT

CORNELIS TROOSTSTRAAT

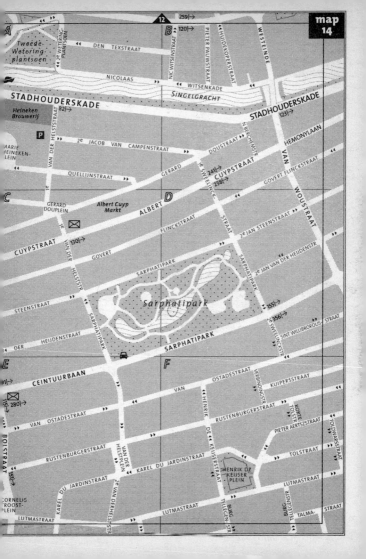

phrasebook

pronunciation

Dutch is generally pronounced in the same way as English, apart from a few tongue-twisting exceptions.

Consonants

ch	as in lo**ch** (coming from your
g	throat)
	as in lo**ch** (never pronounce it as the English g, except when words end in ing)
j	as in **y**es
k	as in **c**at
p	as in a short English **t**
sch	a combination of **s** and **ch** (as above)
w	mixture between the English **v** and **w**

Short vowel sounds

a	as in c**a**rd
e	as in l**a**zy
i	as in l**i**ght
o	as in d**o**t
u	as in fli**r**t

Long vowel sounds

aa	as in fl**a**t but longer
ee	as in s**a**me or f**ai**l
eu	sounds similar to fl**i**rt, but with rounded lips
ie	as in **ea**t
oe	as in l**oo**k
oo	as in g**oa**t
uu	sounds similar to g**oo**d

Vowel combinations

au/ou	as in l**ou**d
aai	as in b**y**e
eeuw	as in f**ai**l (but a much longer vowel sound)
ei/ij	as in f**igh**t
ieuw	as in f**ee**l
ooi	as in **oi**, but with a much longer o
uw	as in ph**ew**
ui	similar to h**ou**se (but say with rounded lips)
oei	pronounced **oo-ee** (as one long sound)

posting letters

telephone	*telefoon*	**tay**-le-phone
telephone box	*telefooncel*	**tay**-le-phone cell
telephone directory	*inlichtingen*	in-lich-**ting**-en
operator	*telefonist*	**tay**-le-phone-ist
dialling tone	*kiestoon*	**kees**-tone
coins	*inwerpen*	**in**-werp-un
phonecard	*insteken*	**in**-stake-un
out of order	*buiten dienst*	**bowten** deenst

phrasebook

essentials

hello	hallo	**hu**-llo
hi	hoi	**h**-oi
bye	doei	dowee
yes	ja	yar
no	nee	nay
thank you	dank u wel	dank i vel
thanks	bedankt	**be**-dankt
sorry	sorry	sorry
excuse me	pardon	pardon
How are you?	Hoe gaat get?	Who gaart et?
good	goed	good
bad	slecht	slecht
okay	ok	okay
open	open	**o**-pen
closed	gesloten	**ge**-slow-ten
entrance	ingang	**in**-gang
exit	uitgang	**owt**-gang
toilet	wc	vhay-say
left	links	links
right	rechts	rekhts
what?	wat?	vhat?
when?	wanneer?	vhan-**eer**
where?	waar?	vhaar?
how?	hoe?	hoo?
I don't know	Ik weet het niet	Ik vayt het neat
Please	alstublieft	**als**-too-blift
Do you speak English?	Spreek jij Engels?	Sprayk yay Engels?
Sorry, I don't speak Dutch	Het spijt me, ik spreek geen Nederlands	Et **spayte** meh, ik **sprayk** khane **Nay**-der-lands
Could you repeat this please?	Wilt u dit een keer herhalen?	Vilt oo dit ayn kir **er**-ha-len?
Do you take credit cards/traveller's cheques?	Accepteert u credit cards/traveller's cheques?	**Ack**-cep-tiert oo credit cards/traveller's cheques?

posting letters

post office	postkantoor	**post**-khan-tour
letter	brief	breef
postcard	ansichtkaart	**ahn**-sickt-karht
parcel	pakje	**pack**-ye
stamp	postzegel	**post**-say-gel
overseas	het buitenland	et **bowt**-en-land

transport

I want to go to...	Ik wil naar .... gaan	Ik wil **nahr** .... gahn
How much is the fare to...?	Hoeveel kost het naar...?	**Hoo**-fail cost et nahr?
Where is the nearest stop?	Waar is de dichtstbijzijnde halte?	Var is de **dickst**-bye-**sayn**-deh holt-e?
bus	bus	buzz
tram	tram	trem
train	trein	trayn
metro	metro	**may**-tro
bicycle	fiets	**feet**-s
platform	perron	**pur**-ron
ticket	kaartje	**kahrt**-ye
airport	vliegveld	**fleeg**-felt
arrivals	aankomst	**ahn**-cumst
departures	vertrek	**fur**-trek
customs	douane	**doo**-ahn-e
baggage-claim	baggage claim	baggage claim
check-in	check-in	check-in
delay	vertraging	**fur**-trah-ging
flight number	vlucht nummer	**vluckt** numb-er
single/return ticket	enkele reis/retour	**ankel**-e reys/ **re**-toor
standard class	tweede klasse	**tway**-de **clas**-se
first class	eerste klasse	**eyr**-ste **clas**-se

hotels

I have a reservation	Ik heb gereserveerd	Ik heb **ge**-res-ur-**feerd**
Do you have any vacancies?	Heeft u een kamer?	Hayft oo ayn **kah**-mer?
What is the charge per night?	Hoeveel kost het per nacht?	**Hoo**-fail cost et per nockt?
single	eenpersoons	**ayn**-per-sowns
double	tweepersoons	**tway**-per-sowns
with bath/shower/toilet	met bad/douche/ toilet	mit baht/doosh/ **twa**-let
breakfast	ontbijt	**ont**-bite
half/full board	half/vol pension	holf/vol **pen**-see-on

shopping

antique shop	antiekwinkel	**an**-tick-vinck-el
bakery	bakker	**back**-er
bookshop	boekenwinkel	**book**-en-vinck-el
cheese shop	kaaswinkel	**khars**-vinck-el
chemist	drogist	**drou**-gist
delicatessen	delicatessenwinkel	delicatessen **vinck**-el
newsagent	tabakswinkel	**ta**-backs **vinck**-el
post office	postkantoor	**post**-can-tour
supermarket	supermarkt	**soup**-er-markt
price	prijs	priys
sale	uitverkoop	**owt**-ver-coup
special offer	aanbieding	**arn**-bee-ding
department	afdeling	**ahf**-day-ling
secondhand	tweedehands	**tway**-deh-honts

smoking

ounce	ons	ontz
gramme	gram	grahm
Have you got a light?	Heb je een vuurtje?	Heb yu ayn **voohrt**-ye?
ready-rolled	kant-en-klaar	cont en **clarh**
rolling paper	vloepapier	**floohr**-pah-pier
tobacco	tabak	**tah**-back
cigarettes	sigaretten	**see**-gah-rat-an

menu guide

dutch specialities

pea soup	erwtensoep	**air**-tun-soop
endive & potato mash	andijvie	on-dive-ee **stamp**-pot
sausage & green cabbage	stamppot boerenkool met worst	**boor**-en-kohl mit worst **hoot**-spot mit clap-stook
vegetable mash with beef	hutspot met klapstuk zuurkool	**soor**-kohl
sauerkraut	cappucijners met spek	**cap**-oo-**sayn**-ers mit speck
beans with bacon	hachee	**hay**-shay
beef stew	pannenkoeken	**pahn**-en-**coo**-cken
pancakes	poffertjes	**pof**-air-tyes
small pancakes	oliebollen	**ow**-lee-bol-len
deep fried batter with raisins & apples		
raw herring	rauwe haring	row-e **hahr**-ring

phrasebook

indonesian specialities

rice table (selection of dishes)	*rijsttafel*	rayst-tarf-el
gado gado (steamed vegetables, egg, & peanut sauce)	*ga~dow*	ga-dow
satay	*saté*	sah-tay
beef stew with coconut milk	*rendang*	ren-dang
boiled egg in hot red pepper sauce	*sambal goreng telor*	sam-bawl go-reng tel-ow
french beans in hot pepper sauce	*sambal goreng boontjes*	sam-bawl go-reng bowr tyes
roast pork with sweet & sour	*babi pangan*	bah-bee pan-gan
roast chicken in soy sauce	*ajam babi ketjap*	a-yam bah-bee ket-chap
chicken soup	*soto ajam*	so-tow ah-yam

eating and drinking

Eating and drinking	*Ik wil graag...*	Ik vil **grarg**...
I would like ...	*rekening*	**ray**-ke-ning
bill/check	*menukaart*	menu carht
menu	*bediening*	**be**-dee-ning
Service included	*inbegrepen*	**in**-bhe-grayp-en
Service not included	*exlusief*	ex-cloo-ceive
	bediening	**be**-dee-ning
starter	*voorgerecht*	**fohr**-ge-reckt
soup	*soep*	soop
main course	*hoofdgerecht*	**howft**-ge-reckt
dessert	*toetje*	**toot**-ye
wine list	*wijnkaart*	**wine**-cahrt
cheers	*proost*	prowst
bon appetit	*eet smakelijk*	**ayt** smar-ke-like
vegetarian	*vegetarisch*	**vay**-ge-tah-ris
glass	*glas*	glas
bottle	*fles*	fles
bread	*brood*	browd
sugar	*suiker*	**souw**-ker
salt & pepper	*peper en zout*	**pay**-per en sowt
garlic	*knoflook*	**knof**-lowk
rice	*rijst*	rayst
eggs	*eieren*	**ay**-r-en
cheese	*kaas*	kaars

milk	*melk*	**melck**
french fries	*patat*	**pah**-tat
crisps	*chips*	chips
potatoes	*aardappelen*	**ahrd**-ap-el-len
carrots	*wortelen*	vort-el-en
asparagus	*asperges*	**as**-pehr-shos
peppers	*paprika*	**pah**-pree-kah
mushrooms	*champignonen*	**sham**-pin-yon-en
broccoli	*broccoli*	bro-col-**ee**
lettuce	*sla*	**slah**
tomato	*tomaten*	**toe**-mar-ten
cod	*kabeljouw*	**kah**-bul-yow
bass	*baars*	bahrs
eel	*paling*	**pah**-ling
halibut	*heilbot*	**hiyl**-bot
salmon	*zalm*	solm
haddock	*schelvis*	**schel**-fis
prawns	*garnalen*	**gar**-nah-len
mussels	*mosselen*	**mos**-sa-len
trout	*forel*	**for**-rel
seafood	*zeevruchten*	**say**-fruck-ten
lamb	*lamsvlees*	**loms**-flays
beef	*rundvlees*	**roond**-flays
chicken	*kip*	kip
pork	*varkensvlees*	**fark**-ens-flays
veal	*kalfsvlees*	**calf**-flays
duck	*eend*	ain't
turkey	*kalkoen*	**cal**-coon
sausage	*worst*	voorts
ham	*ham*	hom
tea	*thee*	tay
coffee	*koffie*	**cough**-fee
fresh orange juice	*jus d'orange*	**shoo**-d'orange
red wine	*rode wijn*	**roa**-der wine
white wine	*witte wijn*	**wit**-eh wine
beer	*bier*	**bee**-ehr
water	*mineraal water*	**mi**-nehr-al **wah**-ter
I have a reservation for..	*Ik heb gereserveerd*	Ik eb **ge**-res-ser- veehrd
Have you got a table for...?	*Heeft u een tafel voor...?*	Hayft oo ayn **tarf**-el for...?

emergencies

help	*help*	help
emergency	*noodgeval*	**nowt**-ge-fall
police	*politie*	**pow**-leet-see
ambulance	*ambulance*	**ahm**-boo-lans-e
fire brigade	*brandweer*	**brahnt**-wir
doctor	*dokter*	**doc**-tur
hospital	*ziekenhuis*	**seek**-en-howse

telling the time

It's five o'clock	*Het is vijf uur*	Et is **fayve** oor
half past five	*half zes*	**half** zehs
five to nine	*vijf voor negen*	fayve for **nay**-gen
five past nine	*vijf over negen*	fayve **o**-ver **nay**-gen

days & months

Monday	*maandag*	**maahn**-darg
Tuesday	*dinsdag*	**dins**-darg
Wednesday	*woensdag*	**woo**-ns-darg
Thursday	*donderdag*	**don**-dehr-darg
Friday	*vrijdag*	**frei**-darg
Saturday	*zaterdag*	**sat**-er-darg
Sunday	*zondag*	**son**-darg
January	*januari*	**jan**-oo-ar-ee
February	*februari*	**fe**-broo-ar-ee
March	*maart*	maahrt
April	*april*	**a**-pril
May	*mei*	my
June	*juni*	**ju**-nee
July	*juli*	**ju**-lee
August	*augustus*	**ouw**-gus-tus
September	*september*	**sep**-tem-ber
October	*oktober*	**ok**-too-ber
November	*november*	**no**-vem-behr
December	*december*	**day**-cem-behr

phrasebook

1	*een*	ayn
2	*twee*	tway
3	*drie*	dree
4	*vier*	veer
5	*vijf*	fayve
6	*zes*	zehs
7	*zeven*	**safe**-en
8	*acht*	ackt
9	*negen*	**nay**-gen
10	*tien*	teen
11	*elf*	alf
12	*twaalf*	twahlf
13	*dertien*	**der**-teen
14	*veertien*	**veer**-teen
15	*vijftien*	**fayve**-teen
16	*zestien*	**zehs**-teen
17	*zeventien*	**safe**-en-teen
18	*achttien*	**acht**-teen
19	*negentien*	**nay**-gen-teen
20	*twintig*	**twin**-tich
21	*eenentwintig*	**ayn**-en-twin-tich
30	*dertig*	**der**-tich
40	*veertig*	**veer**-tich
50	*vijftig*	**fayve**-tich
60	*zestig*	**zehs**-tich
70	*zeventig*	**safe**-en-tich
80	*tachtig*	**tach**-tich
90	*negentig*	**nay**-gen-tich
100	*honderd*	**hohn**-derd

symbols

key to symbols

☎ telephone number
▣ recorded information line
F fax
e email
w worldwide web
❶ hot tips
◑ opening times
♿ wheelchair access
☞ hotel
⊙ frequency/times
♫ map reference
▤ credit cards
   AE = American Express
   DC = Diners Club
   MC = Mastercard
   V = Visa
   all = AE/DC/MC/V
   are accepted

☆ recommended (featured in listings section)

restaurants & eetcafés
  f   cheap (main courses under f20)
  ff moderate (main courses f20–f35)
  fff expensive (main courses over f35)

entertainment
♠ capacity
⬥ dress code

transport
♘ good points
♞ bad points
   tram
▢ city bus
▤ shuttle bus
Ⓜ metro
Ⅲ overground train
✕ airport
⛴ canalbus/watertaxi/ferry
🚗 taxi
ℹ information point

hotels
♣ number of beds
☕ breakfast included
▤ air conditioning
24 24-hour room service
↔ fitness facilities
✎ business facilities
⚘ outdoor area/garden
☕ restaurant/café
♜ bar/pub
P parking

key to map symbols

● sight/museum/gallery/landmark/notable building/shop
● park/garden/square
Ⅲ train station
Ⓜ metro station
⋙ tourist information
▣ bus terminal
▣ airport bus departure point
⛴ ferry/river boat/canal bus

✵ view point
⟳ one-way street
⟫ street number
P car park
🚕 taxi rank
⊕ police station
✉ post office
✚ hospital with casualty unit
Ⓐ grid reference

acknowledgements

Conceived, edited & designed by
Virgin Publishing Ltd
London W6 9HA

Editorial assistance: Tim Brown, Jessica Hughes
Consultants: Rodney Bolt, Steve Korver
Researchers: Daria Birang, Francine Huyser, Laura Martz, Giles Wollenmann
Index: Hilary Bird
Cartographic Editor: Dominic Beddow
Cartographers: Simonetta Giori,
Draughtsman Ltd, London
Tel: 020-8960 1602
mail@magneticnorth.net

Printed by Omnia Books Ltd, Scotland

Features were written and researched by:
Getting Your Bearings: Rodney Bolt | Area Introductions: Sean Condon (Jordaan), Steve Korver (Old Centre, The Canals, De Pijp, Museum District & Vondelpark, Haarlemmer & Westerpark), Clare Tomlinson (Red Light District & Nieuwmarkt) | Area Shopping: Kate Holder | Area Restaurants & Eetcafés: Steve Korver | Area Bars & Cafés, Coffeeshops & Clubs: Willem de Blaauw, Pip Farquharson, Steve Korver, Andy Thompson | Around the Netherlands: Willem de Blaauw, Andrew May | Landmarks: Linda Cook, Brent Gregston, Bart Plantenga | Sights, Museums & Galleries: Linda Cook, Brent Gregston, Bart Plantenga, Nadette de Visser | Parks & Gardens: Willem de Blaauw | Children: Hille Linders | Body & Soul: Elaine Harvey | Games & Activities: Pip Farquharson | Shopping listings: Linda Cook, Nadette de Visser | Restaurants & Eetcafés: Steve Korver | Bars & Cafés: Willem de Blaauw, Steve Korver, Andy Thompson, Pip Farquharson | Coffeeshops: Andy Thompson | Clubs: Andy Thompson | Media: Pip Farquharson | Music & Cinema: Willem de Blaauw | Theatre: Steve Lambley | Dance, Opera & Classical Music: Andrew May | Events: Pip Farquharson | Hotels: Marion Carter | Transport: Pip Farquharson | Practical Information: Elaine Harvey | Phrasebook: Willem de Blaauw

Great care has been taken with this guide to be as accurate and up-to-date as possible, but details such as addresses, telephone numbers, opening hours, prices and travel information are liable to change. The publishers cannot accept responsiblility for any consequences arising from the use of this book. We would be delighted to receive any corrections and suggestions for inclusion in the next edition.

Please write to or email:
Virgin Publishing Ltd
Thames Wharf Studios
Rainville Road
London w6 9ha
Fax: 020 7386 3360
Email: travel@virgin-pub.co.uk

notes